. . . .

"Just call me Hays"

Recollections, reactions and reflections on 42 years of railroading

by

Hays T. Watkins, Jr.

with

Thomas E. Hoppin and Richard E. Bussard

Published by
R.E.B. Communications and Publishing Inc.
16 Hopson Road, Jacksonville, FL 32250

Book design by Suzanne Kochiss and Linda Gould
Typography by David Taylor

Library of Congress Catalog Number: 00-135481
International Standard Book Number: 1-929102-03-8

Printed in the United States of America
May 2001
First Edition

Foreword

. . . .

Some time ago, our grandchildren asked what I did at CSX. I told them I was the chief executive officer, "the boss." As one might expect, that quick answer did not satisfy their curiosity and the realization of that reality was the beginning of what herein follows. From these pages, hopefully, they will finally get their answer, as will others who have expressed interest in the "why" of some of the events and undercurrents that marked my 42-year tenure with C&O, Chessie and CSX.

This effort is not intended to be a management training book; not intended to be a corporate history; and not intended to be a personal diary, although it has elements of each. It, simply put, is a series of recollections, reflections and reactions to what happened, mainly to me and others in the railroad industry, from the time I walked into C&O's offices in 1949 until the day I retired from CSX in 1991.

Along the way I have had the great good fortune of working with hundreds of hard-working, highly skilled and unbelievably dedicated people ... and we all benefited from the equally diligent, honorable and determined efforts of thousands of others. Without them, there is no doubt there would not be an answer to that simple, but complicated, question of the grandchildren.

I thank you all!

H.T.W.

Dedication

. . . .

To Betty
who has and with ease
still masters the toughest job
…managing me

Table of Contents

. . . .

Table of Contents

. . . .

. . . .

Growing Up in Kentucky

Learning the lessons of reality thanks to
The Great Depression

Around 1740, Evan Watkins — my great-great-great-great grand-father — established the first ferry across the Potomac River, located between Hagerstown, Maryland, and Winchester, Virginia, very near where today's Interstate 81 crosses the river. At that time, Watkins Ferry was in Frederick County, Virginia, which included the northwest part of what now is Virginia and the panhandle of what now is West Virginia. Today, the site is located in Berkeley County, West Virginia, opposite Williamsport, Maryland.

Accordingly, while I would not know it until many years later when I began researching my family's history, transportation was a Watkins occupation long before I entered the railroad business more than 200 years later. Evan Watkins, among others, likely also accounts for my appreciation of and proficiency with figures. He kept detailed ledgers of his accounts that survive to this day and contain accountings, as is noted in Parke Rouse's The Great Wagon Road, of "ferriage rates, blacksmithing charges, and prices for such refreshments as wine slings, toddies, and 'cideroyl'."

. . . .

Watkins Ferry, and the related tavern and inn, forge and riverfront store operated by Evan, served most of the travelers moving south along The Great Philadelphia Wagon Road from Pennsylvania and the Mid-Atlantic area into western Virginia, the Carolinas and Georgia. Later, by its connection with the Wilderness Road at Big Lick, Virginia, The Great Road also served the pioneers heading to the western frontier and what was to become Kentucky and Tennessee.

Upon Evan's death in 1765, his son, also named Evan, operated the ferry until 1772, when he sold his lands, the ferry and its associated businesses and moved into the wilds of northwestern Virginia. After serving in the Revolutionary War, the younger Evan moved his family further into western Virginia where they remained until 1791.

In the winter of 1791, he loaded his wife, their 10 children and their possessions onto a flatboat and traveled down the Monongahela and Ohio Rivers to the falls of the Ohio, landing at the then small frontier village of Louisville, Kentucky. From Louisville they followed the Wilderness Road into the center of the state where they were living when Kentucky became a state on June 1, 1792. By 1805, Evan had moved the family to Henry County, where many of his descendants remained for most of the next two centuries and to which my father and mother, with a certain seven-year-old in tow, would return in the early months of "The Great Depression."

. . . . .

My father's mother, whose maiden name was Hays, descended from a family who came to America from Donegal, Ireland, in the early 1700's. After the death of David Hays in Augusta County, Virginia, in 1776, the

. . . .

family sold the home farm, and his son William moved to Albemarle County (near Charlottesville), where he married and began his family. In 1795, William, his wife Charity, and their seven children moved westward to Clark County, Kentucky, where William died in 1801. His wife and most of the by then nine children (two more had been born in Kentucky) remained in Clark County until her death in 1851, but son William, Jr. moved to Henry County about 1812.

. . . . .

Joseph Whiteley (my mother's maiden name) came from Whitehaven, England, to North Carolina in the late 1750s, and went on to Russell County, Virginia, where his son Andrew was born in 1789. In 1811 Andrew and two of his brothers moved west to Henry County, Kentucky. The brothers quickly moved on to Ohio, but Andrew stayed. The following year he married Jennie Watkins, a granddaughter of the younger Evan Watkins who had brought his family to Kentucky 20 years earlier. This was the first Watkins-Whiteley marriage, predating my parents' wedding by more than 100 years.

. . . . .

My maternal grandmother, Nancy (Nannie) Bell Spillman, descended from a German family that originally lived in the Nassau-Siegen district of southern Germany. In 1714, Gov. Alexander Spottswood of Virginia imported a group of German miners (including my ancestor, Johann Spielmann, or John Spilman) to work developing the iron mines on the western frontier of Virginia, in what is now Spotsylvania County.

. . . .

John and his family eventually moved further west in Virginia, and his grandson Henry Spillman, together with his wife Ann (like so many other Virginians), determined to leave Virginia and move to the frontiers of Kentucky. However, Henry died before the family could move. His wife Ann and their nine children traveled with another family to Oldham County, Kentucky, near the Henry County line, in 1829.

. . . . .

Of course there were many other collateral lines of ancestry, and the family names of Abbott, Bartlett, Davis, Downing, Foster, Haggard, King, Miles, Pringle, Smith, White and Winburn frequently appeared in the records of Henry and surrounding counties. In almost every case, these families had been Virginians who had moved west to the wilderness of Kentucky. The Kentucky in which I grew up was far from a wilderness, but many years later I was to reverse the trip, twice making my home in Virginia, where it remains.

. . . . .

My father, Hays Thomas Watkins, Sr., grew up in Henry County and was one of eight children of George Thomas Watkins and Sarah Elizabeth (Sally Bet) Hays Watkins. He graduated from New Castle High School in 1910 and then attended Northwestern University in Evanston, Illinois. Strained family finances, however, forced his return to the farm before graduation.

After being married in 1917, he and my mother, the former Minnie

. . . .

Catherine Whiteley, remained on the Henry County farm for several years.
In the early 1920s, my parents moved to Fern Creek, a suburb of
Louisville, where my father began working at the Bank of Fern Creek.
They made the move at the request of my father's uncle, Fountain Hays
(the younger brother of my father's mother), one of the founders of the
bank.

. . . . .

I was born at home in Fern Creek at 2 o'clock in the afternoon on
Tuesday, January 26, 1926. Fortunately, our next-door neighbor was the
town doctor who delivered me. Later, he would often take me with him
when making house calls. As an only child, I also went many places with
my parents and with many uncles and aunts and cousins. We were never far
from relatives.

By age 4, I could recognize and remember the license numbers on
automobiles. Perhaps this predilection for numbers was an early indication
of my later life's work. It certainly created a bit of a stir in Fern Creek.
When word got around in the community in the summer of 1930 that I
knew everyone's license number, "The Jeffersonian," the local Jefferson
County, Kentucky, newspaper, ran a story featuring "Fern Creek's Four Year
Old Prodigy in Figures," noting I had a "love for reading numbers." It was
my first, and one of my best, experiences with the media.

. . . . .

In the fall of 1931, at age 5, I began attending Fern Creek
Elementary School. Because I knew my ABCs and was conversant with

. . . .

numbers, I was promoted to the second grade after two months. From then on, I was always the youngest person in my class, although being big for my age helped to mask this fact.

My early days in Fern Creek were filled with adventure, many play-mates, and finding challenging paths into the woods, exploring different neighborhoods and visiting relatives on the farm and in Louisville. Even though the far-distant stock market had "crashed," life in a small town, well within sight of the bustling and bursting Louisville, was exciting.

All of this was to end, however, with the inauguration of a new president of the United States, Franklin Delano Roosevelt. On March 5, 1933, the day after he took office, President Roosevelt declared a Bank Holiday and closed all of the nation's banks. Many of the larger banks subsequently reopened, but because of the problems experienced by its correspondent banks in Louisville, the Bank of Fern Creek — even though it eventually repaid virtually all of its customer's deposits — was unable to resume operations.

The owners, officers and directors of the bank, however, never recovered any of their equity. That included my father, who had advanced to being its cashier, and my great uncle, then president of the bank. So the closing of the bank was particularly hard on my Uncle Fount and my father.

. . . . .

With his banking career at an end, my father and mother decided to return to Henry County. In June of 1933 we moved from Fern Creek into the four-room home on the 60-acre farm of my grandfather, William G.

. . . .

Whiteley. My father and grandfather worked together raising crops on the farm, tending the garden and milking the four cows twice a day. Since my grandmother Whiteley had died in 1930 and my grandfather lived alone, this provided company for him and a home for us.

For the next three years, in the midst of "The Great Depression," we survived on hard work and good farm food — the fruits of the garden, fried chicken and country hams — and very little cash. All our farm neighbors were enduring the same circumstances and were in the same financial condition. This narrowed our lives to the essentials and brought us together as a family and as a community. Our lives revolved around and we found great enjoyment and fulfillment in visits to and with neighbors and relatives, community activities, our church and our school. Visits to stores and experiencing commercial entertainment, such as "moving pictures," were exceptionally rare. "Store-bought" bread and meat were unheard of.

. . . . .

Contrasted with life in Fern Creek, life in Henry County was at a much lower key. There was only one neighbor boy in the area — Sammie Lee — and he and I spent many hours building roads in the hog lots and cellar mounds. Our play was not in vain. Sammie became the county engineer for Jefferson County, which includes the City of Louisville, and later became a well-respected consulting engineer and served as president of the National Association of Professional Engineers. (At this writing, I still see Sammie. He and his wife have vacationed the last several years in Naples, Florida, where my family now spends the winter.)

My school experiences at Pendleton in Henry County were quite dif-

• • • • • • • • • • • • • • • • • • • •

ferent from Fern Creek. Pendleton consisted of two rooms, with grades one through four taught by one teacher, and grades five through eight taught by another. My morning began with a one-mile walk across the fields to ride to school with my teacher, Miss Levia Dawkins, who taught the first four grades and was the daughter of one of my grandfather's neighbors.

Our wooden school building, complete with pot-bellied stoves and outdoor toilets, made learning challenging as well as interesting. Since I had completed the third grade at Fern Creek, I began in the fourth grade at Pendleton and had the best of both worlds — Miss Levia as chauffeur and teacher. For grades five and six, my teacher was Miss Kathryn Orem, who was from Campbellsburg, a neighboring town in Henry County.

• • • • •

After nearly three years with grandfather Whiteley (from June 1933 until April 1936), we moved to the farm that had been in my father's family since 1807 and where he and all seven of his brothers and sisters had been born and reared. (The original deed for the farm is signed by Meriwether Lewis, who had completed his famous trip with William Clark and was then governor of the Missouri Territory.) The house had been added on to from time to time to accommodate the growing family and was much larger than my grandfather Whiteley's. And, in 1939, thanks to the Rural Electrification Administration, we even had electric lights.

When my father, his two brothers and five sisters left home, my grandparents stayed on the farm until their deaths in their 60s in 1924 — she in April and he in July. Thereafter, the children kept the 80-acre farm

· ·

and had a tenant family living in the house and sharecropping the land. When we moved to the farm, my father became the tenant sharecropper. He received one-half of the proceeds and he and his brothers and sisters divided the other half. Next to this farm was another 156 acres that my father had purchased in the 1920s.

During the Depression, my father could not keep up the payments on its debt, but the debt was more than the farm would sell for, so no one foreclosed. Thus, he kept it and farmed it (with a tenant farmer) along with his family place.

Mainly we raised tobacco, our "cash" crop, and corn. We also grew hay to feed our horses and milk cows and had the usual assortment of hogs and chickens. Later, my father added sheep, producing wool and lambs. We ate very well from a big garden, a berry patch and on fried chicken and country ham. But cash, as was the case on most farms during the Depression, was always a short commodity.

My days during these years revolved around farm chores and school. Initially, I was enrolled in junior high school in New Castle and I entered high school there in 1938. My morning walk to catch the school bus was only half a mile and attending school in the county seat of Henry County gave me all the conveniences of the big city.

· · · · ·

In 1942 at age 16, I graduated from high school as class valedictorian and hoped I had already seen about all I would ever see of life on a farm. America's entry into World War II had occurred during my senior year, but because of my age, I was not yet draft material. As a result, I began to

• •

search for a college that would give me the education I wanted in business and accommodate my rural background.

This search led to the Bowling Green College of Commerce of Bowling Green Business University (affectionately known as "B.U.") in southern Kentucky, a school with an excellent reputation for training young men and women in accounting, business and the secretarial sciences.

B.U. (now part of Western Kentucky University) also happened to have, because most of the eligible boys had been taken by the military, a student body with a male-to-female ratio of about one-to-20. The only males in school were those too young, too old, or physically unfit for military duty. Those of us in the fortunate minority dutifully endured the rigors of this imbalance as our contribution to th over-all war effort.

• • • • •

Our family finances were stretched to the limit by my entering college. However, my parents firmly supported my efforts. I helped meet the financial requirements by waiting tables at a boarding house, serving as an accounting laboratory assistant at B.U. and, later, working for a local Plymouth/DeSoto dealer as the bookkeeper. The latter experience proved especially interesting and educational.

The dealership was owned and operated by a man named Walter Darby. Since there were no new cars being produced because of the war, he had refocused his business on repair work, his main source of income, and used cars.

He worked hard, especially at keeping up to date on everything that

• • • • • • • • • • • • • • • • • • •

was going on in Bowling Green. He seemed to know everything there was to know about nearly everyone in town, particularly who was or was not a good credit risk. I learned a lot about people from him, which came in handy in later years.

❖   ❖

• • • • • • • • • • • • • • • • • • • •

College Life and the Army

The Japanese language wasn't much help in Panama

During the summer of 1944, when I was 18 and back home in Henry County between my sophomore and junior years at B.U., my draft number was called. I traveled to the induction center in Cincinnati, Ohio, for the required physical and mental examinations, selected the Navy as my preferable branch of service and returned home to await further notice.

When no call had arrived by the end of summer, I returned to college and awaited further instructions. That notice did not arrive until early 1945. Since the school year was almost over, I asked for, and was granted, a month's deferment until the end of my junior year.

When I got to the induction center this time, I was retested and again passed the physical and mental exams. I then learned I was being assigned to the Army. The people in charge were not impressed by my having earlier selected the Navy. "That's tough. As far as we're concerned you are new

. . . .

meat. We need you for the Army and you are now in the Army." That was
it.

The group with whom I had passed through the induction center was
sent to Ft. McClellan, Alabama, which was the hottest place I had ever
been, for basic infantry training. The heat was insufferable and,
of course, those were the days long before air conditioning, not that it
would have made any difference since we spent most of our time in the
field.

During the first few weeks at Ft. McClellan, I was given a series of
language aptitude tests. After completing basic training, a few of my fellow
recruits and I were selected for schooling in the Japanese language, customs
and culture under the Army Specialized Training Program (ASTP). This
training program was part of the military's preparations for the invasion of
the Japanese mainland, which was then projected to take place in the spring
of 1946.

With a few of my associates from Ft. McClellan, I was sent off
to the program. Interestingly, the Army, having subjected us to a
sweltering summer in Alabama, apparently thought that we should be
cooled off — so they scheduled those of us who had been in Alabama into
the ASTP program operating at the University of Minnesota in
St. Paul.

By the time I learned Japanese and completed the program, the war
was over and, fortunately for the country and myself, there had been no

invasion.

With the war over, I had the opportunity to enlist in the regular Army for one more year; thereby assuring that my career in the Army would then end. That was an easy decision. I had no more affinity for the Army than I had for the farm.

After enlisting for the additional year, I got a 30-day furlough and went home to Kentucky before reporting to Ft. Pickett, Virginia, where I was assigned to a group being outfitted for service in Europe. But, when the train left, there were a few extra people who apparently were not needed in Europe. I was one of them, so I went back to Ft. Pickett a bit longer.

The next group put together at Ft. Pickett was to be shipped to the Panama Canal Zone and, as luck would have it, I was included in that group. Upon arriving in Panama, I quickly changed my mind about the weather in Alabama. As I found out over the next year, the tropics are really hot. Of course, I also discovered that my Japanese language training was of little value on a military post overlooking the Miraflores Locks in Panama...where nearly everyone spoke Spanish.

. . . . .

In January 1947 I was honorably discharged from the Army and re-entered B.U. I was able to transfer many of the Army credits from the University of Minnesota, allowing me to graduate in June of 1947 with a bachelor's degree in accounting. There really were few reasons to linger on beyond the one semester anyway, especially since the post-war male-female

• • • • • • • • • • • • • • • • • • • •

ratio was a more normal 50-50. College life was not the same as it had been in my earlier years.

With the G.I. Bill available, I applied for graduate school. Northwestern University in Evanston, Illinois, was my first choice and I was accepted on the condition that I come to Evanston for the summer to take a number of prerequisite courses to the Master's program. With the other choice being 12-to-14 hour days back on the farm in Henry County, and most of that time behind a pair of horses, I picked Evanston and makeup classes so I would be ready to enter Northwestern's master's program in September of 1947.

In August of 1948 I graduated from Northwestern with a Master of Business Administration degree, a fairly rare course of study at the time, and stayed in Chicago to study for the Certified Public Accountant exam, which I passed in November of 1948.

By then, I was 22 years old and it was time to find a job and a career.

❖ ❖

Chapter III

. . . .

Hooked on Railroads at Age 10

Coal miners' strike rings wedding bells, signals new beginning

The railroad industry has always fascinated me. My first visit to a rail yard, at age 10, was with my mother's brother, Alva B. Whiteley, a conductor on the Baltimore & Ohio Railroad (B&O). He lived in North Vernon, Indiana, which is on the B&O's Cincinnati-St. Louis line. When he took us on his caboose in the local yard, B&O's streamlined passenger train, the "National Limited," passed through. This really impressed me because I had been used to the traditionally styled passenger trains with steam locomotives.

Another railroader in the family was my mother's cousin, Robert Whiteley, an engineer on the Chesapeake & Ohio Railway (C&O), operating trains between Lexington and Ashland, Kentucky. He was still working for the C&O when I began my railroad career. After retiring, he moved to Corbin, Kentucky, where he lived until his death in 1999 at age 97.

. . . . .

. . . .

When I was in college at Bowling Green, the Louisville & Nashville Railroad was my preferred travel route from Henry County. When I got to Northwestern, I often visited rail yards in the Chicago area to watch the arrival and departure of the new post-war streamliners, and traveled on the new trains whenever possible to visit family or friends.

The Chicago Railroad Fair in the summer of 1948 also afforded an opportunity to learn about new developments in the industry, as well as view the latest in new equipment. So perhaps it was preordained that my interest in railroads and accounting would be combined into the subject for my MBA thesis, "The Separation of Railroad Operating Expenses between Freight and Passenger Services."

. . . . .

With two accounting/finance degrees and a CPA certificate, it seemed appropriate to visit several accounting firms, and offer my services to the profession after graduation. Hoping to combine pleasure with business, I also decided to interview with several railroad companies with headquarters in Chicago, including the Illinois Central, the Milwaukee Road, the Chicago and Northwestern and the Burlington Road.

In short order, I had job offers from the accounting firms. I heard nothing from the railroads. Then two of my college professors who knew my love for the industry suggested I travel to Cleveland to explore employment opportunities with the C&O. It was a most fortuitous suggestion.

By coincidence, C&O had just acquired a 10 percent interest in the New York Central Railroad, and a small group was assembling in the presi-

• • • • • • • • • • • • • • • • • • • •

dent's office to analyze its new investment. I was offered the chance to be the finance member of an eight-person group, with the high-sounding title of Staff Analyst, with headquarters in Cleveland, reporting to the assistant to the president of the company. Because the C&O's offer of $300 a month was higher than that of other companies and the job appeared to offer greater opportunities, it was an easy choice. Frankly, I would have taken the job at the same salary offered by the other companies. I just liked railroads and, on January 3, 1949, I began my railroad career.

• • • • •

   Living in Cleveland was exciting for a country boy, and after a few weeks in a small hotel room, I found lodging with a family in the western suburb of Lakewood. Boarding at the same place was another relative new-comer to C&O, Alan Cripe. Alan later achieved distinction as the designer of C&O's "Train X," a high-speed passenger train, and a rail-highway vehi-cle known as "Railvan" or "Roadrailer."

   Later versions of the "Train X" concept are being used by European railroads, and the National Railroad Passenger Corp. (Amtrak) is using very similar train sets on its Pacific Northwest Corridor. Built by Talgo Inc., the American affiliate of Spain's Pantentes Talgo SA and known as the "Talgo," this equipment is articulated and operates in a 12-car set that tilts when rounding curves and has a top speed of 125 miles an hour. At the turn of the century, Amtrak tested a later version of the equipment at the railroad-testing center in Pueblo, Colorado. Alan's "Roadrailer" units were used in 1999 and 2000 with great success by several of the nation's railroads in regular intermodal service.

• • • • • • • • • • • • • • • • • • • •

Alan stayed with C&O for several years, designing new equipment and new lettering systems, but later left to form his own company to perfect the "Roadrailer" concept. Like so many brilliant people, Alan — at least in 1949 — was a man far, far ahead of his time.

• • • • •

In March 1949 — just two months after joining the C&O — my career with the company took an unexpected and potentially treacherous turn, thanks to the United Mine Workers (UMW).

The UMW struck the coal industry, which brought a quick halt to nearly one-half of C&O's revenues. Given that circumstance, C&O had no alternative other than instituting significant cost cutting measures, and every department was ordered to cut employment by 25 percent. The President's office was not excused from this and my Staff Analyst position was one of the two jobs cut in our eight-person office. It was a dark day in Cleveland for me when I was ordered to turn in my railroad passes and leave the premises. What I thought and hoped would be a bright and promising railroad career had lasted exactly two months and I thought to myself, "This is a heck of a way to start a railroad career" and, as the old expression goes, "A Hell of a way to run a railroad."

Years later when I reflected on the situation and the circumstances, I realized that I really didn't know what to expect when I went to work for the C&O — other than I sure didn't figure on ever being fired, much less in two months.

With no idea how long the UMW strike would last, what it would mean for the C&O or myself, no job and no money, I headed back to

• •

Henry County and the farm. My timing in that regard could not have been better for my father. Having arrived just in time to help with the spring plowing, I quickly found myself behind a pair of horses and doing other farm chores, all the while hoping (but with no promise or other assurance) that I would somehow be able to resume my career at C&O.

. . . . .

The "hiatus" in Henry County, however, turned out to have a wonderful silver lining that has lasted to this day. One of my former B.U. classmates was living in Louisville. I went over for a visit and he arranged a blind date for me with a North Carolinian, Betty Jean Wright. I had always believed everything happened for a reason, and that introduction and blind date proved no different. Betty and I were married almost exactly a year later.

. . . . .

By the middle of April 1949, the UMW strike had been resolved, and I was thrilled to be recalled to my former position of Staff Analyst at the C&O...with a 10 percent increase in salary. I didn't know then, and I still don't know today, why I received the raise. It never occurred to me to ask. I was just happy to be heading back to Cleveland and off the farm...and hoped it was for good this time.

. . . . .

Over the years, I've been asked if I had any career or job goals in mind in those early days. To varying degrees those asking have found it somewhat amazing that the answer is, "No." In fact, I was just thankful to know that I would soon be back working for the C&O. The only thing I knew for certain was that once I got back I was going to give my best and hope for the best. If anything, I suppose I was simply looking forward to someday having a good job in the Accounting Department. I never dreamed of heading the Accounting Department, or becoming C&O's chief financial officer, much less its chairman, president and chief executive officer.

Some would probably say I was just plain lucky to have advanced in the company as I did and, to a certain extent, they would be right. But I believe there is a much bigger message in my own experience, especially for young people entering the business world — in fact for anyone entering the workplace, regardless of the job. And also for the Human Resources professionals that these days seem to believe everyone at every level should have a planned out career path from the day they are hired.

Everyone would be better off, I believe, if they simply concentrated on doing their very best and then basically let nature take its course. Good people doing good work, it seems to me, almost always are recognized and rewarded with good jobs. On the other hand, I have seen a lot of very talented people get caught up in what I call "running for office." They spent more time working to get to what they thought should be their next job, than they did on the job they had. And it showed in their work, in their ability to work with others, in their relationship with their supervisor, in just about every way one can imagine and almost always to their professional, if not also their personal, detriment.

As for the Human Resources professionals, I would urge they save the career planning for later and concentrate their efforts on helping all employees to do their best in their jobs. The HR folks would better serve everyone's best interests by keeping an eye on equal opportunity while promoting mentoring and diversity and encouraging training and education.

. . . . .

After I received the call asking me to come back to work, I hastily packed my suitcase, prepared to leave the farm duties to my father and began to think about resuming my analysis of the New York Central. But by then, the Interstate Commerce Commission had rejected the C&O's application to control the company through its 10 percent ownership. I returned to find that our group had been reassigned to various other offices and duties, most of which required visits to various parts of the C&O system. For me, it meant a three-month stay in Detroit in the summer of 1949 reviewing accounting systems.

(Not being able to do anything with its 10 percent ownership of New York Central, C&O sold it to two Texans, Murchison and Richardson, for $25 million. Later, in 1954, Robert R. Young was able to get the shareholders of the New York Central to vote in himself and his group of directors.)

. . . . .

In those early days at the C&O, my "big boss" (Carleton Meyer, assistant to the president) would occasionally visit our office and have closed-door meetings with the senior members of our group. Sitting on the outside, I often wondered what great plans were being developed inside, and wished I could be a member of such an "inner group." Later, when I was leading those closed-door meetings, I often wished I could be back on the outside, doing something else.

Being young and single and a devoted railfan, the opportunities to travel over the railroad made my job a great delight, and I availed myself of every opportunity to see the areas covered by the railroad. In addition, and more importantly, I used my railroad pass most weekends to travel back to Kentucky to visit Betty, since our first "blind date" had developed into something deeper and held every promise of being more lasting.

By that fall Betty and I were engaged and, after a year of commuting, we were married — on April 15, 1950 — in Louisville. Betty was soon introduced to the traveling life of a railroad employee. We spent our first summer of married life together in Detroit, sub-leasing an apartment from a local physician whose family summered in Southern Ontario. However, I spent most of the summer on the road studying the passenger operations of the Pere Marquette, the first cost studies of rail passenger services that isolated revenue and expenses train-by-train and line segment.

Chapter IV

. . . .

The Beginnings
of Internal Audit

And...of my experiences with John Edward Kusik

B y the summer of 1950, the need for a separate office of "The
Assistant to the President" had disappeared, and members of the
group were released or reassigned to other departments of the company.

   With my accounting background, I was transferred to the Accounting
Department, headed by an Estonian immigrant named John Edward
Kusik, who had joined C&O a year earlier from General Electric.

   John Kusik, who at this point I had barely met, but would later prove
to have a major influence on my career, had definite ideas about transform-
ing a traditional railroad accounting office into something different.

   One of those differences was the establishment of an internal auditing
function. On September 1, 1950, the office was set up and I became the
first internal auditor employed by C&O, adding many other interesting
studies to those I was already doing on passenger train costs.

   In those days, railroads used traveling auditors to check accounts of
station agents and yard offices, but the idea of reviewing procedures and

• •

headquarters offices was unknown. Under the direction of an acting chief internal auditor, who was on loan from C&O's outside accounting firm, I began the new and novel experience of internal auditing.

• • • • •

With the new assignment came my transfer to C&O's historic operating headquarters offices in Richmond, Virginia.

After having had a delightful summer "honeymoon" in Michigan, Betty and I were transported to the Old Dominion. Once there, Betty again learned about the traveling life of a railroader. We also had a number of other daunting experiences, including renting our first apartment, buying our first automobile, traveling over the rail system, and learning to speak and understand "Virginian."

Work, in the meantime, was going extremely well. The Internal Audit Department expanded in number and scope, and its findings and recommendations became an integral element of the accounting function throughout the company.

• • • • •

One of our more interesting findings was the lack of basic accounting knowledge by officers and key employees of the Accounting Department. Double-entry bookkeeping, concepts of asset and liability accounting, and other elemental accounting principles were virtually unknown in the company, especially in the field offices.

In the fall of 1951, as a result of this finding, I was given the assign-

• • • • • • • • • • • • • • • • • • • •

ment of developing a basic accounting course for railroad officers and employees. Borrowing liberally and literally from my college accounting textbooks, and using the prescribed Interstate Commerce Commission chart of accounts, a 20-chapter Basic Accounting Course was ready for use by the end of the year.

Recognizing these additional duties and my internal audit responsibilities, my title was changed on January 1, 1952, to Staff Assistant.

From January through May of 1952, 24 officers and key employees of the Accounting Department attended twice-weekly classes from 4 to 6 p.m. — in other words half on company time; the other half on their own time — studying accounting.

Having a young college graduate teach veteran accountants a subject in which they had spent most of their business career was a novel experience, both to the instructor and the instructed. But, by the time of "graduation" in May all agreed that the ordeal had been worthwhile, and several additional basic accounting classes were offered in subsequent years in Richmond, Huntington and Detroit, a number of which I also taught.

•   •   •   •   •

One of my Richmond students was the General Auditor, the top accountant in Richmond for C&O, Clarence E. "Buck" Weaver, who reported to the Controller in Cleveland, Roger F. Brown.

Weaver didn't know a debit from a credit and he wasn't unique.

Each department in Richmond kept its own records. Later, when many of the accounting processes were mechanized, they did the same thing by punch card instead of by hand. This was the same routine they had been following for years and years. Nothing was consolidated — the totals were transferred to the head office in Cleveland and that was it. No one in Richmond knew how the accounts all went together, and not at all surprisingly, they didn't really care.

Our basic accounting course started out with simple, double-entry bookkeeping. With that learned, the "students" began to understand how their individual offices and departments fit into the overall picture. Once they understood it, they took to the concept.

Other auditing assignments arose during the year, in addition to the continuing studies of passenger train costs. By late 1952, a monthly Statement of Passenger Train Operations (revenues, costs and net loss), by individual train, had been developed and put into to routine production by the Accounting Department.

These statements served as the underlying data base for many C&O passenger train discontinuance, "train-off" cases before federal and state regulatory agencies, as the development of new highways and higher automobile production and then the beginnings of air travel led to the demise of most rail passenger services.

While developing the source data and the accounting methodology for these statements, I spent considerable time in the C&O's Huntington, West Virginia, accounting office, where several friendly

. . . .

employees were of great assistance to me.

Only later did I learn that these "friends" were actually clerical union officers, who subsequently filed claims with the company alleging that I was performing union work that was covered by their contract. In other words, they sought to be paid for my work.

Even though developmental studies, which was what I was doing, were "exempt" and did not require the use of employees represented by the union, the company, consistent with the union-appeasing milieu of that time, paid the claims...and I learned a valuable lesson.

. . . . .

After three years of internal auditing and the variety of staff work that came with that assignment, it was felt that I needed some "line," supervisory experience. On January 1, 1953, I was appointed Assistant to the Auditor of Expenditures in Richmond.

This was a most welcome change. Clearly it offered me an opportunity to expand my understanding of the business and to test my abilities as a manager. And it brought an end to the extensive travels of audit. With son Tom — Hays Thomas Watkins, III — having been born on December 1, 1952, just a month earlier, I was especially looking forward to spending more time at home.

In my new job, having earlier been chastened by my experiences in Huntington with the clerks' union, I observed the letter and spirit of union contracts as I learned to be a supervisor, improved accounting systems and procedures and coordinated clerical work in the office.

However, it turned out that I really did not need to be overly concerned. The cooperative spirit of the Richmond offices was much more conducive to a well-functioning environment than was that I had encountered just months earlier while doing passenger train studies further west.

There was some travel involved during this period and I distinctly (and very fondly) remember a systemwide departmental staff meeting in March 1953 at The Greenbrier, C&O's legendary resort at White Sulphur Springs, West Virginia. From the moment I saw it I felt it was a special, very special place. To this day I believe it is the crown jewel of our company. In my mind, no other hotel in the world compares to it. Not one.

❖ ❖

Chapter V

· ·

The "Temporary" Return to Cleveland

A three-week assignment turns out to last 28 years

My first sojourn to Richmond ended in September 1953 when I was called to the office of Buck Weaver, my former student and the General Auditor, the top accounting officer in Richmond. Weaver told me I was being temporarily reassigned to the Controller, Roger F. Brown, in the corporate accounting office in Cleveland, and went to considerable lengths explaining that this assignment was to be for just a short while — "three weeks or so."

He did say the assignment could last a little longer, but neither he nor I had any way of knowing that it would last a whole lot longer — 28 years to be exact. Or, that when I did leave Cleveland, on November 1, 1980, that I would return to Richmond. He also did not tell me that he too was being sent to Cleveland — so his concern about my well being was mixed with his own concerns about his future.

After placing our furniture in temporary storage in Richmond, and settling Betty and Tom with my parents in Henry County, I appeared in Cleveland for my "temporary" assignment.

. . . .

In just a few days, though, it was apparent to everyone, including me, that this was no short-term, temporary project. My first tour of duty in Richmond and my time in the expenditures office had summarily ended.

We found temporary quarters in a Cleveland suburb, sub-leasing from a couple that preferred to spend their winters in Florida rather than Cleveland. The furniture from Richmond and Betty and Tom soon arrived in Cleveland, and life resumed back in the city where four and a half years earlier I had started my railroad career.

. . . . .

Shortly after arriving back in Cleveland we learned that my former Lakewood housemate, Alan Cripe, had formed a construction company in his off-duty time and was building houses in the eastern Cleveland suburb of Euclid. The plans looked interesting, the price range seemed to be within our grasp, and there was an opportunity for owner-construction work in lieu of the cash down payment. Papers were signed in the fall, and we looked forward to moving into our first-owned house the following spring.

Like many construction projects, however, unforeseen delays arose, and we were forced to find another home the following summer, leasing from a member of the Cleveland Orchestra whose family spent the summer on a farm in southern Ohio. Construction of the basic structure of the house was barely completed by September when the orchestra member returned for the new concert season. But we proudly moved into our partially completed home with great anticipation.

The subsequent fall and winter necessitated continued work on our

• • • • • • • • • • • • • • • • • • • •

part on the house and the experience of sanding floors, installing electrical and plumbing work, interior and exterior painting, and lawn work furnished excellent examples of the joys of home ownership. We bought other houses, but we never again went the owner-construction route.

Over the years we had three houses in Cleveland. The first was the house we built with Alan that we moved into in the fall of 1954 and where we lived until 1966 when we bought a house in Moreland Hills. Then, in 1972, we had a house built on Quail Hollow Drive, also in Moreland Hills, where we lived until we moved to Richmond in 1981.

• • • • •

My job in Cleveland was to answer a foot-high pile of one-line notes, questions really, that John Kusik, then Vice President-Finance of the C&O, had been sending down to Brown. Kusik had the habit of sending such notes to various people on his staff and he expected answers. Brown, however, had not been answering them and he and Kusik, it seemed, were on the verge of open warfare. In actuality, though, it was Kusik's executive secretary, Mrs. Lillian Prond, who was giving Brown all the problems and he knew it.

Mrs. Prond had a follow-up system that worked. Even worse for Brown, she could really throw her weight around; use her influence. And she had plenty of influence with Kusik. Brown apparently had told Mrs. Prond more than once that he would "Get to those questions when he got around to them." That just led to more complaining to Kusik about Brown.

Finally, in desperation and knowing that Mrs. Prond was going to cause him real problems with Kusik if he didn't do something quickly,

Brown decided he needed someone to gather up the answers and get Mrs. Prond off of his back. Doing that, making peace with Mrs. Prond and then keeping things under control between her and Brown, was my job.

The key to reaching rapprochement between Brown and Kusik was found by developing an excellent working relationship with Mrs. Prond. After a few difficult months, the original stack was cleaned up and future informational requests and comprehensive replies were flowing regularly and quickly. My "temporary" assignment was completed.

Had I not been successful, I am absolutely certain Mrs. Prond eventually would have convinced Kusik to fire Brown. She knew where all the buttons were and how to push them. She was the ultimate executive secrtary, and I had learned where the real power rested in most corporations — in the executive secretaries.

That experience reinforced my belief that being nice and reasonable to people and answering their questions, regardless of how stupid they or their questions might appear, was the way to work. From then on, as far as I was concerned, every question got an answer and it didn't make any difference to me who was doing the asking.

Over the next 10 years, I went through a fascinating series of job changes. The first two years were spent on increasingly complex assignments from the controller, Roger Brown, and also from Kusik.

It was during this time that C&O became the first railroad company to enter the computer era, purchasing and installing a Univac 1 from Remington Rand. This occasioned many visitors from within the rail

• • • • • • • • • • • • • • • • • • • •

industry and prompted one of my more interesting assignments from Kusik.

With so many people coming through to see the computer, to learn how it worked and how we were using it, Kusik asked that a brief booklet be prepared to explain its operation and the work we were processing with it. After rejecting repeated attempts by those in charge of the machine, Kusik gave the assignment to LeRoy Hurt and me.

Roy and I protested that we knew nothing about the computer or its inner workings and Kusik thought that was just fine, suggesting that perhaps such ignorance would be of great value in writing the booklet. We turned to cartoons and "Peter Rabbit" language. The result was a small booklet that comfortably fit in the inside pocket of a suit jacket and explained the computer, its workings and the work C&O had it performing in everyday language. It was a hit with Kusik, but my experiences with the computer were not yet at an end.

• • • • •

With the use of the computer expanding rapidly, Kusik decided that every Finance Department officer should learn computer programming, how to write the instructive code that told the computer what to do. Outside experts were brought in to teach the classes.

After two weeks of intense study it was obvious that my talents did not reside in the area of computer programming. The instructor tactfully, but firmly, suggested that perhaps my time might be more productively spent in other areas of the department. In this manner, my budding career in computers came to an abrupt end and I was returned to the more mundane activity of accounting to await my fate.

• • • • • • • • • • • • • • • • • • • •

· · · · ·

Shortly thereafter I learned that my next career development assignment would be in the C&O's accounting office in Huntington, West Virginia, in some sort of supervisory role. This did not at all appeal to me or to Betty. We had become reasonably well acclimated to Cleveland's weather, had finished our owner-built house, were involved in local community and church activities and starting to feel right at home in Cleveland.

Fortunately, after several tension-filled weeks of discussions at home and in the office, Kevin J. Cahill suggested at lunch one day that we switch assignments. He was unhappy working for A. F. Dell Isola who was then Chief of Budget Services and running the Financial Planning office.

Dell Isola was a very intense fellow. In fact, he later died of a heart attack at age 38. For my part, though, staying in Cleveland under any circumstances beat moving to Huntington, so Kevin and I just switched assignments. And so, effective May 16, 1956, I stayed in Cleveland and became a Senior Budget Analyst, working for Dell Isola, and Kevin went to Huntington.

❖   ❖

Chapter VI

. . . .

An Introduction to Financial Planning

Being one of "those people in Cleveland"

One of the many innovations Vice President Kusik brought with him to C&O from General Electric was the establishment of a financial planning office. Located in Cleveland, it accumulated budget and forecasting data from all parts of the company, summarized this information and then prepared reports and presentations for C&O's top management.

Having switched jobs and cities with Kevin Cahill, I found myself in the modernistic-design "Chart Room" where all the data was gathered and charted.

Life in the Chart Room wasn't exactly dull. For starters, the idea of making short- and long-range forecasts to "those people in Cleveland" was not universally accepted by the top officers of the Operating and Maintenance Departments in Richmond. That fact alone created enough tension to keep life there plenty interesting.

One duty of the Financial Planning office was the issuance of

. . . .

a "Flash Report," an estimate of the immediately past month's results on the first working day of the following month. We followed it with a "final" report of operations by the end of the first week of the new month.

Railroads had traditionally issued results about the 20th of the following month, but Kusik's goal was to advance that reporting date as much as possible. His reasoning was that nothing could affect results after a month ended, and the sooner the results of a month were finalized, reported and analyzed, the sooner everyone would turn their attention to the new, current month.

By the time Kusik retired as Vice President-Finance in 1962, the monthly reports were being issued on the fourth working day of the following month. I pushed it up to the first work day when I was named to head the department in 1964. We were reporting every month in those days, not quarterly. We continued this right through the Chessie/Seaboard merger and the creation of CSX Corporation.

When Seaboard's people found out we were going to continue first day reporting after the merger, they were horrified. But we did and it wasn't until after I retired that my successor, John W. Snow, changed the practice and CSX began reporting financial results like all other companies, a couple of weeks after the close of a quarter. By then, the size and complexity of CSX's worldwide operations had made its continuance impractical.

. . . . .

Getting back to the early days of these reports, the key to their accu-

• •

racy was close communication between the Financial Planning staff in Cleveland and the field operating officers out along the "line of road." In the beginning, the field group was reluctant to share data with us in Cleveland and that caused major difficulties. With the help of the then president, Walter Tuohy, and other top officials, communications gradually improved, but not without forbearance and patience from each group. Learning the mind-set of operating officials would prove invaluable in later years, so the difficulties I experienced in those days tuned out to be of significant benefit.

• • • • •

After experiencing a year of constant challenges and pressures in the Financial Planning office, I got an unexpected call and an offer of employment from a former head of the office, who had left C&O for a key position with W.R. Grace & Company in New York.

While I had no great desire to live in the New York area, the offered position was interesting, and the compensation attractive. The thought of working in the Wall Street area was intoxicating, and there was a certain appeal to leaving behind the stress of Financial Planning at C&O.

Since it did not appear desirable to explain my pending absence, I took a day's vacation and went by train to New York to explore the job. When I returned to Cleveland the next day, several hours late because of a freak late-April snowstorm, I was met at the office by a worried finance official. He immediately offered me a new position as head of the Financial Planning office, actually Budget Services, with a substantial increase in salary.

• • • • • • • • • • • • • • • • • • • •

Whether he knew the purpose of my excursion to New York was never mentioned, but the new challenges — and salary — were more than adequate to keep me in the railroad business.

· · · · ·

The new job was as Chief of Budget Services and I assumed my responsibilities on May 1, 1957. This meant increased responsibilities, new challenges and additional opportunities to develop communication channels around the railroad — and increased patience. In addition, I was given the Internal Audit function, which had increased dramatically in scope and numbers since my days as the first and only Internal Auditor.

However, these new responsibilities didn't last long. Just eight months later, my career development took another direction, and I was "promoted" to General Auditor in charge of corporate accounts in the Accounting Department.

Two weeks after moving back to the accounting area, an executive recruiter called regarding a search for a new controller of Delta Airlines. How my name appeared on his screen was never revealed, but the challenge of a new position on the ground was strong enough to prevent me from flying off to Atlanta even though it was becoming clear that I couldn't hold a job for long on the ground.

· · · · ·

Four months later I was promoted to General Auditor-Operations Accounting, in charge of all payroll and expenditure activities of the sys-

• •

tem. This required additional travel to my old haunts in Richmond, where I had worked earlier; Detroit, where I spent my first summer of married life; and Huntington, where I had almost been sent. It also required that I learn about computer operations and computer-produced statements...but not computer coding and programming.

Having been trained as an accountant in my college days, I decided that this was my area of expertise, and envisioned settling down to a career in railroad accounting.

Alas, such was not to be. Sixteen months later I was returned to staff work as the General Staff Officer of the Finance Department.

Chapter VII

. . . .

A Big,
But Nebulous Job

"You should learn how to be an official of the company.
I am here to help."

M y new assignment as General Staff Officer brought me directly
under Kusik. When I started, I wasn't exactly certain what the job
entailed other than being a high-level assistant to him. I knew it was a big
job, but it also was nebulous.

The job included organizational planning for the Finance
Department, training and a number of other duties involving change in the
way the railroad was being operated and managed. As noted earlier, John
Kusik was one of the forward thinkers in the railroad industry. He had a lot
of ideas about how to run his department and others. He frequently suggested to other departments how they should run their activities. He had
no qualms about giving advice to anyone – whether they wanted such
advice or not.

. . . . .

Just as I was getting comfortable in the job, it was time for another
move — "Broadening my experiences," he said. This time, it was to the

. . . .

Treasury Department, an area completely new to me. As one of two Assistant Treasurers of the company, I was now officially a corporate officer. A year later, I succeeded John F. Kerslake as Treasurer, and another year after that, "Assistant Vice President" was added to my Treasurer's title. But no one ever gave me the combination to the company safe, so I never saw any "real" money.

. . . . .

My relationship with John Kusik was hectic, stormy, close, fearful, and most any other adjective one might choose. Apparently, he felt that I had some potential and that he should challenge me at every opportunity...and he did. In later years he would frequently call me at night at home, generally after he had had a few cocktails, and proceed to deliver long, long lectures.

Probably the most notable of these calls was on a New Year's Eve, when we had a house full of company. He was particularly vociferous that night about my abilities and activities. I had found that the way to deal with his bluster was to listen and, occasionally, agree with him, and say "Yes, you have a good point and perhaps I should have done something differently." Usually, after half an hour or 45 minutes he would run out of steam and hang up. But, this night he ran on for more than an hour.

The interesting thing about those conversations was that he always seemed to remember them the next morning. He would reference some specific point he had made and then say, "I hope I wasn't too strong on the telephone, but I'm doing this for your own good," or "You should learn how to be an official of the company and I'm here to help."

. . . .

. . . . .

In 1964, I was named Vice President-Finance, succeeding to Kusik's title. Actually, he had retired in 1962 as Vice President-Finance, at the age of 65, and then immediately had the board of directors change his title to Chairman of the Finance Committee of the Board. With that title, he continued as C&O's Chief Financial Officer as if nothing had ever happened. That was his style.

C&O didn't have a Vice President-Finance from 1962 until I was named to the job in 1964. All through that time and well after he was calling me at night, still giving me his input.

Most of what Kusik had to say was of value and was well taken. I am certain he never realized the impact, the good influence he had on me. I learned immensely from him. But I never felt completely at ease with him and that was his way of operating.

. . . . .

John Kusik was the son of a Baptist preacher in Estonia. After World War I, he immigrated to the United States, learned English, graduated from the University of Virginia and went to work for General Electric. He overcame tremendous odds, headed GE's auditing department, and worked in China, among other places. He felt that he should instill into other people the same spirit of hard work and dedication to work that he had adopted.

Of course, I wasn't the only person he "adopted." He was always challenging me against Bob McGowan, another young finance officer, and vice versa. We knew it was going on, and accommodated ourselves to it. Bob

．．．．．．．．．．．．．．．．．．．．

was two years older than I. Generally he was ahead of me. In fact, I succeeded Bob in a couple of jobs. I inherited his secretary twice when he
moved on. We did not achieve parity until December 1964 when I was
named Vice President-Finance and Bob was appointed Vice President-
Planning.

．．．．．

All through this period, Kusik basically was still running the department. He asked me to send him copies of every letter I wrote... and I did.
In fact he continued to do that even after I became President.

In 1966, when Walter Tuohy died and Gregory Devine took
over as Chief Executive Officer, Kusik was appointed Vice Chairman of
the Board. It was only with this change that I began to feel the department
was fully my responsibility, even though Kusik remained with the company
another six years. He was not to retire until April 1972, and even then not
voluntarily.

❖ ❖

Chapter VIII

. . . .

The Modern Merger Movement Begins

C&O gains control of B&O

T he railroad merger movement in the modern era began in late 1959 and early 1960, when the Pennsylvania Railroad and the New York Central Railroad first talked about getting together. As soon as word got out about their potential plans, several of the smaller eastern roads also entered into discussions. As I remember, those talks included William White of the Lackawanna, Walter Tuohy of the C&O, Howard Simpson of the B&O and probably one or two others. The Pennsylvania/Central talks shortly fell apart, but the other discussions resulted in Tuohy and Simpson agreeing to the C&O/B&O "affiliation," which also gave me a first-hand introduction to railroad merger studies and railroad mergers.

This time around, while there certainly was plenty of excitement and there would be numerous unexpected turns of events in the years ahead, a coal miner's strike wasn't on the horizon and there was hardly any chance I would get sent packing back to the Henry County farm.

. . . . .

The mergers, acquisitions, consolidations and control proceedings that

• •

took place during the 22-year period from 1960 through 1982 differed greatly from those of earlier generations. The first 60 years of the 1900s mainly were marked by transactions involving a stronger property's purchase of a road experiencing financial troubles, if not one already in receivership, or moves by outside interests to acquire control of rail properties, such as the Van Sweringens' with their Alleghany Corporation that later was used for the same purpose by Robert R. Young.

While passage of the Transportation Act of 1920 signaled a more open-minded public policy on railroad mergers, the industry remained relatively static for the next 40 years despite enactment of the Transportation Act of 1940, largely due to the effects of the two World Wars and the relative financial well-being of the industry. Throughout the 1950s, there were only two mergers of note — the Nashville, Chattanooga & St. Louis into the Louisville & Nashville and the Virginian into Norfolk & Western.

The dawn of the 1960s, however, brought a flood of applications to the Interstate Commerce Commission (ICC), and the industry as we know it today began to take shape. Dozens of applications, including the C&O's for authority to acquire control of the B&O, and, later, the Western Maryland, were decided by the ICC in that decade. In fact, during 1963 alone, 17 applications were filed with the ICC seeking approval of mergers, consolidations, or financial control.

The merger applications filed in the 1960s resulted in creation of the Seaboard Coast Line system and the Erie-Lackawanna; merger of the Nickel Plate into the Norfolk & Western; expansions of the Soo Line, the Burlington and the Chicago & North Western; and numer-

• • • • • • • • • • • • • • • • • • •

ous other mergers and consolidations. The most notable was the merger of the Pennsylvania and New York Central to form the ill-fated Penn Central. As a result of this activity, the number of Class I railroads in the United States declined from 126 to 106 during the 1960s. By the end of 1970, the number was 71. The total stood at 38 at December 31, 1980, and today, for all practical purposes is at seven — CSX Transportation (CSXT) and Norfolk Southern in the east; Burlington Northern Sante Fe, Union Pacific Southern Pacific, Kansas City Southern, Canadian Pacific in the west; and the Canadian National/Illinois Central system in the midwest.

• • • • •

We began the C&O/B&O studies just after I had been named General Staff Officer of the Finance Department in September 1959. After getting organized, the work itself took about six months and the formal announcement of the affiliation was made in May 1960, soon after the studies were completed and approved by the two boards of directors.

Immediately after going public with our plans, Alfred E. Perlman, then President of the New York Central, tried to jump into the deal, urging Tuohy and Simpson to reconsider and do a three-way transaction. Simpson felt this reasonable and encouraged it. Tuohy, on the other hand, wanted no part of it. As a result of our studies, Tuohy was well aware of B&O's shaky finances and saw no sense in adding even more problems by including Central's tremendous passenger service burden and its relatively weak financial condition in the mix. Unable to join on friendly terms, Perlman launched a tender offer for B&O, perhaps figuring the worst outcome would be that Tuohy would change his mind and reverse his position on

. . . .

including the Central in the transaction.

Tuohy, however, stood firm and countered Central with continuation of C&O's tender for B&O's shares. Both offers were a combination of stock and cash and, initially, the value of the Central offer was several million dollars higher than the C&O's. As the solicitation efforts progressed through the summer, though, C&O's stock price rose while the Central's lost value. This shifted the value of the offers to C&O's favor. By the end of the tender offers in the fall of 1960, C&O had locked up more than 60 percent of the B&O stock and the Central had only about 20 percent. Tuohy and the C&O had won the first step.

The Central did not go quietly, however, and threatened to contest the transaction in the courts and before the ICC if the C&O went ahead without it. Tuohy pushed on and we filed for control — not for merger — in February 1961. We filed for control rather than merger because of the strong financial position of C&O and the very precarious financial condition of B&O. In so doing, we avoided imperiling C&O's strong balance sheet, preserved C&O's very favorable debt rating and used our overall financial strength to restore the B&O financially and operationally.

. . . . .

The ICC hearings began June 25, 1961, and lasted the remainder of the year. True to his word, Perlman strenuously opposed everything about the transaction. Other railroads also had objections, but they were limited and, basically, were designed — as was not unusual then or even today — to obtain various concessions from C&O or, failing that, to get the ICC to

• •

impose conditions favoring their interests. I am proud to say that the C&O never resorted to such tactics, but that was unique.

The ICC hearing examiner's report (the examiner was an elderly gentleman named Bradford) came out in early 1962, recommending that C&O be granted control. This proved to be only "Round One," though, as the Central appealed to the courts and to the full ICC. Finally, on February 4, 1963, C&O was granted approval (the Central's protestations gained them nothing) and control was exercised.

After control was granted, most of C&O's senior officers began weekly commutes to Baltimore, headquarters of the B&O. All of us had offices in both Cleveland and Baltimore. We boarded a C&O airplane in Cleveland every Monday morning and spent Monday and Tuesday in Baltimore. Tuesday evening we would reverse the trip and return to Cleveland or go on to other points on the system for the remainder of the week.

• • • • •

As noted earlier, John Kusik was still a major presence and basically continued to run the C&O and C&O/B&O Finance Department during this period even though he had "retired" the previous year. It was not surprising then that he made the trips with us to Baltimore every week, which he continued to do even after I was named Vice President-Finance on December 16, 1964.

One of those trips was particularly memorable, when Kusik called me to his room in the Lord Baltimore Hotel on a Monday night. As soon as I entered, he started saying, "Hays, I think it is time we talked about your

. . . .

future. I know you enjoy your family and your church, but you are going to have to make a choice. You are going to have to decide that your time will be devoted to the company. If you do that, you will advance. If you continue to insist on those outside activities, I have grave concern that you won't advance much further in the company."

To this day there isn't any doubt in my mind that he absolutely believed every word of what he said, but I didn't. "Mr. Kusik," I responded, "I refuse to admit that I cannot advance in this company even dividing my time between work, family, church and community. These are all important to me and I will not sacrifice any of them for the sake of another. If that means I have reached my limit, I regret that, but I will not give up my family life; I will not give up my church; and I will not give up my responsibilities to my community."

It was one of the shortest conversations we ever had — before or since — and it also was the first, last and only time I disagreed with him to his face. But I believed then — and even more so now — that anyone who spends all of his or her time on work and has no personal life; no family life; no community life, is probably not a very well-balanced person. People must have outside interests to gain perspective — to have a balanced view of the world.

I have attempted to make this clear by example throughout my career at C&O/B&O, Chessie and CSX and, also, by stating the fact that people should have outside interests at every opportunity when I met with our employees. I wanted to make certain they would never have pursuing such interests held against them, as clearly could have been the case with myself given Kusik's views.

. . . . .

Most of my efforts during my visits to Baltimore after the affiliation – and those of B&O's treasurer, Edward P. Snyder — were focused on managing B&O's tenuous cash position. B&O had been living "hand-to-mouth" for a good while. C&O eased that problem whenever possible, on occasion even before we got control of the property. In fact, on the opening day of the ICC hearings in 1961, I personally carried a C&O check for $7.5 million in my pocket to the hearing, which was given to B&O President Simpson for the purchase of 1,000 scrap cars that were awaiting demolition on B&O lines.

At one point shortly after the ICC decision, B&O had over $12 million of payment vouchers processed and prepared, but being held in Snyder's office. There simply wasn't sufficient cash to cover them. Every week through the balance of 1963 and well into 1964 we had to decide which bills should be released for payment and which ones we should delay. By the end of 1964, the B&O's cash position had turned around and B&O was paying its bills on time. In my mind I can still see the look of utter relief that came over Snyder's face the day we mailed out the last of the vouchers from the original $12 million.

Chapter IX

. . . .

The Remarkable Cyrus Eaton

"Why don't you stick around after your report?"

I n my early days with C&O and C&O/B&O I dealt with a remarkable collection of individuals. One of the most remarkable — if not the most remarkable — was Cyrus S. Eaton. Eaton was one of the most charming, gracious, avaricious individuals I have ever met.

My first meeting with him came in 1954 after returning from New York, having been sent there to inventory Robert R. Young's office furniture. Young had waged and won a proxy fight for control of the New York Central and given up the chairmanship of the C&O in order to move to New York Central as its chairman. As C&O's Chairman, Young had maintained his offices in New York City, hardly ever setting foot in Cleveland. His office was in the Chrysler Building and the C&O board of directors had agreed to transfer the lease and sell the furniture to Young and the Central.

I had never met Young and I did not meet him on this trip, but I did view and list every piece of furniture in his office. It was fine, fine furniture, of Chippendale and other well-known periods and highly valued

. . . .

styles. Having completed my task, I returned to Cleveland and reported my findings to Eaton. He was 70 then, and hardly a retiring figure. Very tall, erect, impressive were my immediate reactions. And he was exceptionally gracious to me as I gave him my report.

Two decades later I would see another side of him. But during this visit, and many others over the years in between, he was most gracious and considerate of this "young fellow," his standard reference to me.

. . . . .

When I became Vice President-Finance of C&O/B&O I began giving the financial reports at the board of directors meetings. At first, I would be called in to give the reports and then leave. Then, after a couple of meetings, Eaton said to me, "Young fellow, why don't you stick around after your report? You might as well sit there through the meeting."

Eaton was probably being nothing more than his normally well-mannered self and thought I would learn more about the company by staying in the meetings. But the result was far-reaching. Sitting there the next several years gave me the great advantage of quietly observing the C&O board meetings. Most importantly, I got to know the directors, see them in action and gain a good understanding of their individual interests, strengths and weaknesses long before I was to become President and Chief Executive Officer and, later, Chairman of the company.

. . . . .

During these intervening years, Eaton occasionally called me to his office on the 36th floor of Terminal Tower, usually to inquire about some specific facet of the company reports or its operations.

. . . .

I was always apprehensive about these meetings. Cyrus Eaton had been a world-renowned figure for many years before I even went to work for C&O and, frankly, I was in awe of the man. But he had a way of putting me at ease, as he did with most everyone, and after we had finished with the question at hand, Eaton often would reminisce about his early days in Cleveland and his love for his birthplace in Nova Scotia.

. . . . .

Cyrus Eaton came to Cleveland as a teenager, to work for his uncle, Charles A. Eaton, who was pastor of the Euclid Avenue Baptist Church. One of the most active and devoted members of the congregation was John D. Rockefeller, Sr. and Eaton, with the help of his pastor uncle, became a clerk to Rockefeller. Later, Pastor Eaton would move to New Jersey, become a very distinguished Congressman and one of the founders of the United Nations.

In his reminiscences, Eaton told some especially interesting stories about the early days of John D. Rockefeller and how over-zealous Ohio tax officials had hounded him out of Cleveland and out of the state. As a result, New York became the headquarters of Standard Oil. When Rockefeller's wife died, he brought her body back in the middle of the night, fearing he might otherwise be served with an outstanding Ohio sub-poena, and never again returned to the state except in death when his family brought his body back for burial next to his wife.

In 1998, well over 30 years later, I picked up a copy of Ron Chernow's TITAN, the Life of John D. Rockefeller, Sr. Reading it brought back fond memories of Eaton. At times, the book rang so true that I felt he and I were back in his office on the 36th floor of Terminal Tower and he again

• • • • • • • • • • • • • • • • • • • •

was relating to me the stories of his days with Rockefeller.

• • • • •

Over those years I learned much about Eaton's early days in business on his own and his views on local, national and world affairs. He was instrumental in the formation of Republic Steel, headquartered in Cleveland, and for many years one of the nation's largest steel companies.

In the 1920s he assembled an empire of electric utilities and electric traction lines around Chicago, as well as pipelines and other utilities. I remember him telling me about how he had sold them in 1928 to Samuel Insull, a well-known Midwest tycoon of the era. "I told him," Eaton said, "Samuel, I like what I have and I don't want to sell." But Insull insisted, he said. So Eaton sold them to him. "You know," Eaton observed, "I didn't want to sell those lines, but I guess Providence was with me because the following year the stock market crashed. Samuel lost everything and died in disgrace."

Eaton, I later learned, made $160 million on the deal, but lost that fortune, as he would others, in his own business activities. Indeed Cyrus Eaton made — and lost — more fortunes than most of us have in our wildest dreams.

Another of his stories involved a Labrador property he had purchased before or during World War II that was reputed to contain significant iron ore deposits. After buying the property, he commissioned engineering and geological studies and, sure enough, the claims were true. However, the deposits were under a large lake. Eaton hired other experts to

. . . .

determine how the ore could be mined. They made the seemingly impossible suggestion that the lake should be drained. Other experts thought that plan impossible, but Eaton went ahead, having a tunnel built to drain the lake. Steep Rock Iron Mines, which he had acquired for virtually nothing, literally became a "gold mine."

. . . . .

From time-to-time I would have a front row seat on one of his ventures. I especially remember one that involved him and his long-time friend, John L. Lewis, president of the United Mine Workers union. Eaton had a substantial interest in West Kentucky Coal Company, which had a contract to supply coal to Tampa Electric Company. For some reason, West Kentucky Coal had either reneged on the contract or done something else that prompted Tampa Electric to go to court and get an injunction against West Kentucky Coal.

Eaton, of course, appealed the adverse court decision, but doing so required posting a $3 million bond. Eaton asked me if C&O could acquire any insurance dealing with such things that might be structured so that it would satisfy West Kentucky Coal's bond requirements. I made a quick inquiry of our insurance manager, but there was no way C&O could put up the money or otherwise cover the bond. We also found out there simply wasn't anyone in the market that would bond or otherwise insure West Kentucky Coal.

Eaton took all of this in and, knowing that West Kentucky Coal could not afford the $3 million, said we'd just have to go see "my old friend John L. Lewis," and off we went to Lewis' office in Washington.

. . . .

Lewis was in his 80s at the time, as was Eaton. It was fascinating for me to sit and listen to these two grizzled veterans talk about the labor movement, "the old times," and other things of mutual interest for the first hour or so that we were in Lewis' office.

Then, Eaton came to the point of the meeting, "John, I need your advice on something," he said, relating West Kentucky Coal's need for the bond and noting, "I just don't know how to proceed." Lewis, who had listened sympathetically, leaned over and said, "Cyrus, why don't you let us post the bond for you?" Of course, this was exactly what Eaton had come to Washington to get. We exchanged pleasantries and got up and left.

I don't remember how the appeal turned out, but I do know that shortly after the meeting with Lewis, the United Mine Workers became the union representing the employees of West Kentucky Coal. That was Cyrus Eaton diplomacy at its finest.

. . . . .

Throughout the post-World War II period, Eaton remained involved in the many movements and activities that had made him a world figure. He was not highly regarded in Cleveland, for that matter not highly regarded much of anywhere in the United States. His views just didn't fit the times. He felt — and strongly — that the United States should find ways to work with the Russians and with the rest of the Communist world, preferably by opening trade. This, without question, was not a popular position then and, in some quarters in this country, it remains unpopular to this day even though the Soviet Union, as we knew it then, is now long gone.

During these years, right up through the Vietnam era, he would go to

. . . .

Russia, on his own, promoting dialogue and trade and often inviting the Russians to come to Cleveland. Once Anastas Mikoyan, one of the top Russian leaders under Joseph Stalin and himself later chairman of the Supreme Soviet, came to Cleveland to meet with Eaton. The news that Mikoyan was coming prompted vast amounts of criticism and condemnation from virtually the entire Cleveland community and from other parts of the country. Eaton didn't flinch then — or later — when he hosted Russian leaders at his farm near Cleveland.

Those visits to the farm usually resulted in "command" performances for those of us who were officers in the company and that led to interesting — but largely uninformative — evenings. The basic problem we had was communications. The Russians didn't speak much English and we spoke even less Russian, but we both learned to smile a lot.

. . . . .

I vividly remember a number of talks with Eaton after Richard Nixon had been elected President of the United States. Eaton had a great dislike for President Nixon, largely because he had refused for years to accept Eaton's advice on foreign affairs as it pertained to the Russians and the Communist world. Then, to Eaton's amazement, the president he hated so vehemently strengthened our nation's relations with Russia and established diplomatic relations with China, exactly what Eaton had suggested and wanted all along. Eaton, on the occasion of those monumental events — events that vindicated his long, lonely years of work toward the same exact end — was at a loss for words.

. . . . .

Cyrus Eaton in my view was much less interested in the politics of world affairs than he was in the world's economics. He was a businessman and he strongly believed America should be trading with every country around the world, thereby giving American businesses (and Cyrus Eaton) an opportunity to make more money. To be sure, Eaton had a strong desire for peace – no question about that – but he had an even stronger, insatiable desire for profit and profitable business relations. The basis of his political activity around the world was his strong belief, first in capitalism, then democracy. He was a capitalist first, last and always, often saying, "if you are doing business with someone, you're not shooting at him."

Many people criticized Cyrus Eaton for his world peace efforts. I then thought, and now even more firmly believe, that criticism was improper. He was devoted to peace, to capitalism 100 percent, and he was an advocate of the global economy and free trade long, long before it was in vogue.

Chapter X

. . . .

"Mr. Eaton Wants to Speak With You"

When you see Greg, don't tell him I've called...
be properly surprised

In the last year or so before March 31, 1971, the date Gregory S. Devine was scheduled to retire as head of the C&O and B&O, it seemed that if anyone from within the company would succeed him, it would probably be either C. Vernon Cowan, who was Senior Vice President-Operations, or possibly myself. Frankly, neither of us was thought of as a sure thing. Most, though, thought Vernon would get the job as President and Chief Executive Officer. If not, the company might even go outside and bring in someone not associated with the organization.

In 1967, my duties had been expanded from Vice President-Finance to Vice President in charge of the Administrative Group, which included finance, public relations, passenger traffic, purchasing and several other staff areas. I had become familiar with most of the staff functions of the company – but still had no "line operations" experience.

. . . . .

. . . .

Like most others within the company, I was fairly certain the job would go to Cowan. In mid-1970, I was in New York with DeVine for a meeting with financial analysts. We were riding back to the hotel after an evening meeting, when he said, "You know the old man (referring to Eaton) has a high regard for you, even though I think Vernon Cowan should be my successor." I said: "That is understandable. Vern is older, has headed the major department of the company (the Operating Department) for a good number of years and that is no problem with me."

That was about all I heard on the subject from either Messrs. Eaton or DeVine, and I took DeVine's comment to mean that Cowan was the front runner and would probably get the job.

We were dealing with many difficult problems in the last half of 1970 and early 1971 — the Penn Central bankruptcy, the B&O refinancing and other items — and none of us had much time to think about the presidential problem. However, during the last few years of his career I did spend a lot of time in Devine's office. He would call and ask me to come up and then run through a whole series of things that he wanted done. I just assumed he was getting ready to retire and wanted someone else to do most of his work. I still think thatprimarily was the case.

. . . . .

My first indication of the final outcome came in February 1971, a week before the scheduled February C&O board meeting. I had left the office that day for a meeting with Peat Marwick Mitchell & Co., our company's public accountants, going over a number of matters in preparation for the board meeting. It was the first and only time I met with them in

. . . .

their offices. During the meeting, someone came to the door and said to me, "Mr. Eaton wants to speak with you."

Normally, when Eaton wanted to speak to me, he would call me to his office. I thought it very strange that he would track me down out of the office and then call me there.

Someone found me an office and I got on the line. Eaton, in his quiet voice, said, "Hays, when you get back to the office, Greg DeVine is going to call you in and tell you that you have been selected as his successor. But I wanted to tell you first. That's the reason for my call. But when you see Greg, don't tell him I've called, because I want you to be properly surprised." I was pretty stunned, but had enough presence to thank him, assure him I would not let Greg know of his call and continue the meeting without letting the auditors know what had just happened.

After finishing the meeting, I went back to the office. Sure enough, Devine called me to his office. He told me he had recommended to Eaton that I should be his successor. I said, "Thank you very much," and went back to my office walking on clouds, and called my wife.

A week later the C&O board met and elected me President and Chief Executive Officer, effective April 1. I continued to spend time with DeVine for the next six weeks, learning about the job.

. . . . .

After it was announced that I was to become President, Cowan dropped by my office and told me how much he enjoyed working with me, and that he looked forward to working with me in the future. We agreed that he would have a title promotion to Executive Vice President, and that he would work closely with me, because of his background and experience in operations, an area with which I had very little familiarity.

All went well for several months. Then one day Cowan came in to my office and told me he had decided to retire, to move back to Virginia, and live the life of a country squire. And so, not too long after I became President, he took early retirement and left. It was completely voluntarily. There was no push. We had no problems or hard words, and I looked forward to working with him. He knew so many things about the railroad that I did not, so as far as I was concerned, I would have been very pleased for him to continue.

There is no question that he was disappointed at not being selected President. I understood that and why, after an appropriate interval, he would retire. He had a lovely place on the waters of Chesapeake Bay, and he and his wife renovated a beautiful home there. I think he just decided he wanted to live easier, but there was never any disagreement or any problems between us as far as I know.

·   ·   ·   ·   ·

During the latter part of March, before DeVine retired, Betty and I went to Williamsburg, Virginia, to spend a week with our son, Tom, who was then a student at The College of William and Mary. At about 6 a.m. on the Sunday after we arrived, I was awakened out of a sound sleep by a phone call. It was Eaton. He said, "Hays, I hope I didn't awaken you?" I

• • • • • • • • • • • • • • • • • • • •

assured him that he hadn't and he said, "You know we never did talk about your salary, and I think we should have that settled before the first of the month."

He mentioned a number, which was substantially more than I was making, but not what I had hoped for. So I said, "That's OK, but you know Mr. Kusik and Mr. Cowan are making a substantially higher figure. If I'm going to be the President, it seems to me that my salary should be a little bit more than those reporting to me." Eaton responded, "How did they get so high?" but then added, "That's a good idea. What do you have in mind?"

So I named a figure, and he said, "I think that's fine. We'll work out the details when you get back to Cleveland next week." I said, "Fine," hung up the phone and promptly went back to sleep for another two hours.

❖ ❖

Chapter XI

. . . .

The Penn Central Bankruptcy

A mixed blessing for C&O/B&O, the industry... and me

To this day I am not certain how I came to be named President and Chief Executive Officer of the company. Predicting the Penn Central bankruptcy probably helped. Also, I had spent a number of years in the board meetings with Eaton and it seemed that he and the board were comfortable with me. And, while I don't really know if he did or not, I am fairly confident that John Kusik had something to do with my being selected. He was Vice Chairman at the time and probably recommended me to Eaton, who highly respected Kusik's judgment. But, I really have never been sure how it came about.

. . . . .

The bankruptcy of the Penn Central on Sunday, June 21, 1970, cost C&O/B&O plenty, but it also had a silver lining that has been of tremendous benefit to all of the industry. And, it may well have been the key to my promotion the following year.

• • • • • • • • • • • • • • • • • • • •

By 1964, the Pennsylvania Railroad and the New York Central Railroad had resumed merger discussions, culminating in a 1968 merger that formed the Penn Central Transportation Company. As part of the proposed merger, the Pennsylvania agreed to divest its controlling interest in the Norfolk & Western and the Wabash railroads. N&W then moved to acquire the Wabash and the Nickel Plate railroads, completing that merger in the fall of 1964.

Shortly thereafter, in November 1964, merger discussions began between N&W and C&O/B&O. We had been studying and planning for that merger for more than five years when the Penn Central filed for reorganization under Section 77.

There were seven of us, three from the N&W and four from C&O, heading the effort to merge C&O and N&W. From N&W were Herman Pevler, the President of N&W, who came over from the Wabash after Stuart Saunders had gone to the Penn Central; Jack Fishwick, who felt he should have been Saunders' successor and never liked Pevler, since he knew much more about the N&W than Pevler; and Hamilton M. Redman, the Vice President of Finance. On the C&O side were Walter Tuohy, Vice Chairman and CEO; Greg DeVine, President; John Kusik, then Chairman of the Executive Committee of the C&O board; and myself.

The agreement that we worked out after months of study, discussions and negotiations was that N&W would name 10 individuals to the new board, C&O would name seven, and the headquarters would be in Roanoke, Virginia, the N&W's headquarters city. The stock exchange ratio would have given N&W's shareholders about 60 percent of the new company.

• • • • • • • • • • • • • • • • • •

While I am certain other things were going on, I know I was more than fully occupied with dozens upon dozens of financial, traffic and other studies and reams of testimony throughout this period. The ICC hearings themselves were an almost overwhelming ordeal. They were held off and on for nearly two years, from April 1967 through late March 1969.

• • • • •

Had the Penn Central not gone bankrupt and had the ICC approved the C&O/N&W merger, we would have had two balanced systems in the East. In short order, one of us probably would have merged with Seaboard Coast Line; the other with the Southern Railway; and we would have split up the smaller railroads in the region, the "Orphans of the East" as they later came to be called. Thus, we would have gotten to two systems in the East about 30 years before the mid-1999 CSX and NS split of Conrail, the successor to the Penn Central and the orphans. The loss of that opportunity alone has cost the successors of C&O and N&W and the taxpayer many, many billions of dollars. And that is just the tip of the costs.

The C&O/N&W and Penn Central systems would have been evenly matched in terms of geography and markets and, had the Penn Central somehow found a cure for its financial and service ills, there would have been vast improvements in service to the shipper community. We would have been extremely competitive on virtually every route, between every major market in the East outside of New England. Clearly, we would have beaten the trucks to the soon-to-be booming intermodal market. Instead, with the Interstate Highway System then coming together, the trucks grabbed the market. We have been playing catch-up ever since and CSX and NS will be playing catch-up for years to come.

. . . .

. . . . .

Over time I strongly believe we, C&O/N&W, would have emerged as the dominant railroad of the two had the merger gone forward, and that would have presented us with significant regulatory challenges.

Those challenges would have delayed deregulation of the industry. There is no doubt in my mind that we would not have gotten it through Congress in 1980. In fact, C&O/N&W might well have fallen victim to even more regulation because we would have been in such a strong position vs. the Penn Central.

So the silver lining of the Penn Central bankruptcy proved to be the long overdue deregulation of the rail industry. Without the Penn Central bankruptcy it probably still would have come . . . eventually, but not in 1980.

. . . . .

By late 1969, it was apparent to everyone who studied the Penn Central's financial results that the company was running out of funds. As has since been well documented, it was consuming cash at a horrific rate and selling vast amounts of short-term debt to cover operating and other expenses, even the dividend on its stock. And the longer things went, the worse they got.

It also was obvious Penn Central was having terrible service problems. Our customers and we saw it first and up close because we interchanged so much traffic with them. Soon, it was common knowledge as more and more news stories came out relating the woes of lost cars, deferred mainte-

• • • • • • • • • • • • • • • • • • • •

nance and open warfare in the executive suite, and up and down the ranks within the company.

From time-to-time I made it a point to brief Cyrus Eaton and Greg DeVine on my growing concerns regarding Penn Central's financial condition. By the winter of 1969, it was clear to me they would soon have to cease operations, or file for protection under Section 77 of the Bankruptcy Act to stay in business. DeVine would not accept that and kept telling Eaton, "The Penn Central is too big to go bankrupt. It is impossible for a $6 billion company to go under."

Despite his doubts, I kept telling him and Eaton that I hoped he was right, but that I didn't see any other option. Eaton understood the realities. Having gone through The Great Depression and having made and lost several fortunes, he understood the vagaries of business. He also knew a troubled company when he saw one, and Penn Central was in deep trouble.

The last straw for the Penn Central, in my view, came in April or May 1970. It was when Wall Street refused to sell any more of its short-term notes payable (commercial paper). To me, that was it. It would be only a matter of time and I was right. Paul Gorman came in on June 9, succeeding Stuart T. Saunders, and, then, on a rainy Sunday in Philadelphia, June 21, the thought-to-be-mighty Penn Central went bankrupt.

• • • • •

The bankruptcy cost us in many other ways beyond the loss of the C&O/N&W merger. We lost, for example, between $5 million and $6 million of car hire and other payables due us from the Penn Central. And we,

. . . .

C&O, and the rest of the industry had one other major problem … we couldn't raise money in the equity or debt markets. At least that was the conventional wisdom of most of the experts. And that was a big problem for C&O. The B&O had $52 million of debt that was due two months after the Penn Central went broke and we had no choice but to find a way to refinance it.

One of our key financial advisers at the time was Edward V. Milholland, Jr. who was then with Glore, Forgan & Co. (later taken over by Halsey, Stuart). Ed kept saying, "We will find a way to solve the problem," and he had a track record that was hard to argue with, even in those circumstances.

A few years earlier, he was instrumental in designing and effecting the refinancing of the entire debt of the B&O with a $280 million series of bonds — the largest that had ever been done by a railroad.

Early in the year prior to the Penn Central bankruptcy, Ed and I and W. James Price of Alex Brown & Sons, one of our directors, had gone to London to investigate the possibility of selling or refinancing the bonds in Europe.

This was my first experience with Jim Price, and it was an experience I thoroughly enjoyed. He soon became one of my most trusted and respected members of the board.

During the spring and summer of 1970, we continued to work on the refinancing and decided that Glore, Forgan & Co. alone could not swing the $52 million deal. So we brought in Salomon Brothers, then the largest railroad financing house on Wall Street; and we worked with John

• •

Gudfriend, who later became managing director of Salomon.

By the end of August, when the bonds were due, Milholland and Gudfriend had come to the conclusion that we could probably sell about $25 million of bonds, but at a high price, and that we could arrange a medium-term bank loan for the balance of the $52 million.

As it turned out, we were able to sell $27 million of bonds with an 11 percent coupon and borrow the remaining $25 million. The 11 percent coupon was at least two points over what we would have paid had the Penn Central not gone bankrupt. There is no doubt that the rate was unreasonably high.

I always viewed that rate, and the $600,000 or so we paid in extra interest every year for the next seven years, as a sacrifice that our company made to re-establish the credit worthiness of the railroad industry. Many highly respected people on Wall Street said there was no way we could do it at any price, but we did. We deserved a lot of credit for that but paid dearly for it.

• • • • •

Although it was obvious that the proposed C&O/B&O/N&W merger was dead when Penn Central went bankrupt in June 1970, we continued to meet. Those meetings, however, were mere formalities; the merger was a dead horse before it had even gotten out of the barn. Just before he retired, Greg DeVine decided we should formally end the merger proposal and the C&O board acted in March 1991, the month before I became President. DeVine explained, "I wanted to leave you with a clean slate."

. . . .

Many of my colleagues were happy that the C&O/N&W merger had been derailed, fearing that N&W's management would dominate the merged company. I didn't share that concern and even offered to bet that within five years of the effective date of the merger that two-thirds of the officers of the new company would be former C&O/B&O managers.

In my view, and I had been working with the N&W's top managers and officials for all of the five-plus years we were planning the merger, our management strength was deeper. That is all conjecture now, but I had no doubt then, nor do I now, that C&O/B&O people in time would have ended up on top.

. . . . .

So the Penn Central bankruptcy changed everything, probably even my career. It certainly prompted dramatic, everlasting change for our company and our industry. It changed the competitive landscape in the East and taught all of American business a big, big lesson — how not to do a merger.

After the dust had settled and everyone had figured out what really happened, it was very clear the people of companies getting together had to be together. They had to share the same vision and put their petty differences, if they had any, aside and this had to start with the people at the top.

Forever after, that was an axiom. Saunders and Perlman didn't agree on anything from Day One of the Pennsylvania and New York Central merger. And that cost the Penn Central, all the rest of us and the country dearly in many, many ways.

• •

On the other hand, it sped deregulation of the rail industry. It took 10 years after the bankruptcy to get it done, but I have no doubt it would have taken even longer had the Penn Central somehow found a way to stay on track.

❖   ❖

Chapter XII

. . . .

The First Years as President and Chief Executive Officer

Interesting times marked by bankruptcies, a coal strike, suspension of the dividend, the birth of Amtrak... and — not least of all — Mr. Kusik's real retirement.

Being the "new boy on the block" was not quite the picnic I had always envisioned. Those first years as President and Chief Executive Officer of the C&O/B&O were particularly interesting — and definitely most challenging. Even though I had spent much of the preceding months in the office of Greg DeVine, my predecessor (he had decided that I needed some "on-the-job training"), the realization dawned that all decisions of the company were my responsibility. The first year, especially, was a baptism under fire. In it alone, we had railroad bankruptcies, a coal strike, reduction of 15,000 employees and suspension of the dividend.

The Penn Central bankruptcy was followed by a string of other bankruptcies. Within a year of the Penn Central's demise, there were five other Class I roads operating under Section 77 in the East — the Erie Lackawanna, Central of New Jersey, Reading, Delaware and Hudson, and Lehigh and Hudson Valley.

During that period I was out on the railroad, meeting key operating and maintenance officers or visiting key customers and, when back in the office, dealing with mountains of paperwork that never ceased to amaze me. Business was good, and things seemed to be humming along, although there was a slight possibility of a strike in the coal mines. Such threats had been made in the previous years, but somehow they seemed to always be resolved before the deadline, so we did not worry too much about them.

In mid-summer of 1971, our two top coal traffic officers decided it was time to visit our major customers in Japan. We also planned to attend the bi-annual Coal Discussion Meeting (with Norfolk & Western, the other large coal exporter), which also was being held in Japan. The threat of a stoppage in the coal fields was looming larger as our departure drew near, but it was too late to cancel the trip and we left in the final days of September. On October 1, just after we landed in Tokyo, the coal miners strike began. And with it, we lost over 40 percent of our revenue.

It seemed that coal strikes were my doom — the last major strike in 1949 had gotten me fired after two months on the job. This time, it was my job to see us through the difficulties. I wasn't going anywhere... unless we failed and that was not going to happen.

The coal strike forced us to lay off over 15,000 of our 42,000 people and to suspend the dividend. Both were drastic, but essential actions. Sending that many people home "for the duration" was not easy, but I don't think we had anyone in the company who didn't understand that we were in a tough situation. Everyone knew the strike was costing us nearly half of our revenue and that, given such circumstances, business

. . . .

could not go on as usual.

The elimination of the dividend in December 1971 was a rude shock to many people, and a terrible ordeal for us. It was the last — and most reluctant — of the actions we took. C&O had not failed to pay a dividend since 1922, even continuing it through The Great Depression. We received a very strong reaction from our stockholders, despite their knowing how much the strike was costing us. I still remember some of the phone calls from a couple of our larger shareholders — large funds that held our stock — calls of outrage. They went along the lines of "How could you?" "Why didn't you tell us your plans in advance?" or "Why didn't you warn us?" I tried my best to explain that we could not have done that; we could not favor one owner over another, but all that got me were even stronger and nastier comments.

The next spring, when we resumed paying the dividend, we added an extra dividend as a way of thanking the shareholders who had stuck with us, in a small way trying to repay our owners for the income they had lost. I don't think that bought us anything, but the board felt it would make up a bit for the loss of the previous two dividends. Since that time, we have had no interruptions of the C&O — and now CSX — dividend, and I hope that record lasts at least another 50 years and that another disaster like the 1971 coal strike never again befalls the company.

Meanwhile, we were trying to maintain decent service to our customers all through this period without much help in the way of connecting service to or from the major markets in the East due to

• •

the rash of bankruptcies and the increasingly poor condition of
those roads.

But that wasn't all that was happening ... or was to happen. Passenger
service was devouring money on all the nation's railroads and had been for
years. The ICC and state regulatory agencies were being flooded with passenger train abandonment applications throughout the 1960s and that continued in 1970. In fact, before its bankruptcy, the Penn Central filed to
abandon 48 trains all at once. But very few were gaining ICC approval and
the losses continued to mount. Using the ICC's own formula, the losses
were in the $500 million a year range — very serious money — by 1970.

An earnest search for a solution finally resulted in passage of
the National Railroad Passenger Service Act in December 1970, which
President Nixon signed in January 1971. The law became effective May 1,
1971, and Amtrak went into business.

Some have thought that the Penn Central bankruptcy forced
Amtrak's creation. That was not the case. The wheels were in motion for
Amtrak by the late 1960s, well before Penn Central's problems became
known. By the time the Penn Central went under, we were down to working out the details. Perhaps the Penn Central bankruptcy gave the process a
push, but I think Amtrak would have happened regardless.

It also was fairly obvious to all of us in the industry that Amtrak
would never be profitable, even though they abandoned service over almost
half of the passenger route-miles previously operated by the nation's railroads, thereby eliminating most of the deficit, on their first day of opera-

• •

tion. Of course, the government would never have let the railroads do that when we were responsible for the service. Had we been able to do the same, we would probably still be in the passenger business today and, I believe, the nation would have far better service.

There was a "catch" to Amtrak for the nation's railroads. Every railroad that conveyed its passenger service was required to pay Amtrak to take over its passenger service. These payments, in cash, equipment and facilities, were sort of a reverse ransom. If we wanted out, we had to pay to get out from under a business that basically had held us hostage.

C&O and 19 other of the 26 eligible roads paid. In the C&O's case, the price was $44 million: a $9 million cash "fee" that we paid over three years; $13 million in job protection payments to affected employees; and a $22 million write-off of passenger equipment and facilities that were turned over to Amtrak or no longer of value to C&O/B&O. We had far better uses for the cash, but we paid it. The alternative was totally unacceptable. Our 1970 loss from passenger service, on an avoidable-cost basis, was nearly $14 million and our projected loss for 1971 was $17 million. Of course, what C&O/B&O and the rest of the industry paid turned out to be nothing compared to what all of us as taxpayers have since contributed to keep Amtrak running.

Meanwhile, through all of this, I was trying to learn the railroad. I had had no direct experience in railroad operations or engineering and I worked hard at understanding those complexities, especially after Vern Cowan retired. The commercial side of the business presented an equally demanding challenge and required my getting to know our customers and the balancing act our people went through every day trying to match their demands and needs with our abilities and resources . . . at a profit.

By the end of my first year, I was just happy that the company — and I — had survived.

Then, about a year after I had been elected President, Dr. Lawrence A. Kimpton, the former president and chancellor of the University of Chicago and, later, assistant to the chairman of Standard Oil Company of Indiana, who had been brought on the board by Eaton some years earlier, asked me about Kusik and his activities with the company.

And so I spent a lot of time telling Dr. Kimpton about Kusik and how important and valuable he had been to me. But I had to admit that now, nearing age 75, he was not contributing that much to the operation of the company. Dr. Kimpton, having been on the board with Kusik for several years, got right to the point and said he felt strongly that it was time for Kusik to retire again, 10 years after having "retired" the first time, and that he would talk with him about it.

About two weeks before the 1972 annual meeting, as later told to me by Dr. Kimpton, he walked into Kusik's office and said, "John, I'd like to talk with you." Kusik, he said, looked up with a puzzled expression and said, "Of course." Dr. Kimpton then closed the door, sat down and said, "John, I think it is time for you to retire."

Dr. Kimpton said the conversation thereafter was very spirited, but by

· ·

the end of their meeting it was decided that Kusik would retire at the time
of the April 1972 annual meeting of shareholders.

Dr. Kimpton subsequently told me that he just felt it was time for
Kusik to really retire — that it was best for the company. He also arranged
for Kusik to be given an office in another part of the building and staff
support. But, that is not all of the background on Kusik's departure. There
was one more "event" to come.

· · · · ·

Kusik came to the annual meeting in 1972, my second meeting pre-
siding as the CEO. During the question-and-answer period, he rose and
asked to be recognized. I recognized him, and he proceeded to read an
address, which none of us knew was coming. He spoke about his long and
interesting life and career, made a few comments that most would say were
"barbed," although they may not have been, wished us all well and walked
out of the room.

· · · · ·

Even after that I would see him from time-to-time and we
never had a cross word. We would have lunch together, or I would go to his
office and meet with him. After CSX was created and I moved to
Richmond, I went back to Cleveland twice to talk with him. We
had a continued good relationship and there were no hard feelings
between us.

John Kusik always looked upon me as his "prize pupil," and I certainly
looked upon him as my mentor. Without his guidance I am not sure of

. . . .

where, if anywhere, I would have gone in the company. So I owe him a great debt of gratitude. Kusik was an amazing man and, even though it was a hard ordeal at times, what he put me through was for my own good. He made a big difference.

❖ ❖

Chapter XIII

. . . .

Meeting the (Railroad) Presidents

An assessment of the top railroad executives of the 1970s

O n June 10, 1971, shortly after I became the C&O's President and a year after the Penn Central bankruptcy, members of the Association of American Railroads (AAR) board met with President Nixon in the White House. My first meeting with a President of the United States was quite an experience for a country boy. I sat through the meeting in the Cabinet Room in silence, at least as much in awe of the railroad presidents as I was of the President of the United States.

Of this group, I was the youngest by seven years and also its junior member in terms of seniority. We talked with President Nixon about railroad problems in general — the fact that a substantial part of the industry was in bankruptcy, the problems of passenger service (this was just after Amtrak had taken over the service) and the need for some sort of change in the railroad regulatory process.

Looking back, my first experience with efforts to change the industry's regulatory environment was in 1969 with an organization called ASTRO (America's Sound Transportation Railroad Organization).

· ·

ASTRO resulted from a meeting of a small group of railroad officers with Dick Briggs, Vice President of the Association of American Railroads (AAR), in Jacksonville in March 1969 — my first trip to Jacksonville. ASTRO was established as an independent organization and its job was to make the case for deregulation. Shortly thereafter, former Sen. George Smathers (D-Fla.) was hired as its head. During 1969 and 1970 there were additional meetings as the industry attempted to find ways to change its regulatory environment, but those of us that were serious about real change were in the minority. Most of the industry's focus was then on solving the problems of the bankrupts and getting, and then keeping, the industry out of the passenger business.

In those days, as far as deregulation was concerned, most people in the industry were thinking about some sort of modification of the regulatory scheme. Real deregulation wouldn't come for another 10 years — and it came after the airline and trucking industries both had been deregulated, which speaks volumes about how much emphasis the AAR and industry leaders placed on the subject. In those days, as had been the case for many years, the AAR and the railroad industry — even with roughly a quarter of it in bankruptcy — were a powerful force in Washington.

The one area, of course, that the AAR did not handle was pricing. Rate Bureaus served as the mechanism for joint rate making, but the AAR board as such did not have antitrust exemption. Accordingly, marketing and pricing matters were never discussed — only legislative activities, operating practices and finance. The AAR and its various committees dealt with mechanical and other facets of the railroad industry.

Meeting with the President that June day was an impressive group of

• • • • • • • • • • • • • • • • • • •

railroad "giants," including: **W. Graham Claytor,** Southern Railway; **Ben Biaggini,** Southern Pacific; **John Reed,** Santa Fe; **Lou Menk,** Burlington Northern; **Tom Rice,** Seaboard Coast Line; **Jack Fishwick,** Norfolk & Western; **Frank Barnett,** Union Pacific; and **Bill Johnson** of the Illinois Central. It also was a very powerful force in Washington. When the AAR board agreed on something, the railroad industry — and, more often than not, the political leadership of the country — followed. A quick look at the presidents of the then major railroads gives insight into their personalities and suggests why they were so successful in the industry... and in politics.

Frank Barnett of the Union Pacific was very quiet, dignified, a gentle individual, a real statesman who didn't talk much. But when he did speak, he commanded respect. He was a gracious gentleman, representing the richest railroad in the country — the Union Pacific — but very quiet and reserved. He was very active in the creation of Amtrak, working with John Volpe, the U.S. Secretary of Transportation, Congressional leaders, and the industry on the legislation. I always enjoyed being with Frank. He exuded power without the least trace of flaunting it.

Benjamin Franklin Biaggini, Chairman of the Southern Pacific, the then second largest U.S. rail system, was never in doubt on any railroad matter. One of the leaders in the AAR, his forceful manner frequently determined the positions the industry would take. The Southern Pacific had long been the powerhouse in the West, and Ben's personality fit well into this long-established leadership role.

W. Graham Claytor was one of the most voluble members

· ·

of the AAR board. He had an opinion on everything, and shared it with the board, whether the board wanted to hear it or not. I suppose when you are always right it is hard to be modest. Graham was probably the leading advocate of how a railroad should be run. He was a brilliant individual, no question of that. Great charisma, but strong, forthright and never in doubt. A typical railroad president even though he had a legal background, rather than an operating background. He knew how things should be done, and generously shared his thoughts on any and all subjects with us. In all the years I knew him, Graham never changed. He did have one interesting quirk... he talked to himself. I remember one time when a group of us were in Washington National Airport, in the executive terminal, waiting for an airplane. Graham, I noticed, was over in the corner talking — to himself. No one else was around. He was not dictating, just carrying on a conversation. My wife happened to be with me, and she never forgot that Graham Claytor could enjoy his own company of one.

Jack Fishwick by this time had become president of Norfolk & Western after the retirement of Herman Pevler. Jack, like Graham Claytor, was also very voluble and expressed his opinion on every subject that came along. He had very strong opinions on what should happen with the Penn Central and the other bankrupts. Being small of stature, he liked to stand and walk when he talked. I remember innumerable meetings, when we were in merger discussions, at the AAR, and elsewhere, Jack always walked around the table or walked around the group when he spoke. Whether this was his way of getting attention, or whether he felt that he had to stand to be seen, I don't know. Also, Jack usually started his comments with the

• •

expression: "I think we should…" Not "We," but "I."

Bill Johnson, head of the Illinois Central, was president of the Railway Express Agency, headquartered in New York, when I first met him. At one time it had been suggested that C&O should consider buying Railway Express, and operate it as a part of our system even though it was nationwide. We didn't go forward with the suggestion, but I found him to be highly intelligent and a great strategist, traits that benefited him and the IC. Bill had the ability to conceptualize long-term and plan accordingly; to think about where he wanted his company and his industry to go. At the Illinois Central, he became the first railroad president to embrace diversifying into other industries, buying, first, a machine company, and then Pet Milk. Bill was a great individual; one whom I always highly admired and respected -- a great asset to the industry.

Jervis Langdon, the lead trustee of the Penn Central, was someone I had known from his time as president of the B&O when B&O and C&O first affiliated. Jervis was a nephew of Mark Twain and, in the early days of his career, worked as an attorney for C&O, before going to the B&O. When he took over as the lead trustee of Penn Central, it was like getting back together with a long-gone associate. The Penn Central bankruptcy judge, John P. Fullam, was most astute in selecting Jervis, someone who had been active in railroading all of his life and who knew the problems, challenges and opportunities of railroading in the East, as one of the trustees of the Penn Central. He was an excellent choice, a real gem.

Roger Lewis, the first president of Amtrak, joined the AAR board

· ·

after the establishment of Amtrak. He had an airline background and when he took over Amtrak he was determined to show the railroaders that he knew how to run the company. During the first winter of its operation, a number of veteran railroaders offered Amtrak their thoughts on how it might get through its difficulties, but Lewis pointedly ignored them, and the Amtrak system had major problems that first winter. Roger Lewis was a strong-willed individual who refused to listen to railroad people who really did know how to run trains in cold weather and wanted to help.

Lou Menk of the Burlington Northern, another strong individual, became head of the newly formed Burlington Northern just as the Powder River coalfields in Wyoming and Montana were being developed. For many years the eastern coalfields had been the sole source of supply to the Eastern and Midwestern United States. One of the first — if not the first — major movements of western coal was a contract that BN signed to bring Wyoming coal across the country to Lake Superior, and then ship it by boat to Detroit Edison in Michigan. Detroit Edison had been historically a large customer of C&O, and to a lesser extent of N&W.

Naturally we were concerned about western coal making inroads into eastern markets. But when all one needs to do is scrape dirt off the top of 20-, 30-, 40-, 50- and 60-foot coal seams, there's just no way that deep mining (or even strip mining) in the eastern United States can compete. Even though western coal has a lower BTU content, the ease of mining just gives western coal a tremendous price advantage. But the favorable economics of mining the coal do not alter the cost structure of transporting it. When we learned about the BN's contract, it was obvious that there was

. . . .

no way that coal could be railed at those rates for more than a thousand miles and then transshipped into boats to Detroit Edison without BN losing a vast amount of money.

One day at an AAR meeting, I remarked to Lou that we were interested in his new coal movements, saying: "I'm sure this is your way of getting into the eastern market, but you must be losing a lot of money?" He gave me one of his usual snorts, and said: "That is ridiculous. It is a profitable movement and you all are just jealous because we're taking some of your business." My response was: "Well, we are concerned about losing business, and we also wonder about buying into traffic that causes a big loss." "Well," he said, "we're not losing money." Then, years later, after we both had retired, he finally admitted the traffic was a "loss leader," that they did take a major loss in getting that business. Lou was another one who expressed his opinion frequently and widely.

John Reed of the Santa Fe had a financial background, so I always had a special affinity with John. When I was Vice President-Finance of the C&O, John (who was Vice President-Finance of the Santa Fe) and I worked on refinancing the debt of the Belt Railway of Chicago, owned by several railroads including C&O and Santa Fe. John was very retiring, rarely said anything, was obviously highly intelligent and he knew what he was doing, but he did not feel the necessity of expressing himself like many of the other AAR board members. Santa Fe was a good solid railroad, with flashy passenger service — the Chief, the Super Chief, El Capitan, and many others, and was in good financial condition in the 1970s when John Reed was running it.

. . . .

Tom Rice of the Seaboard Coast Line was then, always had been and still is a railroader's railroader, a member of the old operating school — military type, very pleasant, very charming, but very organized — high on hierarchy. I don't know whether the railroad training or the military training came first, but they seemed to go hand-in-hand. During World War II, he was a general and he still looks like a general, acts like a general and operates like a general. He also is a very, very intelligent fellow and a delight to work with.

Our first deal together was in the early 1970s, when the Federal Reserve Bank of Richmond was looking for a location for its new building. They had decided that a location along the banks of the James River was desirable, and they made overtures to the Seaboard Coast Line to use a parcel that had been the site of an idle rail yard. Rice was inclined to sell the land, but he recognized that C&O had a big freight yard on nearby property and, thus, was reluctant to sell Seaboard's land and make the C&O land that much more valuable. Instead, he came to C&O and proposed that he would sell his yard to the Federal Reserve for $1.5 million, if we would agree to put our freight yard, which would be valued at $3 million, into a joint venture. We agreed, and the James Center Development Corporation was formed, with Chessie owning two-thirds and Seaboard Coast Line one-third. Today, the old C&O yard is the site of CSX's headquarters, and the old Atlantic Coast Line yard is the site of the Federal Reserve Bank of Richmond.

❖ ❖

Chapter XIV

. . . .

Bill to Create Holding Company Almost Got Lost

Most other railroad executives thought it was a dumb idea

I n the early 1970s, we at C&O obviously were well aware that
substantial parts of the eastern railroad system were in bankruptcy, and
also recognized that railroads in general were continuing to lose large
chunks of business to truckers. Against this background, it seemed that we
should find some way to diversify our activities, either by getting into other
forms of transportation, or by acquiring companies that might logically fit
within, or compliment and expand, the company beyond our rail interests.

In my first media interview after I became President, I commented to
Steve Aug of the Washington Star that I viewed one of my principal jobs
to be creating a climate at C&O that fostered constructive change. One of
the changes I thought we should explore, I noted, was combining various
modes of transportation within the company, a matter that had been on my
mind for a long time. When the article came out, I got no support of the
idea, or suggestions on it, from any of the other railroad presidents. At best,
I got the impression that most of them thought it a novel and innovative

. . . .

idea, especially coming from a railroader, but I don't believe they thought much of it . . . even that it was workable. And that wasn't all that surprising. The railroad industry had been fighting with all the other modes for more years than I had been in the business, the trucking and barging industries being the principal targets.

To me, however, it wasn't novel or innovative at all; it was obvious and logical. Almost all of our rail customers were integrated companies. Ford and GM, for example, weren't just making and selling passenger cars, or just one or two models of cars. They were making trucks and buses and anything else they could make and get on wheels. GM was even manufacturing locomotives ... and had been for a long, long time. And I had wondered for many years why someone in the rail industry didn't follow suit and get together with another mode or two and see what could be done. To me, it certainly held much more promise than warring with them. If nothing else, it seemed we should be looking for and working toward things that fostered our common good. But, I was alone in the industry in this regard. No one else in the rail industry was of a mind to make peace with long-term enemies.

. . . . .

Getting into other modes required that we establish a holding company, to corporately facilitate prospective mergers or acquisitions. Being a Virginia corporation, we asked C&O's Richmond lawyers to prepare and file the necessary papers with Virginia's State Corporation Commission (SCC). We established Chessie System Inc. as the working name for the new company.

. . . .

The SCC, however, didn't exactly welcome our initiative. Much to our surprise, Judge Ralph Catterall, the senior member of the three-member Commission, refused to accept our application. He pointed out that the Penn Central had been created as a holding company... and then gone bankrupt. He was not about to be a part of any activity that would allow the long profitable C&O, as he said, "to go down the Penn Central route." When our lawyers, both internal and external, argued that Virginia law permitted formation of a holding company, he didn't budge and flatly told them that the SCC would not accept our application. The other two commissioners, Preston Shannon and J.L. (Junie) Bradshaw, privately indicated to us that they felt creating the holding company was possible, but they took a neutral public position, not wanting to openly disagree with their senior colleague.

In an effort to break through, a delegation of C&O officers went to Richmond to see Gov. A. Linwood Holton, then governor of the Commonwealth, and asked for his assistance in obtaining SCC approval of a charter for our new holding company. Gov. Holton tried, but was unsuccessful in his personal efforts to convince Judge Catterall to change his stance.

Our last resort was to ask Gov. Holton to offer a special bill before the Virginia General Assembly that would clarify any and all questions regarding holding companies and Virginia statutes. He agreed (this occurred during the final two weeks of the General Assembly session and the only way a bill could then be introduced was as "special legislation," and it had to be offered by the governor).

. . . .

After the bill was introduced, hearings were scheduled for the last week of the session and several of us testified before a special committee of the General Assembly. We were strongly opposed by the then lieutenant governor, Henry Howell, who made many of the same arguments that Judge Catterall had used to justify rejecting our application. Nevertheless, the committee, and later the Virginia State Senate, passed the bill and sent it to the House of Delegates for its consideration.

On the last day of the session, at 3 p.m., a C&O official was in the Capitol. He made a routine inquiry about the status of the legislation and discovered that the bill had been laid aside in a file without any action having been taken. Fortunately, he was very familiar with General Assembly procedures and was able to have the bill directed to the proper people. In the remainder of the day, the bill was considered by the General Assembly and passed, later being signed into law in March 1973 by Gov. Holton. The C&O official was Edward M. Hudgins, who had been a member of the General Assembly for 14 years before joining C&O to work in our Personal Injury Claims Department. Later, he became Chessie's first Vice President-Casualty Prevention.

Many years later, when I discussed the matter with Gov. Holton, I asked him why he was willing to help us with the holding company. He said he felt that if we were not able to establish it in Virginia, we would go elsewhere, and that the state would suffer in future years. Thus, he said, he felt it was desirable to help us, to keep our charter in Virginia. He was right. Without approval from the Virginia SCC, we would have incorporated Chessie in Delaware. Seven years later his assistance turned out to be very important for Virginia. CSX was created as a Virginia corporation and

• • • • • • • • • • • • • • • • • • • •

headquartered in Richmond.

• • • •

Another interesting and even lesser known fact about the creation of Chessie was the selection of the name itself. We needed shareholder approval after the SCC acted and scheduled a vote for the then upcoming annual meeting. Many of my C&O associates thought we should change the name to something more "dignified," more fitting for a billion-dollar corporation before getting shareholder approval. There were a few of us, however, who thought Chessie was just fine. We had used the Chessie logo and symbols as a short name for the combined C&O/B&O system for more than a year by that time. We saw no reason to change; feeling the name "Chessie System" had become familiar to the shipping and general public. So the named stayed.

Over the years, people gradually got used to the name, although early on I heard many comments about Chessie being a ridiculous name for a major American corporation.

❖ ❖

Chapter XV

. . . .

The Departure of Mr. Eaton

This is a serious matter — highly unusual for a young president to do

Cyrus Eaton, as noted earlier, was one of the most interesting and fascinating individuals of the 20th Century. As chairman of the C&O, his office was on the 36th floor of Terminal Tower, right around the corner from my own after I became President. Yet, he never interfered with railroad matters. He never told me what to do or how to do anything at any time he was chairman. I made a point, both before becoming President and thereafter, to keep him informed. It was my duty, as well as a privilege, to talk with Eaton about my plans, but he never interfered with me, or, to my knowledge, with my predecessor, Greg DeVine, or with his predecessor, Walter Tuohy. He just didn't get involved in railroad matters, other than going over the board agenda items before the board meetings. Basically, he left running the railroad to the President and Chief Executive Officer.

During my first two years as President, with Eaton as Chairman, the C&O board had nine members, the number having been significantly reduced over the years by retirements.

Of those, many were friends or relatives of Eaton. In that group were

• •

his son, Cyrus S. Eaton, Jr., his son-in-law, Fay LeFevre, who was the head
of the Cleveland Clinic, and others who had business dealings with Eaton.
In addition, there was Greg DeVine, the former president, and two distinguished former university presidents: Dr. Milton Eisenhower, president
emeritus of Johns Hopkins University in Baltimore, and Dr. Kimpton, former president of the University of Chicago.

• • • • •

At the August 1973 meeting of the Organization Committee, a board
committee dealing with corporate personnel and organizational matters, Dr.
Eisenhower observed that it seemed Cyrus Eaton had many people on the
railroad payroll and wondered out loud what they all did for the company?
The board members on the committee, in addition to Dr. Eisenhower, were
Dr. LeFevre and Dr. Kimpton. I responded, "That may well be. I'm not
familiar with the payroll of the Chairman's office, but I'd be happy to learn
more and report back at the next meeting."

After the meeting I undertook a study of the expenses of the
Chairman's office and found that there were 13 individuals on his
payroll and that, with the exception of his secretary, everyone else appeared
to be working on non-railroad matters. Also, several offices in the building
were being used by the Chairman's office for his personal files and clerical
support. In total, the company was spending well over half a million dollars
a year for the Chairman's office, with little visible benefit to the railroad.

When I made my report to the Committee, they strongly stated they
felt inappropriate things were going on and their concerns should be brought
to Eaton's attention and changes made. Dr. Eisenhower was par-

ticularly agitated and I well remember his words: "I've worked all my life to earn a good reputation and a little money and I'll be damned if I will let that "blankety-blank" ruin or take away either."

It was agreed that the committee would meet again, after the September board meeting scheduled for Baltimore. Their plan was to have Eaton join them, at which time they would explain the problems as they saw them, layout the potential liability posed by having the company spend such an amount of money on non-railroad matters, and urge that something be done.

Eaton, although not very happy about having such a meeting, agreed and the meeting was set up. Then things began to get interesting. First, Dr. LeFevre came to see me and said, "Since we are talking about my father-in-law's activities, I don't think it is proper I attend this meeting. So I'd like to be excused." Then, the day before the meeting, Dr. Eisenhower called to report he was sick and would not be able to attend the board meeting or the committee meeting. That left Dr. Kimpton and me to meet with Chairman Eaton.

. . . . .

As we began the meeting, Eaton very sourly said, "What's this all about?" Dr. Kimpton, bless his heart, said, "Cyrus, Hays has something he wants to talk to you about," at which point I was ready to go through the floor. In a flash I saw my entire railroad career slipping away, but I had made the study at the request of the committee and had no choice but to go ahead, starting with the prior month's meeting and the committee's request for the study.

. . . .

I went on, very softly noting that the study had been made. I showed Eaton the figures, and indicated to him that the members of the committee felt that having an expenditure of well over half a million dollars that had no relation to the railroad was potentially very dangerous to the company and to him. I also explained that the committee felt there should be some changes.

Eaton did not take kindly to my words, regardless of how softly they had been presented. For the first time in my time with and around him, I saw and felt his full wrath and every ounce of it was directed at me. "Young man," he began, "number one, I don't believe your numbers; number two, I am worth it; and number three, when I bought control of this company from Robert R. Young he told me I could spend any amount of money and have any amount of staff that was necessary. This is the end of this meeting."

With that, Eaton got up and walked out. Dr. Kimpton and I just sat there for a few seconds and looked at each other, both of us wondering what would happen next. Then we left.

By coincidence, my wife and I had planned to leave Baltimore immediately after the board meeting for a week's vacation, driving to North Carolina to visit some of her family. As we drove out of Baltimore an hour or so after the meeting, we couldn't help but wonder what, if anything, would happen while we were away, but not worrying too much about the possibilities.

. . . . .

When Eaton got back to Cleveland, he and his personal, non-railroad lawyer met with several members of my railroad staff and declared,

. . . .

"That young whipper snapper cannot tell me what to do with my company." During the week I was away, I had a call from John Hanifin, who had become Vice President-Executive Department and was one of my closest associates. He told me Eaton had told him about "the ridiculous activities," had indicated he was very unhappy, and had stated that some things had to be changed.

When I got back to Cleveland the following week, Eaton stormed into my office and told me how valuable his staff was to him, and how hard they worked. Then he said, "I work and think about railroad matters all the time — I never take vacations, listen to the radio or watch television. I am always thinking and planning about what's good for the railroad. All of this concern about stockholders suits and Internal Revenue Service audits is a lot of rubbish. The IRS has reviewed my expenses, and their only comment was that I wasn't charging the railroad enough."

"I've always," he added, "supported you, left running the company to you, and approved or supported your salary increases. Now, what do you make, and how much company stock do you have?" Then he turned and left.

During the next few days I saw nothing of Eaton, but I did spend plenty of time on the phone with members of the board of directors, explaining about the Organization Committee meeting and the report, and asking for direction. The only member of the board I did not talk with was Cyrus Eaton, Jr., who happened to be in Russia. The other members of the board were virtually unanimous in suggesting there should be a special meeting with Eaton so the matters could be discussed fully by all members,

. . . .

rather than just those of the Organization Committee.

Later in the week Eaton came back into my office and announced that he was planning to "get more active in affairs of the company" and asked for a list of officers, saying he wanted to know "whom to call in case of urgent problems." As the week ended I found out that he in fact did call members of my staff into his office and ask specific questions about railroad activities.

. . . . .

While this was all going on, I was talking with the railroad's outside (not company officers) lawyers, asking them to review the company's bylaws, Virginia's corporate statutes (C&O was a Virginia Corporation), and related case law.

Their conclusion amazed me. First, even though I had been elected Chief Executive Officer two years earlier, the bylaws clearly stated that the Chairman of the Board was actually the CEO and the President was only the Chief Administrative Officer. In view of that, they said the President did not have the authority to act against the Chairman's wishes, especially as to the Chairman's own office. On the other hand, there was little legal exposure for me personally for not acting sooner and, likewise, the board of directors had little legal exposure unless they knew of some improper action.

The lawyers also suggested that under the company by-laws, I, as President, should call a special meeting of the board to fully review the matter and to discuss what, if anything, should be done. In line with that advice, on Monday, October 1, I wrote the Corporate Secretary directing

. . . .

him to call a special meeting of the board for the following Friday after-noon. He immediately sent out telegrams calling the meeting for Friday afternoon in Baltimore and followed them with confirming Special Delivery letters.

. . . . .

The next morning first brought a telephone call — not an office visit — from Eaton. "What is this all about?" he demanded. I told him it was to discuss his office situation and he replied, "This is a serious matter — high-ly unusual for a young president to do." I tried to explain that it was the will of the board and was being done in accordance with the recommendations of our lawyers. That didn't impress Eaton at all and he repeated, "For a young man to take a great corporation and get it involved in a thing like this is a serious matter. We'll see about this, and I'll be there Friday after-noon."

Later that same day, Eaton did come to my office. Charging in, he announced, "I want that special board meeting on Friday called off. You tell the other directors that I am opposed to the meeting and that I demand it be called off. If you don't call it off, I'll seek to have the meeting enjoined. I want your answer by 10 o'clock tomorrow morning," and then charged out of my office. About all I had time to do was say "Yes, sir" as he cleared my door, but I knew the fat was now really in the fire.

Shortly after leaving my office, Eaton departed for Washington, announcing he was to meet with Members of Congress "on important rail-road matters." I gathered our railroad lawyers and held more discussions with them and with our outside counsel. Everyone was in agreement that the meeting must be held and could not be called off and we prepared to

. . . .

"batten down the hatches," and anticipate anything Eaton and his lawyer might try.

On the day before the scheduled meeting, I received a letter from Eaton's Staff Assistant announcing that "Mr. Eaton has asked me to advise you that he regrets that it will be impossible for him to attend the meetings in Baltimore tomorrow." That was it.

. . . . .

As was our custom, the company plane left Cleveland early Friday morning and went to various locations around the country picking up our out of town directors en route to Baltimore. Once there, we all assembled in the board room of the old B&O Building, fully expecting Eaton and his lawyer to drive up from Washington, despite the letter I had gotten from his assistant. The only absent director was Cyrus Eaton, Jr., who was still in Russia.

We waited some time, but Eaton did not appear. We went ahead and convened the meeting, with me as President acting as Chairman. A full discussion of the matter followed, including a recap of Eaton's reaction and what steps might be taken. After an extended period of discussion, one member of the board, I can't remember who, moved that Cyrus Eaton be removed as Chairman of the Board. The motion was unanimously passed. Then there was an additional motion, that I be elected Chairman of the Board and remain as Chief Executive Officer. That also passed unanimously. Finally there was a third motion offered, that John W. Hanifin be elected President, and it also passed unanimously. With those actions taken, the meeting adjourned.

. . . .

. . . . .

We made our way to the airport and flew back to Cleveland, giving everyone a few hours of quiet. That all ended as soon as we landed at Lakefront Airport. When Dr. LeFevre, Eaton's son-in-law, stepped off the plane, he was immediately besieged by the Cleveland press and asked for an explanation of the events just passed in Baltimore. I have never known how the media got the word, but I assume a press release must have been issued after the meeting and the press just staked out the airport to await our return.

I remained on the plane, which was going from Lakefront Airport to the company hangar at Cleveland Hopkins Airport where my car was parked, and did not actually see what happened, but the press apparently mercilessly attacked Dr. LeFevre. Later, I was told, even members of his family berated him for having part in such a dastardly thing.

The headlines and stories in the Cleveland Plain Dealer the next day indicated that Eaton had been replaced as C&O's Chairman at a special meeting of the board the day before and that neither Eaton nor his son was present at the meeting. Dr. LeFevre was quoted as saying, "I can't give you any comment. No comment at all." And Eaton, according to the paper, was unavailable at his home in a Cleveland suburb.

The next week speculation ran rampant in Cleveland and elsewhere, but there was nothing public until the following Sunday when another article appeared speculating about what had happened. No one, as far as I know, made any public comment or statements about the affair then, or later.

• • • • • • • • • • • • • • • • • • • •

• • • • •

What actually happened on the Monday after the special meeting and thereafter was fascinating. I received a visit from a local Cleveland attorney who was representing Eaton. The attorney suggested that he and I should "work out the details of the changeover." I pointed out that this would be better and more appropriately handled by our Vice President-Law, Owen Clarke, and suggested arranging a meeting between the two of them. The attorney declined, indicating that Eaton wanted to keep his office and staff and that "something had to be worked out." With that, he got up to leave and, as he headed for my door, I again urged that he discuss the matter with Clarke.

Later in the week I received a telephone call from the lawyer. After consulting with Clarke, I suggested to the attorney that Eaton could continue in his present office, with an office staff of up to six people, as compared to the 13 he had, and that he would receive an annual salary of $100,000 in recognition of his long and valuable service to C&O. Shortly, the attorney replied that this was insufficient and that something more had to be done.

The following week, another call came from the attorney, asking what we had worked out? I told him the company's offer was now three employees and a salary of $50,000 a year. This was summarily rejected.

When the next call came from the attorney, I gave him the company's final offer: one assistant, a $30,000 annual salary, and company-paid expenses of up to $30,000 a year. Apparently, this got the word through to Eaton that negotiations were not advancing in a desirable manner ... and

. . . .

the final offer was accepted.

. . . . .

After all arrangements had been completed, the board felt
Eaton should be appropriately recognized and so another special meeting
was called for the end of the week, to be held at the home of Dr.
Eisenhower in Baltimore. At that meeting, Eaton, who was then 89 years
old, was elected Chairman Emeritus, loudly praised for his valued contribu-
tions to the company and the country, and a "love feast" was held by all.
From that time on, Eaton continued to be a very valuable member of the
Chessie Board.

Cyrus Eaton remained on the board and participated fully in its activities until March 20, 1978. In all his discussions with me throughout those
intervening years — and those he had with others as far as I knew — he
never mentioned the unpleasantness of October 1973. He never uttered a
cross word or made any other reference to those events. He was a perfect
gentleman.

At age 94, Eaton's health had begun to decline rapidly, and he
announced to the board at his last meeting that he felt it necessary to give
up his duties. At that meeting, the board accepted his resignation as a director, elected him an Honorary Director and re-elected him Chairman
Emeritus of the company. He lived another year or so before his death on
May 9, 1979 at age 95.

When Eaton died, we were in the latter stages of our planning
for the Chessie-Seaboard merger and the creation of CSX. Eaton's
secretary, Raymond P. Szabo, had been a long-time and valuable employee

of Eaton's and the company. My secretary at the time had indicated that she would not move to Richmond and I asked Ray if he would have any interest in going to Richmond with me? Much to my surprise, and delight, he said, "Yes, I would love to do it." So, when we established CSX's head-quarters in Richmond a year and a half later, Ray came with me as my secretary and valued assistant. Thus, my long relationship with Cyrus Eaton continued, indirectly, long after his death. Ray remained in that position for two years until being promoted to Vice President-Administration of CSX and assuming responsibility for overseeing CSX's charitable activities.

Chapter XVI

. . . .

Secrets of
The Greenbrier's
Bunker Revealed

Diversification of other railroad properties begins

After the creation of the new parent company, Chessie System Inc., our first steps of diversification were to separate our coal lands, which the railroad had long owned but was legally prevented from operating and were leased out to mining companies and others, into Western Pocahontas Corporation. We also moved The Greenbrier Hotel, in White Sulphur Springs, West Virginia, into a separate, non-rail company. Real estate that we owned, but which was not needed for railroad operations, was placed into a new company named Chesapeake Realty Development Corporation, with Bob McGowan in charge.

When The Greenbrier Hotel was returned to C&O by the U.S. government after World War II, it underwent extensive rehabilitation and reopened in April 1948 to considerable acclaim. In 1950, E. Truman Wright was brought in from the Lake Placid Club in New York, and he remained president and managing director of The Greenbrier until his retirement in 1973. At that time, The Greenbrier was operating at about a break-even point, and not contributing much money to the company. We engaged out-

• •

side experts to advise us on what to do about this, asking them to look at a possible sale, operational changes, or reorganization.

Fortunately, because I would never have agreed to sell it, the consultants concluded that a sale was not feasible because of the hotel's marginal financial performance. They did feel, though, that the hotel could be made more profitable by improving on its ability to market itself to conferences and other large groups and make other operational changes under new leadership. After a long search, John S. Lanahan, who had operated The Breakers in Palm Beach, Florida, was selected as the new Managing Director of The Greenbrier. A few years later he moved to Cleveland as Chessie's Vice President-Sales, and his assistant, William C. Pitt, III, was made President of the hotel. Pitt continued after the formation of CSX, and when we acquired Rockresorts, he became head of all CSX Resorts. Ted J. Kleisner, his assistant manager, took over The Greenbrier and remains President and Managing Director as we move into the 21st century.

• • • • •

To me, The Greenbrier was and still remains very special. This goes way beyond the fact that it is profitable, is a first-class hotel and is managed and operated by wonderful people. The Greenbrier is in a class by itself. It reflects quality, refinement, and the best of everything. It is one of the few things that sets CSX, and before it Chessie, apart from other companies. I think we all like to be associated with the best, and when one speaks of The Greenbrier to someone, you immediately get a very special reaction. This has happened to me all around the world.

The people at The Greenbrier long ago learned that service is the name of the game and they go out of their way, routinely, to give good service. They are the greatest asset of The Greenbrier and know good service brings people back. These feelings go far beyond every one of the employees — it extends to their families. Generations after generation of these great people have worked at The Greenbrier and they take great pride in "their" hotel. This is very, very special. Our job was to make certain that we encouraged and did what needed to be done to protect that attitude; that heritage. The Greenbrier also serves as a role model for the rest of the corporation. If the employees of other CSX companies had the same dedication and the same spirit, we — and our customers — all would be much better off.

. . . . .

For many years, there was an air of mystery about The Greenbrier. That mystery is out in the open now and actually has become something of an attraction for our guests. I'm talking about the "bunker," of course, the government hide-away that would have accommodated the legislative branch of the Federal government in the event of a nuclear attack on our nation.

As Assistant Treasurer of C&O, I first learned about the government bunker at The Greenbrier in 1960, when construction was underway.

Early on, I learned that $12 million had been placed in various C&O bank accounts for the construction of a new wing of The Greenbrier. I did not immediately learn the source of those funds, but found out soon thereafter, when the construction and disbursement of funds began, that it was the U.S. government.

• • • • • • • • • • • • • • • • • • • •

C&O President Walter Tuohy later told me he had negotiated the deal with government representatives in the late 1950s under President Eisenhower's administration. Since I was not involved in those discussions, I have no idea who was involved on the government's behalf.

• • • • •

From time-to-time over the years, C&O and CSX had been approached by various hotel chains and others wanting to purchase The Greenbrier. We were always polite and listened to the offers, but knew we could not sell the hotel because of our arrangement with the government for the use of the "bunker."

The existence of the facility and the contract led to an interesting ruse in 1988 when CSX announced a major restructuring. We had completed a review of all our holdings that summer and decided in September of that year to divest our non-transportation holdings. As part of that plan, we included The Greenbrier and our other resorts in the offering. We privately assured the government representatives that The Greenbrier really was not for sale, and that there was no need for them to be concerned. However, we had to "include" it in the restructuring announcement that we were planning to sell all of our non-transportation assets — to do otherwise would have raised too many questions.

This led to a spirited debate at the CSX board meeting when we discussed and sought board approval for the restructuring. During the time the bunker contract with the government was in effect (and the facilities were maintained at the ready, on standby), the C&O, and later, Chessie and CSX, Chief Executive Officer and the President of The

Greenbrier were among the few company employees with the appropriate security clearances. In addition, one company director was cleared and had knowledge of the bunker. For many years, the designated director was Frederick Deane Jr. from Richmond. So when he went along with the ruse and argued against sale of The Greenbrier during our discussions of the restructuring, he was aware of the arrangements and the impossibility of selling it. Other directors, however, were not aware of the security matters. In particular, I remember Jim Price arguing against the sale because he felt The Greenbrier was an integral part of Chessie and CSX, and should not be sold under any circumstances.

A few weeks after the announcement, we pulled The Greenbrier from the list of assets to be sold, citing shareholder objections. In reality, I think we had gotten only one or two letters of concern from shareholders and maybe a couple of phone calls. But no one questioned us on the change and we were able to take the hotel off the block without raising any concerns about the legitimacy of the balance of our plans. Even without the government's bunker, I would not have sold The Greenbrier; it is one of those very rare and priceless assets that one doesn't part with.

. . . . .

Initially, the contract with the government provided for an annual "inactive lease payment" of $25,000 that later was raised to $50,000, where it remained until the end of the arrangement. Each year the check was hand delivered to the President of The Greenbrier, and he delivered it to me as C&O Treasurer, and later as Vice President-Finance, and I always endorsed and personally deposited that check into The Greenbrier's bank

. . . .

account. These were the only funds that I actually saw or handled for the company in my entire career. It was classified as "Miscellaneous Income" to avoid any undue attention.

. . . . .

Audits of The Greenbrier presented problems, especially after the establishment of CSX. Josiah A. Stanley, who had been Chief Internal Auditor of Seaboard Coast Line before our merger, headed the new CSX Internal Audit Department. As a part of the department's routine internal audit duties, Stanley and his associates audited The Greenbrier.

At his first audit, he raised questions about certain expenditures at The Greenbrier. Under arrangements between the government and The Greenbrier, a few selected Greenbrier employees would spend part of their time maintaining the government facility.

Entries in The Greenbrier's books covered this activity, but they were purposely unclear. Stanley and his people could not understand the nature of the entries and asked the hotel's staff for an explanation. Not receiving what he considered a reasonable response, he then went to The Greenbrier's president. Again, the explanation was not satisfactory to Stanley, and he appealed to me, after making the comment, "Something fishy is going on at The Greenbrier." We then had an interesting series of discussions, but nothing I could say cleared up the issues to his satisfaction. Finally, I was forced to tell Stanley that these particular entries dealt with "private matters," and his audit notes, if he felt it necessary, should indicate that the Chief Executive Officer of the Company was personally responsible and further examination was not warranted. As I had expected, he felt it necessary...and we ended up having his appropriate exceptions filed in the company records. I assume they are still there.

Joe Stanley was a "bulldog," and was not about to accept any explanation that he did not fully understand. I would not have wanted him to be otherwise. I don't think he ever completely forgave me for not telling him about the nature of the entries. Of course he later found out what was really going on, but only after the existence of the "bunker" became public knowledge ... thanks to *The Washington Post*.

Chapter XVII

. . . .

Penn Central Doomed by Personality Clash

A great opportunity was lost and later proved costly.

In my opinion, the merger of the Pennsylvania Railroad and the New York Central into Penn Central was doomed from day one. Most organizations are a reflection of those at the top, and that was definitely the case at Penn Central.

With two strong-willed individuals, Stuart Saunders and Alfred E. Perlman, each so dominant in his own railroad, and with their inability to work together, the problem spread throughout the two organizations. If Perlman and Saunders had worked together in a genuine spirit of cooperation, I believe that system would have worked and the railroad industry would be vastly different today.

As to whether Section 77 was the answer to Penn Central, I didn't know, but I always felt that some new type of reorganization or recapitalization plan would have to be developed. I was involved in the search to find a solution to the Penn Central's woes from the early days, because Chessie was operating in the same area as Penn Central. So we fol-

· · · · · · · · · · · · · · · · · · · ·

lowed developments very closely, since this was our primary competition in the Northeast. Jack Fishwick, President of the Norfolk & Western, suggested the creation of a "firewall," having the Federal government take over and subsidize the eastern portion of the Penn Central. Our concern was that the government would put so much money into Penn Central that it would create problems for the rest of us.

There was no question that Penn Central had special concessions — in cutting out a lot of track and being able to reduce its operations — that the solvent railroads did not enjoy. On May 20, 1975, Secretary of Transportation William T. Coleman asked Jack Fishwick and me (as President of C&O/B&O) to meet with him and his Deputy Secretary, John Barnum. His goal was to see if he could find a way that our railroads would agree to take over the entire Penn Central and the other bankrupts, with some type of governmental help.

After a full day of discussions, the Secretary proposed a suggestion. He said he felt he could obtain a $500 million grant for each of us, plus another $2 billion each in what he termed "a soft loan" (a low interest rate with delayed repayment terms) if we would agree to take over the entire Penn Central system. I indicated that I felt the Chessie board could accept those terms (after appropriate study), but Fishwick rejected the idea, and would have nothing more to do with it.

During the next month, we continued to talk with Secretary Coleman and his staff, and in June we reached agreement with the United States Railway Association (USRA) that C&O would be willing to buy the Erie-Lackawanna Railroad, and most of the Reading Railroad, for $115 million cash. One of the alternatives we suggested, if the acquisition of Erie and

• • • • • • • • • • • • • • • • • • • •

Reading was not acceptable to USRA, was that we would be willing to buy only the Reading and some Penn Central lines leading from Columbus, Ohio, to Charleston and Deepwater, West Virginia.

USRA Chairman Arthur Lewis immediately declined this alternative. His feeling was that the purchase had to be all of the Erie and Reading, or nothing. He was unwilling to make any reduction or concessions, saying that USRA was only concerned about establishing some type of competition for Penn Central. He felt that adding the Erie-Lackawanna to the Chessie System would provide a viable alternative between Chicago and New York and between Chicago and Philadelphia, the main lines of Penn Central. However, he strongly believed that any reduction in that plan, which would leave out Erie-Lackawanna, would not provide the competition he felt was necessary in rebuilding or reconstituting Penn Central.

We pointed out that Chessie would get into New York through the Reading, but it would not be a direct service from the Midwest, because the B&O goes through Pittsburgh and then south into Maryland before turning north to Philadelphia and into New York. Lewis felt that having the Erie-Lackawanna line, which was relatively direct from Chicago through Akron and the southern tier of New York State, was a more viable, competitive alternative. When he said we should take the whole thing, or nothing, we agreed to further study.

I testified before a Senate committee twice, and we promised to determine if it would be possible to structure a deal that was financially viable to Chessie and acceptable to USRA.

We spent most of the summer and fall of 1975 in further studies. In

· · · · · · · · · · · · · · · · · · · ·

November 1975 we made an offer of $54.5 million to acquire the Erie-Lackawanna from Ohio east, plus the Reading and parts of the Central Railroad of New Jersey. The USRA board accepted that offer on November 6, 1975.

Meanwhile, the N&W was expressing no interest in buying any part of the bankrupt estates. Jack Fishwick continued to urge a demarcation along what he termed "the firewall." This partitioned the Penn Central and the other bankrupts into two parts. The first part, which was to be behind the "firewall," fell roughly east and north of a line from Buffalo, New York, and Harrisburg, Pennsylvania, to Washington, D.C. As N&W envisioned things, the government should have nationalized those lines. The lines west of the line were to be sold or otherwise disposed of by the bankrupts' trustees.

Norfolk & Western never altered its position. It never made or agreed to any proposal that would have it acquire any part of the Penn Central or the other bankrupt roads.

Our offer to USRA was contingent on reaching satisfactory agreements with the labor unions of the Erie-Lackawanna and Reading. We proposed to operate the acquired lines under the labor conditions then in effect on the B&O. The B&O agreements were more costly to us than were those of the C&O, but since the Erie-Lackawanna and Reading would connect with the B&O, we were willing to extend the B&O labor agreements to the newly acquired lines. The railroad unions rejected this offer outright, insisting that the to-be-acquired lines only would be operated under their then existing labor agreements. Since the union agreements on the Erie-Lackawanna and Reading were more onerous and even more

. . . .

costly, we felt we could not profitably operate these new lines under their existing labor rules.

Negotiations continued through the end of 1975 and early into 1976, but the unions would not budge. They had a great arrangement (for them) with the Erie-Lackawanna and the Reading. Even though these costly labor agreements were one of the reasons Erie-Lackawanna and Reading were bankrupt, the unions refused to make any changes, and we reached a stalemate during January and February.

. . . . .

Secretary Coleman, however, wasn't quite ready to give up on finding a private sector solution. In early February 1976, he called W. Graham Claytor, president of the Southern Railway, and me, to his office in Washington.

The Southern had agreed to purchase Penn Central lines on the Delmarva Peninsula, from Norfolk, Virginia, to Wilmington, Delaware, about the same time Chessie had agreed to acquire the Erie-Lackawanna and Reading, but they too were having difficulty in reaching labor agreements.

The meeting began at 9 a.m. in the Secretary's conference room with Claytor, the heads of the major railroad unions and myself in attendance. For about an hour, Secretary Coleman explained the vital importance of reaching agreements and finding some resolution of the Penn Central problem to all of us. Then he suggested that the Southern purchase was far less complicated than the Chessie purchase, and thus it would be desirable for him to meet with Claytor and the union people first and get that prob-

• • • • • • • • • • • • • • • • • • • •

lem resolved. Then he could meet with me and with the labor union representatives on the Chessie part. So, around 10 a.m. I was sent to the office
of his Deputy Secretary, John Barnum, with Coleman commenting that,
hopefully, they would finish their negotiations regarding the Southern by
noon, and could start after lunch with me.

Lunchtime came and Secretary Coleman reported that they had not
reached agreement. He suggested it would be best for me to have lunch
and come back for our discussions. I returned after lunch and the afternoon
passed with me still waiting in Barnum's office. At about 6 p.m., Secretary
Coleman reported that they were still negotiating with the Southern, and
perhaps I should go out for a bite of dinner, and be back prepared to reach
agreements after dinner.

I did that and then returned to Barnum's office, remaining there until
2 a.m. Secretary Coleman came into the office at that point and reported
that they "had not quite finished their negotiations on the Southern" and
suggested it might be best if I found a place to sleep for the remainder of
the night.

Since I had flown down on the company plane from Cleveland that
morning with the expectation of flying back in the afternoon, I had not
brought any clothes or toilet articles. Secretary Coleman prevailed upon the
desk clerk of the L'Enfant Plaza Hotel to find me a room, and I was sent
off at 3 a.m. to spend the remainder of the night.

The next morning I returned to the Department of Transportation,
and about noon Secretary Coleman indicated that they had not been able
to reach any meeting of the minds regarding the Southern, and in view of

• • • • • • • • • • • • • • • • • • • •

that I might as well return to Cleveland and wait for a later date.

During the next two weeks, we were pressured by several governmental representatives to accept the Erie-Lackawanna and Reading properties with their own labor agreements, and not insist on B&O terms. When I explained that this would not be financially feasible, I was told it was my duty as a patriotic American to have the railroad sacrifice something in order to resolve the Penn Central crisis. William J. Ussery, at that time the head of the U.S. Mediation Service and later Secretary of Labor, was particularly strong in his insistence that we must take the deal. We did not "take the deal," and after a period of time, negotiations stopped. Thus ended our proposed purchase of the Erie-Lackawanna and the Reading.

• • • • •

When Conrail was proposed later that same year (1976), the labor unions apparently felt they could pressure the government and USRA into accepting the existing labor agreements in any restructuring of Penn Central, feeling they did not have to make any concessions in order to resolve the problem. As a result, they took a "feet in the mud" attitude and just would not budge. They ended up paying a terrible price later, but then felt they were "in the driver's seat" and did not have to make concessions.

Once Conrail was created, there were huge buyouts of labor on the Penn Central and other bankrupt properties, but with the government paying the bill. A lot of people lost their jobs, but the termination payments were very liberal, far more liberal than was normal in general industry. Looking back, I suppose the labor chiefs felt they could either continue their expensive rules or get the costly buyouts. That is exactly what happened.

. . . .

. . . . .

Conrail started operations on April 1, 1976, April Fools' Day. I never questioned the activities of the United States government, but there were grave doubts as to how long Conrail would last. When Conrail was formed, large segments of the former Penn Central and other bankrupts were immediately abandoned, large numbers of employees were eliminated, and the slimmed-down system certainly had every opportunity to operate efficiently and profitably — opportunities that other railroads did not have. The question was whether anyone could rehabilitate the remaining physical properties, and, more importantly, could Conrail re-establish confidence in its customers and the employees that remained.

. . . . .

The property Conrail took over was in horrific condition. There had been very little maintenance for many years, and it required tremendous amounts of funds to rehabilitate the tracks. We had seen reports of freight cars derailing while sitting still in a yard, and similar problems. That was pretty bad.

Right after Edward G. Jordan was appointed President of Conrail, he made his first appearance at an AAR board meeting. I had several dealings with Jordan, as he was the president of one of our main competitors. His background was in insurance and he was very pleasant. I spent a considerable amount of time in his office, trying to find ways — unfortunately without much success — that we could work together for our mutual benefit.

Over the years, he spent a lot of government money... about $7 billion in all. But he did not find a way to operate profitably and continued to ask for — and obtain – more government money until late 1980.

. . . .

Then L. Stanley Crane, who had been head of the Southern Railway before retiring, moved to Conrail and a new era began. Conrail started making money under Crane. All we really knew about Conrail's activities was what we read in their financial records, and how they handled inter-change business with us. We knew they had serious problems when Crane arrived.

We had well-founded hopes he would bring improvements. Crane had been very effective and efficient as head of the Southern and was con-sidered an operations expert. So, we hoped things would get better — and they did. Conrail and Chessie had innumerable inter-connections, all the way from Chicago and St. Louis on the west, throughout the industrial Northeast, and any breakdown in Conrail's service impacted strongly on us and the N&W. The turnaround Crane engineered was most welcome.

. . . . .

It has turned out that labor conditions and costs since that time have been ameliorated throughout the industry, and perhaps that would have occurred regardless of Penn Central. It may have been in a different form, but competitive pressures and the push toward deregulation — and then general business conditions — may have made it possible later for railroad costs to be reduced merely for the railroads to stay in business. So I can't say that the Conrail labor conditions were the only reason railroad labor costs have been reduced in recent years; the changing competitive balance was undoubtedly another reason.

. . . . .

Looking back, one cannot help but wonder what would have happened had Chessie been able to reach agreement to acquire the Erie-

• • • • • • • • • • • • • • • • • • • •

Lackawanna and the Reading. That would have brought more competition in the east, but with the major reduction in Conrail employment and its ability to eliminate branch lines, Chessie may have had difficulty in maintaining service in the New York market.

If Chessie had acquired those lines, it would have been a benefit to the country, and to Chessie, but it certainly would not have been a bonanza.

The most interesting retrospective analysis of the whole experience, in my mind, has to be what would have happened had Jack Fishwick not issued what surely is the most expensive "No" in American corporate history? Just consider the financial implications.

Each of us would have received a $500 million grant and a $2 billion soft loan as was offered by Secretary Coleman. Instead, the country spent $7 billion of taxpayer money subsidizing Conrail's operations and funding the extensive rehabilitation of the bankrupts' lines from 1976 through 1980, just four years.

Then, in 1997, CSX and Norfolk Southern spent well over $10 billion acquiring Conrail, dividing the property between the two. Had we taken Secretary Coleman's deal, rather than having spent the $10 billion, we would have received a billion dollars in cash, plus $4 billion in soft loans.

I will always believe – as I would expect would most others — that would have been a much better deal.

So, I think we can easily say that Fishwick's "No" cost somewhere between $15-20 billion. And that's without considering a present value calculation as to what the $5 billion would really be worth today, considering

• • • • • • • • • • • • • • • • • • • •

the market opportunities that were foreclosed and won't be realized until after 2000, if ever, in terms of their entirety, or allowing anything for the headaches we all suffered through and the opportunities we all lost in the ensuing years.

❖   ❖

Chapter XVIII

. . . .

First Choice for Chessie President Didn't Work Out

Partnership ended over proposed purchase of Erie and Reading Railroads

Another of the very interesting people with whom I worked over the years was John William Hanifin. My first experience with John came in the late 1960s, when C&O purchased the Washington & Old Dominion Railroad, a short railroad of about 50 miles from Alexandria, Virginia, west to Purcellville, Virginia, at the base of the Blue Ridge Mountains. The W&OD was originally planned in the mid-1800s, with the idea of going all the way west. But, like so many other early rail lines, the money ran out and the line was built only to the foot of the Blue Ridge. C&O bought the W&OD in 1954 and later decided to abandon one of its branch lines. As the Chief Financial Officer of the C&O, I was sent to testify before the Interstate Commerce Commission and John Hanifin, who was Assistant General Counsel of C&O in Richmond, was assigned to the case as the lawyer.

When I became President in April 1971, one of my first requests of the board of directors was the election of three executive officers. Hanifin

• • • • • • • • • • • • • • • • • • • •

was elected Vice President of the Executive Department; Jack Ford, who had been Assistant Vice President in the Finance Department, was elected Vice President-Finance, and George Sandmann, who had been Assistant Vice President-Coal, was elected Vice President-Coal Traffic.

Hanifin was very familiar with the legal issues facing the company and also had worked with the traffic and sales departments. These were areas with which I had little familiarity and I felt he could be of great help in his new role, which proved to be the case. In recognition of his work, he was elected Executive Vice President and also was elected as a director of C&O in 1972. He clearly was my chief assistant and worked very closely with me on everything. Hanifin was very intelligent and had a keen insight into things that I might not pick up. Throughout those early years, we had a good relationship.

When I succeeded Cyrus Eaton as chairman in 1973, John Hanifin became President, continuing our partnership. The next year, in October 1974, at my recommendation, the board elected him Chief Executive Officer of the railroad. I was Chairman and President of Chessie System Inc., the parent company, and Hanifin became President and CEO of the railroad. So again, we continued our close relationship.

Over those years, it seemed that John's methods of operation increasingly began to rub some of our associates in the railroad the wrong way. However, since he was the President of the railroad and obviously worked closely with me, people did not openly complain. During 1975, however, problems between him and the railroad's staff continued to expand, with claims that he kept pressing for more and more authority and wanted everything his way. Over the summer, my relations with him began to

. . . .

strain and he and I began to have problems; conflicts would flare up from time-to-time. Nevertheless, I still felt he was doing a good job and had much valuable insight into the problems and opportunities of the company and that made me willing to put up with his personality even though by this time things were becoming increasingly difficult.

At the October 1975 Chessie board meeting, most of the day was devoted to discussing the possibility of Chessie making an offer to the United States Railway Association to purchase parts of the Erie-Lackawanna and the Reading Railroads. Hanifin did not feel this was a good thing and expressed his opinion to the board. On the other hand, I felt it was advantageous and recommended it for necessary board action.

At the end of the day, the board accepted my recommendation and voted to make the offer to USRA. This seemed to trigger something in John. He said, in very loud terms to the board, "You are doing the wrong thing!" Then, very forcefully and red in the face, he proceeded to shake his finger at members of the board saying, "You people should recognize that I am the President and Chief Executive Officer of this railroad and you should listen to me."

Trying to cool things down, I commented that the board obviously recognized there was a difference of opinion between us, but the board had acted. I then said that he and I would discuss this privately and that "we didn't need any more discussion of it here, before the board." This brought an end of the meeting.

As soon as I got home that evening, my telephone started ringing from directors of Chessie calling, saying, in effect, "We don't appreciate any-

• • • • • • • • • • • • • • • • • • • •

one shaking their finger at and lecturing us. As a board of directors, we'll have to do something." There followed a great deal of discussions that night and it was agreed, before the night was over, that it was time to ask for John's resignation.

The next morning I asked Owen Clarke, who was Vice President-Law and had been in the board meeting, to join me in my office. We discussed the matter and I explained to him that the board and I felt it was appropriate for John to resign. Then we went to see John in his office.

Explaining that I had received calls from members of the board the night before and it was agreed that he should leave the company; I said I was there to ask for his resignation. That upset him. He said to Owen Clarke, "You can't do this and I will have you disbarred for even suggesting such a thing." We said, "Well that's too bad, but that is what the board wants." I also told him it was what I wanted. I said I'd leave it up to him and Owen to work out the details and went back in my office.

John left the office, went home, and called his lawyer. His lawyer got in touch with Owen and after considerable discussion they agreed on John's resignation and the details of his departure.

In my opinion, his departure was a great tragedy for the company. John was highly intelligent, but very sensitive. In retrospect, he obviously felt that people were picking on him, ganging up on him, and his way of dealing with this insecurity was to demand to have things his way or else.

The scene with the board brought everything to a head and made it clear to all of us that things had gotten to the point where it was not possible for him to continue with the company.

There is no question that I was the person who kept recommending that John be moved up in the organization. Along the way, especially after he became President and Chief Executive Officer of the railroad, I knew he had become difficult to deal with. But I felt he was making a good contribution to the company, as did the board until things just got out of hand at that last board meeting. I have not seen or talked with him since the day after that board meeting.

Chapter XIX

. . . .

A Day of Terror at Terminal Tower

Apprentice accuses Chessie of cheating veterans; makes frightening visit

One of my most unusual and frightening experiences as President occurred on August 29, 1976, in Terminal Tower in Cleveland, even though I was miles from the office. When I got up that morning and saw it was such a beautiful day, I decided I would just take the day off. I had never done anything like that before and told my wife, "Let's take the day off and go somewhere."

About 10 a.m., someone at the office called my home, saying a former employee, Ashby Leach, had come to the offices with two guns, demanding first to see Eaton, and when he wasn't where, demanding to see me. When he was told we were both away, he got very agitated. Leach then asked to see an officer of the company and Vice President Bob McGowan voluntarily went to talk with him, even knowing that Leach was armed. Bob should be praised for that; it was a brave thing to do. Once my wife Betty and I learned that Bob had volunteered to see Leach, Betty went over to see Bob's wife, Jean, who was a neighbor, and stayed with her.

. . . .

There were a number of tense moments throughout the day
and at one time Leach held 13 people (some employees, some visitors)
hostage at gunpoint. He demanded radio and television coverage to tell his
story of how Chessie was cheating Vietnam veterans. This was denied him,
but the armed standoff did make that evening's national network news
shows. After seeing that on television sets that he had demanded be
brought in during the day, he surrendered around 6:30 p.m. to the SWAT
team that was surrounding the office.

As background, Leach was hired in May 1970 as a machinist at the
Huntington Locomotive Shop. For some reason he thought he was being
cheated out of on-the-job supplemental veteran's benefits. He accused
Chessie of "cheating thousands of veterans out of millions of dollars."

The accusation was absurd, of course, because Chessie had a very
aggressive policy of hiring Vietnam era veterans. In the years 1973-76, for
example, Chessie hired 4,928 Vietnam veterans – 37 percent of 13,269 new
hires during the period. Chessie far exceeded the government's goal for hiring Vietnam vets.

Later, Leach left Chessie and went to work for the Cotton Belt
Railroad in Pine Bluff, Arkansas, where he was earning the salary of a jour-
neyman, not an apprentice, and also receiving $300 a month in veteran's
benefits by attending a vocational school.

Apparently he still felt strongly about Chessie's record, because in
January 1976, Leach wrote a threatening and abusive letter to me, which I
did not see until many months later, saying: "You had better get the details
worked out because time is running out on you. You know I have the guts

• • • • • • • • • • • • • • • • • • • •

to do it." In April that year he quit his job as machinist in Pine Bluff and returned home to Huntington, West Virginia. He was next heard from when he showed up armed in the Chessie offices.

It was later revealed that he had left Huntington the day before, intent on driving directly to my house to confront me at my front door with his accusations. Since I had always answered my doorbell without any hesitation, the thought of such a confrontation still leaves me with a cold chill. On his drive to Cleveland, however, his car broke down en route, and his arrival in the area was delayed until the next morning.

From then on, I have always looked out my front windows before answering any unexpected doorbell ring.

Chapter XX

. . . .

The First Trans-continental Railroad... that didn't Happen

Biaggini kills a deal — and what would have been a great railroad — with his demands

E ach month in Washington, the railroad presidents customarily had an informal dinner on the Thursday night prior to the AAR meeting on Friday morning. At one particular meeting in late 1976, I happened to be sitting next to Ben Biaggini, the chairman of the Southern Pacific Company. He said they had been considering the possibility of combining the Southern Pacific with other roads, and wondered if Chessie would have any interest in talking with them? My answer was: "Sure, we would talk, even though nothing may happen." So we agreed to have our respective staffs study the possibility of putting Chessie and Southern Pacific together. We at Chessie would study Southern Pacific data, and SP would study Chessie data.

A couple of months later we got together again, but we had found in our studies that there was only one connection between the two roads. Chessie was in the northeastern United States, while Southern Pacific was in the west and southwest.

• •

The only point of connection was St. Louis, Missouri. We both wondered if having only one interchange point between the two systems would
be practical, so we went back for more analysis and planning.

For our next meeting, we both came armed with railroad maps and
plastic overlays and found there was one railroad in the middle that would
be an ideal fit between the Southern Pacific and Chessie. That was the
Rock Island Line that came into Chicago, St. Louis and Memphis on the
east, and extended to Denver and Tucumcari, New Mexico on the west.
The only problem was that the Rock Island was bankrupt, had been bankrupt for many years, and probably was on its last legs.

Nevertheless, we made studies of a three-way combination of SP,
Rock Island and Chessie, but soon determined that the Rock Island would
be more of a liability than an asset. So we gave up on that and started looking for another system that might serve as an intermediary connection
between the two of us. That other system proved to be the Seaboard Coast
Line, which in a three-way merger would have given us great coverage in
the United States, from Oregon and Washington in the Northwest down
the Pacific Coast, across the southern United States, and into the industrial
east. When one looks at a map of the three railroads, it forms a great system. So Biaggini and I invited Tom Rice to join in our discussions.

Rice agreed to join in our explorations and this prompted additional
studies and meetings in Washington, Jacksonville and Cleveland. Jack Ford,
Chessie's Vice President-Finance and I represented Chessie; Ben Biaggini
and Alan Firth, SP's Vice President-Law, represented Southern Pacific; and
Tom Rice, Chairman, and Prime F. Osborn III, President, represented

. . . .

Seaboard Coast Line. By the spring of 1977 we all had determined that such a three-way system might well be workable. We were still working without any public announcement. However, we all knew we were getting close to the point where some announcement would have to be made.

As our final private step, I suggested that each of the three of us offer a range of the maximum and minimum percentages that our particular company would need in a three-way merger, recognizing that the total of the three maximums would be well over a hundred percent. But, I was hoping that the three minimum numbers might be close enough to 100 percent that we could start talking in more specific terms. Personally, I felt that such a combination might work with Southern Pacific having about 40 percent of the combination and Chessie and Seaboard having roughly 30 percent each. This would mean that no one system would have a majority of the new company, and would give us some working room.

After we wrote down our maximum and minimum percentages and showed them to each other, Biaggini said his minimum percentage of a new company had to be at least 55 percent, and that Seaboard and Chessie could divide the remainder in any way we wanted. Both Rice and I felt this was unreasonable. We told Biaggini this and suggested that unless he would agree to something under 50 percent, there was no longer any need for discussions. Biaggini, in his customary outspoken way, said there was no way he would take less than 55 percent of any new company and that he naturally would be the controlling senior officer and the Southern Pacific would be "calling all of the shots." That ended the three-way discussion between SP, SCL and Chessie … and any thoughts any of us were having

· ·

about announcing and moving forward to pull off the nation's first transcontinental railroad merger.

· · · · ·

After the three-way talks had broken off, we spent a period of time looking for other possible merger partners. In May 1977 we began discussions with Ashland Oil, one of the largest companies in Kentucky. It had an oil business, a coal business, a strong brand in Valvoline, and was just launching a new concept, the convenience store/gas station combination. They were at the forefront of that concept and from it sprang a whole bunch of companies, like the 7-11s.

The Chairman of Ashland, Orin Atkins, and I decided the best way to explore the possibilities would be to take the key officers of Chessie and Ashland away for an in-depth discussion. At the Royal York Hotel in Toronto, we spent three days going over every division and every detail, financial, operational and otherwise of Chessie and Ashland.
It appeared that there would be advantages for a combination and it seemed a good idea to move ahead. So we undertook more serious merger discussions, working together over a period of several months.

Finally, in January 1978, Adkins and I met with our respective financial advisors in New York to see if we could devise a structure and a plan of merger for presentation to our respective boards of directors. After two days in a weekend of intensive negotiations, we arrived at an exchange ratio for the stock of between 1.05 and 1.10 shares of Chessie to a single share of Ashland. We haggled over the difference between the two numbers, the .05 of a share, for three hours. Neither one of us would budge; we could not

• •

close the .05 gap. After getting that close, we decided that if we couldn't agree on that, we might as well end the discussions.

We later exchanged "regret" letters, expressing disappointment that we could not come to agreement, but we had gone as far as we could go in terms of the exchange ratio. We would just have to move on to something else.

That "something else" turned out to be a merger with Seaboard and the creation of CSX, but that didn't appear very likely at the time. After SP, Seaboard and Chessie had agreed to disagree, I learned that Biaggini had gone back to Rice and said, "Now that Chessie is no longer interested, why don't we get together and the two of us talk about a combination of Southern Pacific and Seaboard Coast Line?" It would have been a very effective system stretching all across the southern United States. So those two roads, unbeknownst to Chessie or anyone else, began discussions.

Rice and Biaggini, initially, didn't get very far. Then Southern Pacific bought 10 percent of the Seaboard stock, and Biaggini called Rice and said: "Now that we are your largest stockholder, let's sit down and talk." Rice didn't have much of an alternative, so they discussed a merger for about 10 months. It is my understanding that the Seaboard was not overly enamored with the combination, or with being taken over by the Southern Pacific, but continued the discussions until May 1978 when the Seaboard decided that further merger discussions should be terminated.

Prime Osborn delivered that message, calling Biaggini in San Francisco at the exact hour that Biaggini was conducting his annual meeting of shareholders. After getting him off the floor of the meeting, he

• • • • • • • • • • • • • • • •

informed him that as far as Seaboard was concerned, the merger was off. I understand Biaggini had strong words in reaction to that news. Publicly, the Southern Pacific-Seaboard merger discussions were terminated in May 1978.

The Watkins family home in Fern Creek, Ky., near a suburb of Louisville as it appears today. (Charles Castner photo)

The Watkins family home in Henry County, Ky., near New Castle on Sept. 3, 1948. (Watkins Family photo)

Hays T. Watkins Sr. (center) and two unidentified gentlemen in front of the Bank of Fern Creek. (Watkins Family photo)

Attending the organizational meeting of the CSX Corporation Board of Directors at the Federal Reserve Building in Richmond on Nov. 1, 1980, were seated, left-to-right, J.J. Daniel, director; Dr. Fay A. LeFevre, director; Dr. Mary T. Kimpton, director; Hays T. Watkins, director, CSX co-CEO and president; Prime F. Osborn, III, director, CSX co-CEO and chairman; Nicholas T. Camicia, director; James L. O'Keefe, director; Buck Michel, director; and Frederick Deane, Jr. director. Standing, left-to-right, Edwin E. Edel, vice president-corporate communications, CSX; H. Furlong Baldwin, director emeritus; Philip Lanier, vice president-law and public affairs; John K. Stevenson, director; John R. Eck, director emeritus; Robert H. Radcliff, Jr. director; Norman G. Halpern, senior vice president, Chessie System Railroads (Chessie); Edwin L. Hatch, director emeritus; James L. Cremins, associate general counsel, CSX; Gregory S. DeVine, director and retired president and CEO, C&O/B&O; Richard A. Hollander, general counsel, Family Lines Rail System; W. Thomas Rice, director and chairman emeritus, Seaboard Coast Line Industries; Roland W. Donnem, senior vice president, Chessie; Alvin W. Vogtle, Jr., director; John W. Snow, senior vice president-corporate services, CSX; A. Paul Funkhouser, president and CEO, Family Lines; Garth E. Griffith, general counsel, CSX; William B. Sturgill, director; Gerald L. Nichols, vice president and executive assistant, CSX; Charles P. Lykes, director; Kenneth R. Daniel, director emeritus; William R. Carmichael, manager-office services; William E. McGuirk, Jr., director; J. Lee Williams, assistant corporate secretary, CSX; and Richard D. Sanborn, senior vice president-administration, Family Lines. (CSX Corporation photo)

• • • • • • • • • • • • • • • • • • • •

At their Henry County Home,
Hays T. Watkins Sr. (left), Hays T.
Watkins Jr. and Minnie Catherine
Whiteley Watkins. (Watkins
Family photo)

Sitting, left-to-right, are Betty J. Watkins, and daughter-in-law Wendy R. Watkins.
Standing, left-to-right, are Catherine R. Watkins, Hays T. Watkins Jr., Hays T. Watkins
IV, Hays T. Watkins III, and Caroline S. Watkins. (Greenbrier photo)

Prime F. Osborn, III, director, co-CEO and chairman, CSX Corporation, left, with Hays T. Watkins Jr. (CSX photo)

A. Paul Funkhouser, then president of CSX, left, and Hays T. Watkins Jr. (CSX photo)

• •

Ronald Reagan shakes hands with John W. Snow at the White House as Hays T. Watkins Jr. looks on. (White House photo)

On June 10, 1971, a year after the Penn Central bankruptcy, President Nixon discusses the railroad's dilemma with industry's top brass. Left-to-right: AT&SF's John Reed; AAR President Stephen Ailes (behind Reed); SCL's Thomas Rice; N&W's John Fishwick; C&O/B&O's Hays Watkins; PC's William Moore; IC's William Johnson; UP's Frank Barnett; White House staff's Peter Flanigan; DOT's John Volpe; President Nixon; SP's Benjamin Biaggini; SR's Graham Claytor; and BN's Louis Menk. (White House photo)

Chapter XXI

. . . .

First Chessie–Seaboard Talks Begin

Lessons learned from Penn Central fiasco helped CSX

T wo weeks after the merger talks between Seaboard and Southern
Pacific ended in May 1978, I called Tom Rice in Jacksonville from
my office in Cleveland with a simple question. "Now that you and the
Southern Pacific have terminated conversations," I asked, "could you and I
get together to see about the possibility of merging Chessie and Seaboard?"

Rice was not too excited about this, having just spent 10 months with
Ben Biaggini, but he agreed that we could get together. We met at the
Commonwealth Club in Richmond on June 3, 1978. We had a nice lunch
and talked about the possibility of making merger studies. While we were
sitting there, a friend of Tom's came by and said, "Are you two fellows talking merger?" We both looked up with complete innocence and said, "Why,
no, we are just having lunch and talking about railroad matters." After
lunch we agreed that we would get together again to talk further. Tom told
me that he was retiring as chief executive and that Osborn would be taking
over shortly, either that month or the next, and that he and Osborn would
get together, talk about this and get back to me.

. . . .

He obviously was not too excited, because when Osborn called he said that the first available date on their calendar was at the end of July — some two months later. Nevertheless, we met and decided we should start putting figures together. We also agreed that we would meet again with additional representatives of the two railroads.

That meeting was held on the Eastern Shore of Maryland at the picturesque home of Mike Kelly, a director of Seaboard Coast Line, and went very well. At its end, we agreed to meet again about two weeks later for further discussions.

Since Osborn had become CEO of Seaboard during the summer, he was the key executive involved in our discussions. Assisting him, along with Tom Rice, was Philip Lanier, Seaboard's Vice President Law and Public Affairs. For Chessie, Jack Ford and Ron Donnem, Vice President-Law, supported me.

Of course, both railroads were thinking about possible exchange terms, but we did not get to those matters at these first two meetings. Things were going so well that in early September we asked four members from the Seaboard Board and four members from the Chessie Board to meet with us.

We met again at Kelly's home, to explore things in greater detail. That meeting also went well, and based on earnings, assets, and other criteria, it seemed like some type of exchange ratio that would give Chessie in the area of 50 to 55 percent of the new company and the balance to Seaboard, was in order.

. . . .

However, keeping in mind the experiences of the New York Central and the Pennsylvania Railroad, I suggested we split everything down the middle 50-50. In that way, neither railroad would feel that it had been taken over, and neither railroad would feel it was in the superior or inferior position. I felt it would give us a good chance to work cooperatively together. When I suggested that, everyone agreed immediately. Our "merger of equals" was in place. We went back to the two boards shortly thereafter, made the public announcement and began planning the merger — the first of what were to become known as the "mega-mergers."

One thing we were most concerned about was the reaction of Southern Pacific, which still owned 10 percent of Seaboard. We agreed that I would be the one to call Biaggini. And so, with great trepidation, I called. I recounted the three-way discussions we had, reminded him that he had his chance with Seaboard, and now we wanted to have our chance. I told him we recognized he would be the largest stockholder of the combined company and that I hoped this was satisfactory with him and that we could work together without any major difficulty. Biaggini was very gracious, said, "Thank you for calling," and "We will have to go back and study our options and I will let you know."

Biaggini called me a few days later and said "We regret not being able to be a part of the combination, but we recognize that times move on. We do not propose to have any problem with this, and will look forward to being your largest stockholder." So that "specter on the horizon" disappeared. I don't remember exactly when SP sold its 10 percent, but it was not too long thereafter.

. . . .

After the merger announcement was made, there were some expressions of opposition, which resulted in our having a series of discussions with other railroads. I remember that the N&W wanted a few things, and the Southern wanted a few, and one or two of the midwestern roads also wanted some concessions. But, none of these demands were major. I have to think that the railroad industry, by that time, had matured and recognized that practicing such warfare as had Al Perlman back in our C&O/B&O days really was not productive and did not, in the final analysis, result in much gain for anyone.

. . . . .

Looking back, the decision to split everything in our Chessie/ Seaboard merger on a 50-50 basis was probably the wisest decision of my business life. Of course, we had seen the disastrous results of Penn Central, and the problems caused when there were two strong personalities who were not willing to work together for the common good. Early on, Osborn and I decided we would have complete agreement on every item, and any differences would be private and without outside interference. To quote Osborn: "If we ever have a disagreement, we will go into a room, lock the door, and not come out until we are in agreement." Fortunately, we never had the need to test that process.

The 50-50 concept carried us to decisions no one ever dreamed. First of all, we fashioned the stock exchange ratio so owners of Chessie and owners of Seaboard would each have one-half of the new company's stock. Next, we agreed that each company would name half of the board of directors of the new company.

This presented somewhat of a problem, since Chessie had 11 directors at the time and Seaboard had 24. I suggested we have 11 from each company, but Osborn felt he could not get below 15 or 16 from his group. We finally agreed on 12 each. It was no problem for us at Chessie to add one director, but Osborn spent many sleepless nights trying to decide who of the Seaboard directors would be "in" and who would be left "out." Some of those not chosen by Osborn were quite offended, and bruised egos remained for many years.

Both railroads operated in essentially different parts of the country, with only one parallel line, the 12 miles between Lexington and Winchester, Kentucky. For this reason, we felt it best to continue separate operations of each railroad, with minimal direction from corporate, the holding company. At the holding company we agreed we would concentrate on what we called the "Three-P's" concept – Policy, Planning and Policing. At the corporate level, we would establish overall policy and strategy, plan for the future and work with the business units on their annual and longer-range plans, and police the results, insuring compliance with our policies and plans by the operating units.

Both railroads, the realty and coal lands companies, The Greenbrier — in fact, each of the businesses — would operate independently. The only areas we would really manage at corporate were auditing, accounting and the treasury functions.

In addition, we agreed to select key executives of CSX with an equal number from the two railroads; to select a "neutral" city for our headquarters; and to have two chief executive officers — one from each company. This concept was novel, to say the least, but we were determined to carry the 50-50 concept through in every detail. We were not going to repeat the managerial and image problems of the Penn Central.

. . . .

Selecting an outside auditing firm also required compromise and a new beginning. We released the two firms that had independently audited Chessie and Seaboard, and conducted an exhaustive review of services with each of the then "Big Eight" national accounting firms, selecting Ernst & Whinney, which had not been associated with either Chessie or Seaboard.

In every decision, large or small, we were always conscious that one company could not be favored over the other. And that included how Osborn and I comported ourselves. Every organization reflects the policies, personalities and attitudes of the top executives. We were determined to show, in everything we did, that there was no partiality toward either group. I believe we succeeded in sending that message throughout the company... and beyond.

Even the selection of the name of the new company was designed to show no preference. "CSX" was the code name we selected for the incorporation of the new company for purposes of the ICC application. The letters simply stood for Chessie (C), Seaboard (S) and everything else and the growth we expected to result from the merger (X). Later, we planned to hold a contest among employees to select a permanent name from their suggestions. By the time the ICC finished its deliberations, the CSX name was well accepted and we saw no reason to change.

Chapter XXII

. . . .

Country Boy Goes to Washington; Meets the Presidents

Reagan most impressive; Carter most intelligent

As head of the railroad, I had an opportunity to meet with a number of United States Presidents. My first meeting with a President of the United States, as noted earlier, was with Richard Nixon, shortly after I became president of C&O/B&O. This was with the group of railroad presidents in the Cabinet Room of the White House just after the Penn Central bankruptcy and the establishment of Amtrak.

President Nixon had an impressive knowledge of the industry and its problems and displayed a genuine interest in finding solutions. He was very personable, and I found that meeting very interesting. After the meeting, we were invited to a reception in the White House, and he greeted each of us as we entered. I especially remember that when he shook hands with an individual, he faced you directly and completely. You felt you had his complete and undivided attention for that short period of time and that he was genuinely interested in what you had to say. Then, but only after you moved on, he greeted the next person with the same intensity. He was not

• •

the type that was always looking over your shoulder at the next person in line. When I met him at this time and commented about being from Chessie, he immediately recalled some very pleasant times he had had at The Greenbrier, and so we found an item of mutual interest.

The next president I met was Gerald Ford. Since his home was Grand Rapids, Michigan, a key point on Chessie's northern lines, we again had a point of mutual interest. President Ford was very pleasant, very friendly and very neighborly. He also seemed to have a genuine interest in those that he met. When he was Speaker of the House of Representatives, he was frequently entertained at The Greenbrier by Owen Clarke, Vice President-Law for Chessie, and former chairman of the Interstate Commerce Commission. In my conversations with him then and later, President Ford always got back to his pleasant memories of The Greenbrier and his times there.

Meeting President Jimmy Carter at the signing of the Staggers Act, in the East Room of the White House, and then standing behind him with other railroad presidents and the smiling Chairman Harley Staggers as the President signed the landmark bill, was one of my most satisfying times at the White House. President Carter and I also had a point of mutual interest. He is from Plains, Georgia, and one of his offices there was in the Seaboard Coast Line depot. At the reception following the signing, I had another opportunity to chat with him, and found him to be a very pleasant conversationalist.

President Carter was one of the most intelligent individuals to ever be in the White House, although he apparently did have difficulty in delegating and managing a large organization.

. . . .

President Ronald Reagan hosted several receptions for railroad presidents in the White House, and I found him to be a delightful individual. In his second presidential race in 1984, CSX operated a campaign train for him in Ohio. The following year John Snow and I were able to meet with President Reagan, and present him with a book containing pictures of the campaign special. In our conversation at the White House, I mentioned being a longtime fan of his, particularly in the early days of television when he was the host of the "General Electric Theatre."

He said he had always been a railroad fan, and that he had always traveled across the country by train when he was hosting the GE Theatre. He said, "I do a lot of flying now on Air Force One, but there's still nothing as pleasant as having a long enjoyable train ride." We both commiserated on the problems of rail passenger traffic in those days, and joyfully recalled the long-gone days of the luxury streamliners. He was a delight to meet, and it is a tragedy to find him in difficulties in these, his later days.

My meeting with President George Bush was through the auspices of J.J. Simmons, Chairman of the Interstate Commerce Commission. He and I had lunch with President Bush and some of his staff. President Bush was a delightful individual, very pleasant, warm and friendly and well versed on transportation problems, as well as many other things.

Of all the presidents that I met, I would say that President Reagan stands out as being the most impressive – although each one in his own way possessed and portrayed great stature.

. . . . .

• •

Of course, there were many other notables I encountered in Washington over the years. Just to mention a few:

If Elizabeth Dole had ended up on the Republican Party's ticket, I would have voted for it. When she served as Secretary of Transportation in the Reagan cabinet, I had many opportunities to meet with her. While we did not always agree — particularly on her recommendation to sell Conrail to Norfolk Southern — she was a most gracious and charming hostess. One of her goals at that time was a desire to resolve the Conrail problem. We all were in favor of getting it out from under the government, but for 16 months during that time she would not meet with me to discuss our alternative to her plan to sell it to Norfolk Southern. Of course, she knew where we stood and probably didn't feel she needed to hear our views in person. John Snow and I were spending a lot of time meeting with senators on the Conrail problem and everyone knew we opposed the administration's plan. Eventually, with the good help of many people, the Senate turned down the sale to Norfolk Southern and opted to let the company go private. This was our preferred course if we couldn't work out a joint deal with the government and Norfolk Southern that would have allowed us to split the property. In later meetings with Mrs. Dole, we frequently talked about Conrail, but never brought up our earlier differences. I thought it best to let bygones be bygones.

• • • • •

The two prime political movers in the rail deregulation efforts were James J. Florio and Brock Adams:

. . . .

Jim Florio (D-NJ) was a very able committee chairman. I worked closely with him for many years, and our Washington representatives worked with his legislative assistants while Conrail and deregulation legislation was being drafted and crafted. I always felt that he was a forward-looking Congressman, who was concerned about the railroad industry, and he recognized — far better than most of his associates — that some changes had to be made. At times, he, like most other legislators, would engage in "horse trading" and putting up "strawmen" in order to have something to trade, but that's how legislation is crafted. It is much like sausage — you should not learn about how it is made, or what is in it; just enjoy the results. Florio was a very dedicated and hard-working legislator, and I enjoyed working with him.

Brock Adams (D-Wash) was another very crafty politician. He was a bit more aggressive and a bit more vociferous than Jim Florio, but equally as effective and a long-time friend of the railroad industry. He also understood the industry's problems and worked hard on our issues, doing his best to help the industry. Adams was an expert in transportation and had been for many years before later being named Secretary of Transportation. It was a pleasure to work with him, as well as Florio, but Adams was a bit more temperamental, a bit more outspoken, and at times it was more challenging to resolve problems with him. Later, as U.S. Secretary of Transportation, he continued to be very able, very knowledgeable, very dedicated and a very conscientious public servant.

. . . . .

. . . .

Other individuals with whom I worked closely on railroad matters included:

Fred Rooney (D-Pa.) was a delight, and I always enjoyed being with him. Our mutual concern with Chairman Rooney was Bethlehem Steel Corporation, headquartered in his district. Bethlehem Steel was Chessie's second largest customer. We handled coal from most of their coal mines, and were a big purchaser of Bethlehem Steel rail, and sheet and plate products for freight car construction, so there were a number of common interests between Chessie and Bethlehem Steel that transcended our ties with any other steel company. He was well versed on railroad matters and railroad issues. We were always very pleased with his cooperative spirit. He listened with patience and asked good questions. He clearly was concerned about the future of the industry and, with Conrail headquartered in his state and with considerable operations in his district, that was only natural. He was a pleasant, delightful individual and I can recall many entertaining evenings with Chairman Rooney and his wife at functions in Washington and other rail functions around the country.

John Dingell (D-Mich.) was a unique individual, a real "piece of work," and a great legislator. As the head of the Commerce Committee under a Democratic Congress, and the ranking Democrat under a Republican Congress, Chairman Dingell was — and still is — a powerful member of Congress. He was well versed in transportation, about the automobile industry and its problems. Since General Motors was Chessie's largest customer, we had in Congressman Dingell an individual who was very concerned about rail transportation. He was a major force in Congress and we endeavored to convince him of the need for a strong rail industry, how deregulation would help us better serve our customers and the nation. Chairman Dingell scared off a lot of people because he appeared and sounded gruff, but he was never anything but very pleasant and gracious to me. It was always a pleasure to visit with him to discuss mutual problems.

Wendell Ford (D-Ky.) was a long-time senator from my home state of Kentucky. More important, Ford's home was in Owensboro, the home of Texas Gas Resources Corporation. We met with him a few times in the early years before we acquired Texas Gas and were warmly welcomed. After we added Texas Gas to the CSX family of companies in 1983, we were even more warmly welcomed. Sen. Ford at times seemed to have an aversion to Woody Price, our representative in Washington. Woody, mindful of this, often would suggest that I meet with Sen. Ford without his joining me. I never knew what the problem was between them. Sen. Ford never mentioned it and he certainly wasn't hesitant about expressing his opinion on any subject. Neither did Woody, so I didn't pry with either of them. With us having so many mutual interests in the Commonwealth of Kentucky, I always enjoyed meeting with Sen. Ford, especially after Texas Gas, which made things even easier. I always admired Sen. Ford, and felt he was a very dedicated and conscientious senator who well represented the people of Kentucky.

Vance Hartke (D-Ind.) was chairman of the Senate Commerce Committee when several of us from Chessie met with him to discuss railroad matters. That meeting was my first with him and it was memorable and told me a lot about him. After being kept waiting for some time after our scheduled appointment, we were ushered into his inner office and seated as he designated. Shortly after getting settled, his assistant brought in a

. . . .

tray of coffee cups. The first cup and saucer, trimmed in golf leaf, was cere-
moniously given to Sen. Hartke. Then, the rest of us received our coffee in
ordinary plain white cups and saucers. I suppose this indicated his lofty
position as chairman of the committee. In my opinion, he was too concerned with what could advance Sen. Hartke, and I never had much regard
for his ability or his dedication to the best interests of the railroad industry.
When we met years later, he was the representative of the bondholders of
the Georgia Railroad. He was not quite as proud, but was still more
impressed with his own importance than anything else.

*Barbara Mikulsk*i (D-Md.) is a great lady. We first met shortly after
C&O and B&O got together, when she was in her early days in
Washington as a member of Congress from Baltimore. She always made
quite a point of having an all-female staff, and frequently pointed out to us,
long before the days of the Women's Movement, that she made sure that
women had important, key roles in her congressional office. She also was a
knowledgeable representative for her district, particularly about Baltimore
and port matters, and always worked closely with B&O, and later Chessie,
on matters of mutual interest. Being under five feet in stature, she seemed to
compensate by being eternally loud and vocal, but I always enjoyed working
with her, and we had some mutually beneficial activities regarding
Maryland port matters. Later, when she became a senator, we met several
more times. She is one of the many dedicated individuals in Washington
working very hard for their constituents, and is an excellent public servant.

❖ ❖

Chapter XXIII

. . . .

When Two Votes First Outweighed Ten

The beginning of a beautiful friendship

O ne of the treasures of the B&O for many years has been the B&O
Railroad Museum in Baltimore. It contains a great collection of
memorabilia, equipment and other items originally accumulated for the Fair
of the Iron Horse in 1927.

At the time C&O and B&O came together in 1963, B&O was in
financial difficulties and the Museum, although open, was not functioning
well and had a minimum staff. At times it had been closed to the public.
After I became president in 1971 (and after we had gotten through the first
year with the coal strike and other problems), Howard Skidmore, our Vice
President of Public Relations, suggested that it was time to do something
with the Museum. He suggested we should reopen it, sell it, give it away to
the Smithsonian Institute, or close it entirely. He felt it had a very valuable
collection, though, and his strong preference was that the Museum be
reopened to the public. But first, he noted, the roof of the roundhouse had
to be repaired. It was leaking badly and putting the museum's priceless col-

• • • • • • • • • • • • • • • • • • • •

lection of railroad equipment in danger of being destroyed by the elements.

The question as to the future of the Museum was the subject of a staff meeting of C&O/B&O officers in Baltimore in early 1972. We had just weathered a major coal miners' strike, temporarily suspended the dividend and furloughed 40 percent of our people during that time. Even so, Skidmore began the meeting by recommending we should repair the roof of the roundhouse. And making matters worse, Skidmore said we couldn't repair the roof in just any way — it had to have slate, just like the original slate, and it would cost about $1 million. A million dollars in 1972 was very, very big money.

The matter was discussed fully and, at the end of the day a vote was taken on whether or not to divert $1 million of the company's money to fix the roof of the roundhouse. The motion carried by a vote of 2-10, the two being the president, Watkins, and the vice president, Skidmore. That was the first of our famous 2-10 votes. (The second one was when deregulation carried with John Snow and myself voting in favor.) We always said that everyone's vote was equal, but the president's vote was a smack more equal.

Having decided to repair the roof and do whatever was necessary to open the museum to the public, we turned our attention to other problems with the museum. One was the residential area around it, including some houses that were rather run-down. Also, a public street ran through the property. Since there were a number of tracks on the site and we wanted to set up permanent equipment displays on them, we needed to improve security to protect the public, the property and the equipment. The best solution was to build a fence around the property, but that required closing the street.

. . . .

Someone would have to go to the City of Baltimore and get the proper approvals.

An appointment was made for me to see the mayor, W. Donald Schaefer. On the appointed day, I made my first trip to City Hall in Baltimore. I was taken to the mayor's office and greeted by his secretary. After telling her who I was and that I had an appointment with Mayor Schaefer, she responded, "Oh, yes, we've been expecting you, please come in."

The mayor's secretary led me into a huge, magnificent room with very high ceilings and ornate furnishings. Mayor Schaefer was sitting at a desk in one corner of the room. He got up and the secretary introduced us. We exchanged pleasantries and sat down. As an opening comment, I said, "Mr. Mayor, I'm here to give the City of Baltimore a million dollars." He gave me a very quizzical look and said, "I beg your pardon?" So I told him again, "We want to give the people of Baltimore a million dollar gift." There was silence for a while after that. Then, in a very low voice, he said, "That's nice."

After more silence I began to explain, noting that we had decided to reopen the B&O Museum. To accomplish this, we were going to spend $1 million to repair the roof and do some other things that needed to be done so it could be reopened to the public and again be an important tourist attraction in the city. Again, he said, "That's nice," and then asked, "What do you want from me?" I told him we would like to put a fence around the property to protect it and that this would involve closing a city street, but other than that, we didn't want anything. Learning this broke the ice with the mayor. We then had a great discussion about the museum and it turned

. . . .

out he was a rail fan. I was there an hour and a half, and left promising to keep him informed on the progress of the project. About a month later, when I called for another appointment to let him know we had the cotract to repair the roof, I was warmly greeted.

From these meetings, we formed an association that developed into a genuine friendship that continues to this day.

Later, after I got to know him, he told me what he had expected at our first meeting. He said he expected the president of the railroad to come in with a half dozen or so assistants, with an entourage. When I showed up by myself, he said he was surprised. Then, when I told him we were going to do something for the city without asking for anything, he said he could hardly believe it. Of course, the more times the mayor tells the story, the better it gets and he still delights in telling it...at least as much as I do hearing it.

These meetings and subsequent meetings about the museum, as the work progressed, led us into the habit of getting together at least twice a year. On these occasions, I would brief him on what the company was doing in Baltimore.

He always had a list of things he wanted us to do and delighted in taking me around the city to show me what he was talking about. I've probably seen as much of Baltimore as many of the citizens of the city.

One of our visits was particularly memorable. B&O had a building in the port area that was becoming disreputable. He took me to see it and asked if we couldn't do something about it? I went back and asked our people to check into it, but our people didn't do anything to fix the problem.

The next time I saw him, he was full of fizz and vinegar and he didn't have a kind word for B&O and what we were doing for "his" city. I think that was the only time I ever heard any strong words from him. Of course, he was right, we should have done something. Shortly thereafter, we did.

Later, when he became governor of the state of Maryland, I frequently traveled to Annapolis to have lunch with him at Government House. After his two terms were over, I resumed going to Baltimore every year to have lunch, just to sit and chat about things. I found he is a delightful individual, gruff on the outside, but a very warm, considerate, concerned individual. We always have a great time together. He is one of my very favorite people and I count him as a dear friend.

Fortunately we got to the point that we could discuss things very frankly. When there were things that did not please him or were not advantageous to Baltimore, I could tell him about it and he would understand. He would not be happy, but he understood.

One of his great disappointments with me was his desire for Baltimore to be the headquarters of CSX. It was painful to tell him that we were going to Richmond, but I explained to him that Baltimore was just too closely associated with Chessie, that we had to pick a neutral site and that it would be Richmond. Of course, before CSX came along, Chessie kept headquarters in both Cleveland and Baltimore, although the vast majority of our people were in Baltimore and, for all practical purposes, Baltimore was the headquarters.

· ·

· · · · ·

Don Schaefer was and is a special individual. He has been totally dedicated to the city of Baltimore and building it up, and he did whatever was necessary to improve the city. If it meant challenging the corporate community against neighborhoods, the labor unions, the port administration, he did it. We all knew that and respected him for it. I can truly say that, of all the people I have worked with during my entire career, no one ranks as high in my regard, admiration and respect as Don Schaefer. He was an excellent businessman. As mayor and as governor, he was the chief executive and he knew how to get all constituencies working together. It has been a real pleasure to work with him.

Chapter XXIV

. . . .

The Hiring of John Snow, 1977

Chessie led push for railroad deregulation

A s the head of Chessie living in Cleveland in the 1970s, I would peri-
odically travel to Washington to meet with members of Congress or
regulatory agencies, but usually only if we had a problem or needed some
form of legislative or regulatory relief or assistance. These were sporadic, "as
needed" visits, and generally with large state delegations or groups such as
the AAR board, or state businessmen. During the bankruptcy of the Penn
Central, and the subsequent creation of Conrail, there were many meetings
with various groups or administration officials, but, again, they were primarily to deal with specific subjects or problems as they arose.

Gradually, it dawned on many of us that there should be a more
organized approach to meeting with our elected representatives and governmental agencies.

Most railroads (and most large companies), including Chessie, had
maintained a Washington representative for many years, but with varying
frequency of contact on a regular basis by the chief executives.

. . . .

In 1977, our railroad representative in Washington,
Charles Van Horn, who had worked for the B&O for many years and was
most able, announced his plans to retire. In searching for a successor, we
determined it would be helpful to find someone with prior governmental
experience who was capable of putting into practice some of our ideas
regarding establishing a planned and more regular schedule of visits.

After reviewing many possible candidates, we selected John W. Snow
to become the understudy, and eventual successor, to Van Horn. Snow had
been a key U.S. Department of Transportation official under Secretary
William T. Coleman, as well as having had experience in other areas,
including practicing law in the Washington area.

About this time, we were still concerned whether Conrail could survive, and the possibility of reduced regulation — or deregulation — was
accelerating. The airline industry had been deregulated under Alfred Kahn
and the railroad industry was right behind the airline industry in pushing
for some type of deregulation. So, it was very apparent that we had to be
adequately represented in Washington. When Van Horn retired, John
Snow went on point for us there and he turned out to be a great choice for
that job...and others that neither of us knew were to follow.

. . . . .

When the push for less regulation of the railroad industry began to
pick up steam, a few of us in the industry felt the time was right to press
for major changes. It was interesting over time to watch the reactions of
people both within Chessie and outside the industry as those of us who

· ·

wanted to push forward tried to build momentum. Within Chessie, all during the late 1970s, we had continuing staff discussions regarding the
Chessie position. Finally, in 1978, we devoted a full day staff meeting to the
subject, thoroughly considering the advantages and disadvantages of deregulation.

At the end of the day, we voted on whether we should adopt
a corporate position on complete deregulation. The vote, in favor of deregulation, was 2 to 10 and it carried, despite the margin, because the two
people voting for deregulation were President Watkins and Vice President
Snow. Every other department head, while agreeing that some form of
reduced governmental regulation was desirable, was unwilling to go so far
as to say that government regulation of the industry should be ended.

On the AAR board, the general feeling was very similar to that
of Chessie's officers. Most railroad presidents agreed that some
reduction in government regulation was desirable, but very few of them
went so far as to advocate full deregulation. So I was pretty much alone on
the board. There were some that were leaning toward less regulation, but I
don't remember any that wanted outright deregulation, at least not initially.

Frankly, in the beginning of our discussions, most of the presidents
did not think we could prevail if we went for more than modest modifica-
tions. However, the industry was in such a perilous condition in the 1970s
that all agreed something had to be done. Complicating the issue was the
fact that the railroads had antitrust immunity and were able to collectively
set rates. The various rate officers of railroads in different geographic
regions of the country would meet and, through organizations called rate

. . . .

bureaus, jointly set rates.

I remember very clearly our Chessie representative to this group saying that without collective rate making, the industry shortly would be in
chaos. I don't think his views differed from those of any of the other rate
officers. Generally, they all thought that unfettered competition, which
worked very well for every other industry, just wouldn't work in the railroad
industry. In their view, there was no way an individual railroad, left to its
own devices, could compete in an open and free marketplace. According to
most of the inside experts, thinking of doing so, much less actually doing it,
was impossible.

This resulted from a long-established mindset that tracked how the
industry had been managed and regulated over the years. It was not at all
surprising that the people who grew up in such an environment just could
not comprehend having the freedom to really operate a business as it
should be, rather than depending on mutual agreements and government
approvals.

This attitude was endemic in the industry and was very hard to over-
come. Even customers were comfortable with the then-current regime.
With the rate bureaus, even after rates were justified, customers knew they
could appeal to the Interstate Commerce Commission and at least delay
their implementation. Normally, however, the ICC would impose various
restrictions or concessions. Thus, customers found ways to operate under the
system to their own advantage and, like the railroads, had learned to live
with it. Deregulation, to the customers and the vast majority of the industry, represented the unknown — a major change. And no one likes change.

. . . .

After airline deregulation was enacted, it was obvious that the railroad industry might hope for more than just "some relief." There was a real possibility that we could get some form of deregulation. It was at this point that the railroad presidents really began to push. By the fall of 1979, the AAR board had voted overwhelmingly for full deregulation, and was behind the proposed legislation. As someone once said, "Success has many fathers; defeat is an orphan."

Draft legislation was circulated, discussed, worked, reworked and vehemently argued under the so-called Florio-Adams bill, named for Congressman Brock Adams, later senator from Washington and Secretary of Transportation, and Jim Florio, later governor of New Jersey. These two led the charge on the Hill and I worked closely with both of them. When the legislation passed in 1980, it was renamed the Staggers Act, in honor of the longtime chairman of the House Commerce Committee, Harley Staggers, from West Virginia. But Chairman Staggers was never in favor of deregulation, and had no part in its passage other than voting in the affirmative for the bill. The bill was named in his honor because of his long government service and (so it was then rumored) to secure his support.

I firmly believe the entire railroad industry would have gone bankrupt — yes, even the profitable roads — had we not been deregulated. I am equally confident that this, in time, would have led to nationalization, or some form of government-subsidized operation. Either would have been of much detriment to the country. The trucking industry always was the strongest competitive threat to the railroads. Even before its deregulation, it had far greater freedom in establishing rates and operating competitively.

. . . .

The fact that the airline industry — then the trucking industry — were deregulated helped foster the feeling in Congress that the railroad industry should receive similar treatment.

❖ ❖

Chapter XXV

. . . .

Politics in Virginia is of a Higher Order

Gov. Dalton helped land CSX for his state

John N. Dalton was elected governor of Virginia in 1977, shortly before Chessie and Seaboard started exploring the possibility of merger. By early 1979 it appeared that the merger would move forward. As a result, we started getting invitations from states to locate our headquarters in one of their cities. Maryland Gov. Harry Hughes, for example, entertained us with a group in Annapolis, hoping to get us to locate in Baltimore. Kentucky Gov. John Y. Brown and his wife, Phyllis George, entertained us twice, trying to get us to locate in Louisville or Lexington. The Browns had two small, intimate dinners, each with about 300 of their closest friends.

Then we got an invitation from Gov. Dalton for a dinner in Richmond. We had visions of another small, intimate dinner with 300 people. The night of the dinner, Prime and Grace Osborn, Tom and Jackie Rice, John and Patty Collinson and my wife and I went to the Governor's Mansion not knowing what to expect. Mrs. Dalton met us at the door, welcomed us and invited us in. One of us asked where the rest of the guests

• • • • • • • • • • • • • • • • • • •

were? She said, "This is it, John and myself." So four of us from Seaboard, four of us from Chessie and Gov. and Mrs. Dalton had a wonderful dinner. They completely charmed us all.

When we had final approval for the merger, we had a series of meetings within the company to decide where to locate the headquarters. It came down to Richmond or Louisville. Osborn favored Louisville. He had lived in Louisville when he was president of the Louisville & Nashville Railroad, a subsidiary of Seaboard Coast Line, and liked it. I was leaning toward Richmond, although Louisville was all right with me, too, since I was born in a Louisville suburb. In the end, as we discussed all relevant factors with the two boards, we tentatively decided that Richmond was the most logical location. It was closer to Washington and New York, had better rail and air service and the business climate seemed to be better. Virginia, for example, had a right-to-work law.

We asked our real estate people to look around and see what they could find in Richmond that would work for a headquarters office. We hoped for some space in one of the newer buildings. The word came back that the only place available was an old cigarette company warehouse. They said they could get it fixed up, but both Osborn and I agreed that would not work and asked them to find something else. They tried, but couldn't come up with anything.

So I called Gov. Dalton and told him we had tentatively selected Richmond, but were having problems finding suitable space. I explained we were looking for space in a building like the VEPCO building or the Federal Reserve Building. I told him we were coming to Richmond if we could find space; otherwise, we were going to Louisville. Our people had

. . . .

already located a new building in a beautiful area of Louisville on the waterfront. The owner was a friend of Osborn's and offered us the building rent-free for the first few years.

After I explained our dilemma to Gov. Dalton, he asked for a little time. Two days later he called, saying the 15th floor of the Federal Reserve Building was available and asked if that would be suitable? Of course, we said, that would be just fine.

Later, we found out that Gov. Dalton had called Bruce Gottwald, the president of Ethyl Corporation. (Gottwald's brother Floyd, then Chairman of Ethyl, was on the Seaboard board.) Ethyl Corporation had three floors leased in the new Federal Reserve Building. Gov. Dalton called him and told him he had a chance to get CSX if he could get space and then he asked for one of Ethyl's floors in the Federal Reserve. Gottwald agreed, giving up the 15th floor, and we moved to Richmond. That was pure John Dalton. Because CSX Corporation became the largest corporation in Virginia when it chose Richmond as its headquarters, there has continued to be substantial contact between the chief executive of CSX and the chief executive of the Commonwealth of Virginia — its governor. I was most fortunate to work with Gov. Dalton and each of his successors, and count those experiences among the most memorable of my career.

Following Gov. Dalton came Gov. Charles S. Robb, who got me involved in the creation and early problems of the state's Center for Innovative Technology. I met with him quite a few times on CIT matters and, later, he appointed me to the Board of Visitors of the College of William and Mary where our son had gone to school. Gov. Robb had a lot of new ideas, especially on education and technology. With CSX being new

• •

in the state, he hardly missed an opportunity to get us involved. I found him very able, very personable and a very easy man to deal with — indeed; he was one of the best governors I had ever dealt with.

Then came Gov. Gerald L. Baliles. My contacts with governors continued with him on CIT and general business items, especially the problems of the presidency of CIT. After the first CIT president left, another was selected but quickly resigned when a more lucrative position was offered in California. That prompted a complete review of CIT, and Gov. Baliles was able to persuade former Gov. A. Linwood Holton to come in and put CIT on the right track. I thought Gov. Baliles was very able, very effective. He was an especially thoughtful individual and, in my opinion, an excellent executive.

L. Douglas Wilder was lieutenant governor under Gov. Baliles. During that time, I had gotten to know him and found him interesting, if unorthodox. Very few gave him much of a chance at being elected governor. Being African-American was not thought to be an asset when running for political office in the Old Dominion. At a fund-raiser during the campaign, he asked me if I would work with other business leaders and help him select his cabinet if he was elected. I told him I would and in September of that year, I was amazed to read that candidate Wilder had announced a committee to be appointed if he were elected governor to help him select his cabinet. One of the names on the list was mine. This caused surprise among some of my friends. They didn't know I was an active supporter of the lieutenant governor and I explained I wasn't, but that I had agreed to help should he be elected.

After he won the election, he activated the committee, composed of 12 business and political leaders from all over the state. It was a very distinguished group, even if I do say so. In a series of meetings over six weeks, we reviewed lists of candidates that had been suggested for every post. With only one exception, Gov. Wilder accepted our recommendations, naming them as his cabinet. The only exception was his appointment of the chairman of the Democratic State Committee to a cabinet post, and he turned out to be an excellent choice, doing a great job.

In my opinion, politics was just a big game with Gov. Wilder. If one thing didn't work, he would back off and try something else. This made for an interesting period in Virginia politics. My only major disagreement with his style occurred fairly early in his administration. CSX had reached agreement to buy the outstanding shares not already owned by CSX of the Richmond, Fredericksburg and Potomac Railroad, our connection between Richmond and Washington. The deal was structured as a stock swap, making it tax-free for RF&P shareholders. The governor had the idea that the RF&P had a lot of valuable real estate. He felt our bid was low and wanted the state retirement system, which owned about 20 percent of the RF&P, to buy it for the real estate. Later, the state retirement system did buy the company, selling CSX the railroad and retaining the real estate.

This proved to be a great disservice to RF&P shareholders. The transaction by the state retirement system was for cash, which was all taxable, and the value of CSX stock, which the stockholders would have received tax-free, virtually doubled within a few months. So rather than getting a tax-free exchange that would have doubled in value, the RF&P sharehold-

• • • • • • • • • • • • • • • • •

ers got a smaller, taxable transaction. Apparently he had some advisers who kept telling him that the RF&P real estate was worth a whole lot more money. Unfortunately, he listened to them instead of to his own good, common sense.

While all of this was going on, he remained very positive with CSX on everything else. In fact, during this time I was named the "Virginia Businessman of the Year" and the governor introduced me at the awards dinner at the Science Museum of Virginia. Before the dinner, we chatted and I asked him what he was trying to do to us. He really didn't respond. Later in the evening he got up and introduced me as his "great and good friend."

By the time George Allen succeeded Wilder as governor of the Commonwealth, I had retired from active service with CSX, so my visits to the Executive Mansion were generally related to community and civic matters.

• • • • •

My political philosophy has changed very little over the years. I have always supported the individuals who I felt would be best for the office and I still do. I've never expected to receive any special favors for my support. As citizens we have a responsibility to support good government wherever we see it, or think we see it.

The political leadership in Virginia has always impressed me as being at a higher level than most other states within which CSX operates. There are probably several things that make politics in Virginia different. One is tradition. Virginia has a long tradition of great statesmen, and a little of that rubs off on all its candidates. Also, the fact that the governor is allowed only one term in office and cannot succeed himself or herself, makes the governor focus more on getting things accomplished. Otherwise, that person would be running for re-election all during the first term. The minute one is elected governor of Virginia, one becomes a lame duck, so there isn't much time to get moving.

This does have disadvantages. For the first two years, governors usually are operating under budgets that were the products of the prior administration. So it is not until the last year or two that they can make any impact on financial and fiscal policy. Finally, I think there is a general feeling in Virginia that politics is not a dirty word. Over the years, political leaders in Virginia have generally been politicians of a very high order. They play politics, but by and large, they have been very honorable people. Virginia, in my view, has been very fortunate.

❖　❖

Chapter XXVI

. . . .

Partnering with Prime Francis Osborn III

Merger led to mutual respect and true friendship

P rime Francis Osborn III. Let me start by again relating the
agreement concerning the new company, CSX, that we had regarding
his being Chairman, my being President and the two of us sharing the
Chief Executive Officer duties. This all went back to the meeting with representative directors of both companies at Mike Kelly's house on the
Eastern Shore in 1978 when we first discussed the possibility of a
Chessie/Seaboard merger.

Having made the 50-50 financial agreement, we decided that everything else would be split down the middle. And, "everything" included the
top job, so we decided that we would be joint CEOs. Osborn, since he was
older, became Chairman. From that time on, we worked together. We
agreed, for example, that the corporate staff should be split 50-50. When
we met, whether it was outside the company or at meetings in the company, the two of us always made certain that we approached things as equals.
We didn't know each other that well at the start, but we quickly developed a

real friendship. The more we worked together, the more we found that we had similar ideas and values and this, along with our determination to demonstrate that CSX was a true partnership, resulted in the arrangement becoming a way of life. We simply would not do things unless we were in agreement.

That included key meetings in the company and any outside appearances. Company meetings were not scheduled unless we both could be present. The same rule applied to outside events; neither of us would participate unless both of us were present. The thing that was in front of us all the way was the horrible example set by the Penn Central. Stuart Saunders and Al Perlman couldn't agree on anything…. ever. They had the red team and the green team and spent much of their time trying to "one up" each other instead of paying attention to the business and so did their people. We were determined that would not happen at CSX. We were not going to give anyone, insiders or outsiders, an opportunity to think CSX was anything other than a true partnership.

There were more than enough problems with putting the merger together — different cultures, different backgrounds, different operating practices, different regions of the country and different customers, just to name a few. We didn't need anyone thinking we had two different personalities at the top. We just wouldn't have it. We never had it in writing. I don't remember even discussing it at any length with Osborn. We just had an intuitive understanding with each other.

We agreed that if we ever had a disagreement we would go in a room and lock the door … just the two of us. And we would not come out until

. . . .

we had an agreement. We never had the need for that. We didn't always agree on everything, but after a few minutes of discussion, we always arrived at common ground. And after a time, this just became a way of life, became second nature. When we relocated to Richmond, we lived in the same area, in identical condominiums. We rode to and from work together. When we were in our temporary quarters in the old Seaboard building on West Broad Street in Richmond, we stayed in the same motel and ate breakfast, lunch and dinner together every day.

We became genuinely close, and no one ever doubted it, certainly not within the company. I'm not certain people outside the company really understood what was going on, but people inside the company understood and that was the whole idea. Our relationship went far beyond business. It became a friendship, a very close friendship.

. . . . .

Prime Osborn was a genuine, good man. He was good in every sense of the word. He was concerned, caring, intelligent, decisive, a pleasant fellow to be with whether you were in the office or out to dinner. He had a patent on southern charm and a grace about him that instantly endeared him to everyone. He had a great sense of humor and, yet, he knew what he wanted and how to get it done. He had a legal background and was a crackerjack lawyer. I had a financial background, so we meshed well together. Bookkeepers and lawyers, it has facetiously been said, are going to take over the world. In fact, they already have. We relied on and deferred to each other's judgment. If I didn't have a strong opinion on a legal or administrative matter, for example, I would defer to him. By the same token, he

. . . .

would defer to me on financial matters.

Osborn was a very thoughtful, concerned individual. I think the two of us were equally determined to make the CSX merger work and genuinely took the feelings of each other into consideration when we got together. Our personalities fit very well. We both had southern heritages. We both had worked our way up to heading major companies and we both knew that companies reflected the character and temperament of the people at the top. We always kept that and, therefore, each other in mind.

There seems to always be one common reason why mergers fail, or succeed. It is the way that the key people decide to go about implementing the merger. If the top people don't get together, that sends a resounding signal throughout the organization and beyond that the way to succeed is to fight. That is not the way to run a company. In such circumstances, people inside and out, try to play everyone off of each other and that doesn't work.

As in everything else, Osborn and I worked closely together in selecting the people for the corporate office. We first tried to visualize what we would need.

We had agreed that the two railroads were going to stay separate, at least for a while, so we made no changes on either of them. At corporate headquarters — where we would focus on what became known as "The Three P's" — we needed a chief legal officer, a chief financial officer, a general administrative head and an internal auditor. We looked at the people involved in these functions at Seaboard and Chessie, dividing the jobs between the two organizations.

. . . .

Bob Hintz was picked for finance; John Snow for law and public affairs; Joe Stanley for internal audit; and Gerry Nichols as the chief administrative officer. I didn't know Nichols, but Osborn was very high on him, having worked with him when Prime headed the L&N back in Louisville. I did know Joe Stanley from my finance days and I had a very high regard for him.

Choosing members of the new CSX board was very difficult for Osborn. Seaboard had 24 directors, Chessie 11, so we agreed that CSX would have 11 from each. Osborn tried and tried to pick just 11, but, finally, after a lot of agony, he said he just could not get below 12. So we added one Chessie director to give us each 12. We also agreed that if anything happened to any of the 12 from either company, then the remaining directors from that group would get together and select a new director. Greg DeVine, my predecessor as C&O president, died suddenly on December 24, 1980, barely two months after the company was formed. I told the former Chessie directors they had the right to name another board member if they wanted to do so, but it seemed to me that things were working well and they should waive that right and go on with 23 directors. All of the former Chessie directors readily agreed and announced their decision at the next board meeting to the full board. I think that was an important step for the board, really bringing it together.

Deloite, Haskins and Sells had been the Seaboard auditors; Peat Marwick Mitchell served for Chessie. In order to assure objectivity, a committee was formed, headed by Bob Hintz, the Chief Financial Officer, and it requested presentations and bids from each of the Big Eight firms, asking them to outline the scope of work they would propose and its cost.

• • • • • • • • • • • • • • • • • • • •

The top three were called in for personal presentations and, at the Committee's recommendation, Ernst & Whinney was selected by the board to be CSX's outside auditors.

After the four top officers had been selected, others were added to the CSX general staff. Bob McGowan was brought in from Chessie to head the real estate operation (CSX Resources Inc.); there was no comparable Seaboard counterpart. For office staff, we interviewed people who had worked for Seaboard in Richmond before its offices were consolidated to Jacksonville, but had not relocated. That worked out well, allowing us to fill the support staff jobs with people who were familiar with the business. They were all very good and we didn't have to relocate anyone.

After the merger, Chessie moved its administrative offices from Cleveland to Baltimore, while Jacksonville remained headquarters for Seaboard.

The one CSX office that caused Osborn and me many sleepless nights dealt with the law and public affairs position. Chessie had a well-respected, able head in Ron Donnem; Seaboard's Philip Lanier was equally well qualified and also highly regarded. Either would have served CSX well, although their two strong-willed personalities at times did clash. After studying the pressing needs of the two rail organizations, we determined that their talents could be best used in rail affairs, rather than at CSX head-quarters.

CSX's needs, we determined, lay more in the public and governmental affairs area, as compared to the law, and this led us to select John Snow, then Chessie's Washington representative for the post. The more we dis-

•   •   •   •   •   •   •   •   •   •   •   •   •   •   •   •   •   •   •

cussed our needs, the more we realized Snow's political and legal back-ground was ideal for the corporate staff. As we all now know, things could not have worked out better.

In fact, that move also solved the problem as to who would head our Washington office. The job, since Snow came to Richmond, went to Woodruff M. Price, who was already there representing Seaboard. Price proved to be just a great choice… with everyone except Sen. Wendell Ford. As mentioned earlier, I never found out why, but when we had an appointment with Sen. Ford, Price would always say, "Well, I think you would be better off without me."

❖   ❖

Chapter XXVII

· ·

Blazing New Trails

Merger, deregulation came at the same time

C SX Corporation began operations on November 1, 1980, 16 days after the effective date of the Staggers Act deregulating the industry. Thus, Osborn and I were launching the first major rail merger since the Penn Central and we're doing it in a totally new regulatory environment. There was excitement and, of course, uncertainty, at every turn. Economically, our timing wasn't all that great. By late 1981, the country would be in a deep recession.

Our first few months were devoted to getting the parent company concept organized, insuring that the two railroad units were on a coordinated path, and integrating the realty unit. We talked with a number of people about our future direction, exploring whether we would expand the company's reach in transportation, or move into other areas. Early in 1981, we had discussions with Alco Standard, a conglomerate headquartered in Valley Forge, Pennsylvania, which was about the same size as CSX and had a widely diverse set of holdings outside of the transportation business. We

. . . .

considered the possibility of putting the two companies together. In addition, there were talks with others that came to us and suggested they might be a logical part of CSX, but none of those discussions appeared advantageous to CSX. In the end, we decided to sit tight those first two years, focus our attention on coordination activities at the two railroads, sell off assets that didn't fit our transportation vision, and make the most of deregulation.

Most days, the issues surrounding deregulation presented more than enough in terms of challenges. For the first time, we had the freedom to set rates, but on the other hand, there were a number of open questions that prompted challenges to virtually all rate adjustments that went to the Interstate Commerce Commission. Anytime either railroad changed a rate in the first two or three years of deregulation, the customers challenged it...and this was all unplowed ground. So we were spending a lot of time trying to determine a number of things, such as, "What is a captive shipper?" That term had been used in the Staggers Act. Another was "market dominance." It took two or three years to get these things settled so the shippers and we knew what could and could not be done under deregulation. This kept the sales and marketing people, and the lawyers, very busy in our company and, I am certain, also those of our customers. It also kept Wall Street on its toes. The analysts had a hard time with their forward-looking valuation models with CSX and with the rest of the industry in those early years.

. . . . .

Just as our CSX "birth pains" were resolving and the organization was settling into a comfortable — and profitable — pattern, Osborn's scheduled retirement date of May 1982 was upon us. While this was recognized from the early days of our merger discussions, it nevertheless came as a shock to the organization — and, especially, to me. Osborn and I had previously agreed that when he retired, I would assume his title as Chairman, become the sole Chief Executive Officer, and that the 50-50 concept would continue by naming A. Paul Funkhouser, who had become President of Seaboard on merger day, as CSX President.

This action did indeed reaffirm for everyone the Chessie/Seaboard "partnership" concept. In fact, although he never discussed it in those terms, that may well have been Osborn's primary reason for wanting Funkhouser named president of CSX after his, Prime's, retirement in 1982. And, if for no other reason than that, the years with Funkhouser were worthwhile.

Thus, in May 1982, CSX began operating with a different management team. Paul Funkhouser had a very pleasant personality, but he was not Prime Osborn — no one could have been — and we developed a different relationship from the one that Osborn and I had enjoyed. He was emotional, like Osborn, but not nearly as aggressive or as strong-willed. Yet, while we didn't have the same chemistry, I think we worked well together.

After about two years, Funkhouser decided he wanted to take early retirement. I don't know if I was too over-bearing or our relationship prompted that decision or not; we never discussed the "why" of his decision. All I know is that he decided to have a more leisurely lifestyle, and that with his decision all the chips were in front of me, I was again the Chairman, President and CEO of the company. Where CSX went and how we did would be my responsibility.

❖   ❖

Chapter XXVIII

. . . .

Learning New Ways in Washington

We usually wanted nothing, bringing looks of relief

T he deregulation of the industry and the creation of CSX all came within a month in late 1980. John Snow moved to Richmond as a member of the new CSX management team when we opened our offices there in November 1980, and Woody Price, who had been Seaboard's Washington representative prior to the merger, became head of the CSX Washington office. Price had a long career in Washington, having been an assistant to Congressman Brock Adams before coming to the Seaboard to head its Washington activities, and was well known to government and agency personnel at all levels.

One of the high priorities Osborn and I established for the new company was a more aggressive and orderly method of visiting key Washington officials. And so, about twice a month, Osborn, Snow and I would travel to Washington early in the morning for a day of visits. This contrasted sharply with our old way of visiting Washington only as a member of an industry or other group and even then only when we wanted or needed something.

Implementing our new strategy, Price would schedule a series of
meetings with congressmen, senators and agency heads, primarily for the
purpose of meeting them and discussing areas of mutual interest, but without having a specific agenda. During these visits, once we got beyond who
we were and who we represented, we made a point of letting our host know
that we had no problems, needed nothing and merely wanted to have the
chance to meet them.

Usually, our operations were either within their district or state, or our
business touched areas of interest to their agency. After these assurances,
we would be greeted warmly, and generally have a delightful conversation
about matters of mutual interest or other matters of the day. Upon leaving,
we would always express our thanks for their time, and state that we would
be back to visit them again, noting that we might (or might not) want
something next time.

There usually was a look of relief on their face when we said we wanted nothing. Most of these people only had visitors when the visitor wanted
something, or had a problem. Often, our conversations went far afield from
our specific business. And we would invite them to call our Washington
staff or us if any problems arose concerning our business or if we could be
of assistance to them.

In scheduling our visits, Woody Price would set a very aggressive pace.
It was usually a very tiring, strenuous day, but at the end of the day, we
always felt exhilarated by what we had accomplished and who we had seen.
Price and I have often laughed at his scheduling ability and his sense of
direction. He seemed to always set appointments in every House and
Senate office building and, frequently, back-to-back meetings were at

. . . .

opposite ends of Capital Hill. Going to the meetings, we often traveled in the tunnels connecting the various buildings. After our first few times in Washington, I found that Price, despite his many years in Washington, often would make a wrong turn in those tunnels. As a result, I learned to find my own way around them very well.

In addition to visiting key long-time members of Congress, we made it a point, whenever possible, to also meet with newly elected members. Our logic was that the new Congressmen, first of all, normally did not have as many visitors as those of longer duration. So, it was easier to get an appointment. By the same token, he was more interested in seeing us. Also, if we could meet with them early in their career, we felt we could better establish a relationship that, at some later date, would be beneficial to both ourselves and to them. Sometimes, we were a freshman Congressman's first visitors, even arriving as he was still moving into his offices.

I have often stated that more decisions affecting our company are made in Washington than are made in our own boardroom. Government is here to stay; it is intrusive in all business, and the more we understand about the process, the people involved and the inner workings, the better off the company will be.

Over the years, we found that these periodic visits were of great value to both the company and the government representatives. As we developed an understanding of each other's issues and problems, we more objectively evaluated the pressures each of us felt from our constituencies and we worked together much better as we sought a mutually beneficial outcome.

One illustration of the value of these visits came in 1982 when the

• • • • • • • • • • • • • • • • • • • •

Reagan administration recommended that Conrail be sold to Norfolk
Southern. We at CSX recognized the detriment to our traffic that such a
combination would bring, and undertook to express our opinion to anyone
who would listen. During that time, I met with dozens of Senators and
Congressmen, and had no problems getting in to see any of them. I always
reminded them that I had warned them at the end of earlier visits that I
might be back someday and want something. Then I would say, "Here I
am, and I would like to tell you about our problems with this proposal and
why we think this is a bad idea." We did not always get agreement, or their
support, but I felt we always got a sympathetic hearing.

Thus, in my mind, it is important to all companies that the legislators
of their city, their state, and their country, understand how their business
works, its issues and all the possible outcomes. This requires building trust
through relationships. People who ignore government, especially
Washington, do so at their own peril. More businesses are learning this
every day, that communications is the key to solving most problems. Those
with special interests are going to communicate. If businessmen don't join in
that effort, they are in for lots of trouble.

❖ ❖

Chapter XXIX

• • • • • • • • • • • • • • • • • • •

A Period of Sales and Acquisitions

CSX focused on its core business, transportation

Despite a general feeling of increasing cooperation between the two rail units, the nation's economy was not helpful to CSX in its early years. Record high interest rates, soaring unemployment and generally stagnant business levels caused problems for all businesses. In view of this, and recognizing the need to concentrate on integrating the two railroads, Prime Osborn and I decided we should consider divesting some of our non-transportation assets and concentrate on the transportation business. Our first unit for review was Florida Publishing Company, which published Jacksonville's two daily newspapers, the *Florida Times-Union* and the *Jacksonville Journal*, as well as the *St. Augustine Record*.

The publishing company had been a subsidiary of Seaboard Coast Line for a long, long time. Initially, Seaboard Air Line Railroad owned a third of Florida Publishing, the Atlantic Coast Line Railroad owned a third, and an estate associated with the Florida East Coast Railroad owned the other third.

After the Seaboard Air Line and Atlantic Coast Line merged in 1967

· ·

(becoming Seaboard Coast Line), they acquired the other third, bringing their ownership to 100 percent.

Osborn and I, especially Osborn because he was more familiar with it, felt that newspaper publishing was not an especially good fit with our transportation interests. We thought of CSX as a transportation company, not strictly a railroad. The newspaper was a distraction, taking management time, and we agreed we would divest if we could get a good price. Also, as was often pointed out, it seemed the newspaper went out of its way to prove to its readers and the Jacksonville community that it was independent, not at all beholden to the railroad. But, neither that issue nor the recession drove our decision. The sale was just a good economic move and based largely on a general feeling that newspaper publishing was not a logical part of the company.

The sale was undertaken through a bidding process and we ended up selling to Morris Communications, for what proved to us to be an attractive price. An interesting background to the sale was the fact that, for many years, the head of the Morris company (William S. Morris, Jr., father of the current chairman) had tried — unsuccessfully — to purchase the papers. When his son, William S. Morris, III, learned they finally would be available for purchase, he priced his bid liberally in order to hopefully insure it would be highest, which proved to be the case. He conditioned the bid on only one requirement — that CSX would never reveal the spread between his bid and the other bids, or the actual purchase price. We never did.

❖ ❖

Chapter XXX

· · · · · · · · · · · · · · · · · · · ·

Along Comes Bill McGowan

Fiber optics — having your cake and eating it, too

At the same time CSX was exploring possible sale of some of its non-transportation units, it also was reviewing methods of making its rail properties more productive. One of the proposals involved a proposal to bury fiber-optic cables, then in its infancy of development, along railroad rights-of-way.

That idea first came to us from William G. McGowan, founder and chairman of a then fledgling communications company named MCI. At his request, a small group of us went to his suburban Washington offices and met with him. This meeting resulted in an agreement to further explore the idea. Then, when it began to look like it was actually feasible, McGowan got cold feet. He told me, "I don't know why I want to deal with you. Railroads are the worst bureaucracies in the world and you all will never get anything done." I responded, "Bill, let's continue to work on this and if there is any delay I guarantee you it will be your problem, not ours." He laughed at that, but eventually agreed to go ahead.

After months of study, discussion and argument, we finally reached agreement on the terms. Our lawyers promptly reviewed and signed the agreement; then sent it on to MCI, only to have MCI's lawyers sit on it for a couple weeks. When MCI finally signed it, I enjoyed reminding McGowan that it was his lawyers, not ours, who had held things up.

Our lead executive in those discussions was Gerry Nichols, who at various times was, or would become, an officer of Seaboard Coast Line, CSX, Seaboard System and CSX Transportation. Legal work was handled for us by a then newly hired lawyer, Mark Aron — who became Vice President-Law and later Executive Vice President of CSX. Terms of the contract provided for payment of $8,000 per mile for the 4,000 miles of right-of-way to be used by MCI — a total of $32 million for otherwise unused property.

Later we were approached by Sprint communications group, and were able to work out an identical deal. An added bonus in the MCI contract gave CSX the rights to two pairs of fiber-optic cables as part of the consideration. Today, they are the backbone of the communications network MCI-World.Com operates for CSXT.

❖   ❖

Chapter XXXI

. . . .

Offer to Build
Slurry Pipeline Ignored

T. Justin Moore just laughed; I was serious

I n the early 1980s, just after CSX was formed and had selected
Richmond as its headquarters, a group of Virginia electric utility and
coal companies began a campaign for construction of a coal slurry pipeline.
Virginia Electric Power Company (VEPCO) led this "warm welcome" to
Virginia — the state's largest user of coal and a big customer of CSX and
the then newly formed Norfolk Southern. The plan put forward by the
group called for the pipeline to connect the coalfields in the southwestern
part of the state to Hampton Roads, in the City of Portsmouth. As was the
case in other efforts by utilities and coal companies, this proposal was
designed primarily as a "wedge" to drive down freight rates on the coal-
hauling railroads — in other words on CSX and Norfolk Southern. The
foray prompted a series of studies, meetings and rounds of newspaper
advertisements for and against the concept. Since the group needed the
right of eminent domain in order to build the slurry line, the issue eventually wound up in the Virginia General Assembly.

The interesting thing about the proposal was that it would not have affected CSX that much; most of our coal traffic originated in West Virginia, and would not have been subject to diversion to the pipeline. Norfolk Southern, however, would have been hurt badly. Still, Norfolk Southern, having just been formed by a merger of the Norfolk & Western and the Southern Railway and apparently not wanting to badly rile a major customer, took a less active role in the fight than did CSX. We knew that construction of a slurry line anywhere was bound to encourage demands for construction of others.

Thus, we at CSX were quickly thrust into the midst of Virginia politics, and employed former Gov. John Dalton to lead an active opposition. Meetings with groups of Virginia senators and delegates, appeals to environmental and other groups, and more studies followed. In his 1982 State of the Commonwealth message, Gov. Robb indicated that he did not support the pipeline, but if the General Assembly saw fit to pass authorizing legislation, he would sign it. As a courtesy to the new-established CSX, he called me several hours before delivering his address, reading me the part of his speech dealing with the proposal.

While this battle was going on – as is often the case in business, especially in Virginia — T. Justin Moore, the chairman of VEPCO, and I were working together with Gov. Robb traveling across the state on the formation of the Center for Innovative Technology. On one of our CIT trips I said to Moore, "Look, if you want to build a slurry line, let's you and I get together and build it. We've got the right-of-way. Just pay us for its use and you can forget all this stuff in the General Assembly about the right of eminent domain." That was the whole thrust of the legislation, getting the right of eminent domain to cross our right-of-way.

• • • • • • • • • • • • • • • • • • •

Moore just laughed my comment off and never did directly respond. His implied response indicated that we would just have to battle things out, which we did…to his and VEPCO's loss. Later, he told me he thought I was kidding him and thus did not seriously consider my proposal. But I wasn't kidding. Our railroad competitors would not have been happy, but if there was going to be a coal slurry pipeline, I really did believe we could provide the right of way, in the same manner as our fiber-optic cable deals with MCI and Sprint.

Chapter XXXII

. . . .

More to Corporate Citizenship than Giving Money

Involvement by companies, employees essential to success

Corporate America, generally, does a very poor job with corporate citizenship. I think every business has a responsibility to work with elected officials to do whatever the company can to protect the environment, provide employment and anything else that improves the relationship between business and government. I feel very strongly about that; always have. I have tried to work with local, state and national officials with that in mind, doing what we can to be good corporate citizens.

But, doing it right really requires much more than working with political leadership on matters of mutual interest. It also requires contributing to important causes and working with citizens and civic organizations. I always encouraged our people, both at Chessie and CSX, to get involved in civic and cultural activities. We can give money, but I think it is more important for us to give of our time and talents.

Of course, we gain from these efforts. Companies that are involved are viewed as being cooperative and helpful and that improves the relation-

. . . .

ships. Even if that didn't happen, I would still feel that corporations have a responsibility to do things to improve the community.

When CSX came to Richmond, we wanted to become good corporate citizens and participate in as many civic and cultural activities as we could. We contributed time, money and talent. It was nothing new for any of us. Whether from Chessie and Cleveland, or Seaboard and Jacksonville, we all had been active in community and civic affairs long before CSX and Richmond.

I found out later that we had a substantial change on Richmond corporate culture. Our activities challenged other companies in Richmond to do more than they had been doing in the past. Several business leaders in Richmond told me that CSX had cost them a lot of money. I think we raised the level of corporate involvement and corporate giving significantly when we came to Richmond in 1980.

A number of us served on a variety of boards and study commissions. We had other people on the Arts Council and worked with virtually all of the cultural organizations. We also took a great interest in educational institutions and social services organizations. One group of spouses, Dolly Hintz, Nan Hawk, Jackie Nichols and others, raised the money for the Medical College of Virginia's Hospitality House.

Then they went out and found a house and oversaw its rehabilitation and operation as a guesthouse for families of MCV patients. In more recent years, they and their successors oversaw the purchase and conversion of an abandoned downtown hotel into what surely must be one of the most extensive guesthouses for patient families of any hospital in America.

So I think CSX did then and continues now to make a difference in Richmond and in a lot of other cities. It goes back to balancing one's life. Business people live in these cities. They should have and enjoy a good non-business life. Doing that requires that they actively participate in and be part of the community.

One of the most interesting challenges for me personally came shortly after we moved to Virginia in 1980. Gov. Robb had recently been elected governor and one of his campaign planks was to bring new technologies to the Commonwealth. Early on in his administration he appointed a committee to study ways to do this, headed by local businessmen T. Justin Moore and James C. Wheat.

This committee recommended that some sort of organization be established in the Commonwealth to facilitate development of new technologies. About this time, Gov. Robb appointed a number of businessmen to a committee, including myself, to attract a microelectronics consortium to Virginia.

We were not successful, but the governor soon recommended establishment of a committee on innovative technology to the General Assembly. He asked me to head this group, made up mainly of university presidents and businessmen in the state.

Out of this grew the Center for Innovative Technology. Our mission was to set up groups at most of the state's leading universities to work with small technology businesses, attracting them to the state. After a

. . . .

nationwide search for someone to lead the new organization, Robert Fry
was selected as the first president of CIT. An office was established in
Northern Virginia, but Fry's leadership style was not suited to the organization and he left after about one year. Later, former Virginia Gov.
Linwood Holton was selected, and succeeded in developing CIT into a
well-functioning asset for the state.

In addition to the personnel issues, there were many legal problems.
Most of them dealt with intellectual property questions that were forced by
the state's involvement. The issue was — Who owned what? Was the
knowledge gained, public or private? Eventually, these issues were all
worked out, hopefully to everyone's satisfaction.

This organization, which had severe birth pains in its early years,
today is functioning quite well. It has turned out to be a great thing for the
state, bringing a number of electronic and other technology-related businesses to the state, especially to the development of the strong base of technology companies in Northern Virginia.

. . . . .

The Grace Commission was established by President Ford to study
governmental operations and to recommend ways to improve government
and make it more efficient. Peter Grace, the chairman of W.R. Grace at the
time, agreed to head it. I was involved with a group dealing with the
Department of the Interior.

The main work of the commission lasted about three years and
its report and recommendations developed potential savings of several billion dollars per year in various areas. Like most such reports, some recom-

• • • • • • • • • • • • • • • • • • • •

mendations were adopted, but others were politically difficult or unappealing and were never put into effect. Overall, the effort was worthwhile and did help the government reduce inefficiency to some extent.

One of my principal associates on the Grace Commission was John Snow, who had just joined the Chessie organization. Since he was far more familiar with governmental methods than I, he knew where to find information and get the answers we needed. In addition, it was a great way for me to become acquainted with John, and to learn of his great potential. He did most of the work. I got the credit.

❖   ❖

Chapter XXXIII

. . . .

The Acquisition of Texas Gas

Kentucky's "Kitchen Cabinet" connections put CSX in pipeline, barging

J ust before CSX was born, John Young Brown, a most colorful politician, was elected governor of Kentucky. One of his campaign promises, which he quickly instituted after the election, was to assemble a group of leading businessmen in Kentucky, or having Kentucky connections, to meet with him as a Business Advisory Committee. Through the urging of one of his close associates, William B. Sturgill, a director of Seaboard Coast Line (and, later, of CSX), Gov. Brown asked me to join the group.

This committee met with the governor several times, generally at his residence. Frequently, the group also included Mrs. Brown, Phyllis George, a former Miss America and a charming lady. Also in the group was Dennis Hendrix, Chairman of Texas Gas Resources Corporation of Owensboro, Kentucky. Since Texas Gas owned a barge line, we would compare notes from time to time, especially with regard to coal traffic. One time as we were having lunch one of us suggested that maybe we ought to put the two companies together and have a true, multimodal transportation

• •

organization. We talked about it several times at these meetings, but nothing happened.

Later, the Chairman of Coastal States Gas Company in Texas, Oscar Wyatt, indicated he was interested in acquiring Texas Gas. As soon as Hendrix heard this, he called me in Richmond. He reminded me that we had talked about getting together and asked if CSX really had any interest. I assured him we did, and we began negotiations in New York. After two days of nearly non-stop discussions with CSX's Chief Financial Officer Bob Hintz, a legal team headed by Bob Burrus of McGuire, Woods, and other outside experts, we reached an agreement.

We at CSX were very impressed with the people at Texas Gas and it seemed to be a very good fit for both companies. Texas Gas had three primary units – a natural gas transmission pipeline from Texas and Louisiana northeastward to the Ohio Valley and eastern consumers; an oil and gas exploration company operating both domestic and international fields; and the country's largest inland waterway barge line, American Commercial Lines.

When the proposed merger was announced, the inland waterway industry immediately went to war, and pledged strong opposition to our plans. This led to our decision to put the barge line in a voting trust with an independent trustee until we could get the necessary authority from the Interstate Commerce Commission and the courts.

It was more than a year before this was completed.

During this time, we at CSX were very confident that the ICC would approve the application, despite certain wording contained in the

• • • • • • • • • • • • • • • • • • • •

Panama Canal Act. I had always been in favor of coordinated transportation and it seemed it was especially appropriate, with the passage of deregulation, to start putting transportation units together. As my ICC testimony pointed out, and I believe we fulfilled this, we would find ways to work together. But if another railroad was a better fit for a move on ACL, or if another barge line was a better fit for us on another piece of business, it would be in our own self interest to do whatever worked best for ourselves and our customers. If we could make more money by keeping things separate, or working with another barge line, or railroad, we would do it. The Panama Canal Act did seem to have restrictive language, but our lawyers felt it was time to clarify and, if needed, modify the wording.

Once the deal was complete, Bob Best was appointed head of Texas Gas and Dennis Hendrix moved to Richmond as Vice Chairman of CSX. At age 42, Hendrix became an active member of our planning group and made good progress in learning the other aspects of our business. But after just a few months, he decided he didn't want to be a part of the railroad industry. He said he had never realized the power that labor unions and governmental entities had over the railroad industry; it was just too restrictive and he didn't feel he would be happy working under such restraints. And so, he tendered his resignation to return to the oil and gas industry in Texas.

For a lot of us, his departure was a disappointment. Hendrix was a very likable, very able fellow. It seemed to most of us that he had a bright future with our integrated company, and he worked well with other key CSX officers. Considering my age and his relative youthfulness, he well could have been my successor. But he was determined to leave, and we had to adjust our future plans accordingly.

There were others from Texas Gas who remained with CSX and made significant contributions to CSX. Foremost of those was Richard Leatherwood. He had run the barge line and a trucking company that Texas Gas owned before the merger. He headed the CSX non-rail companies for some years, and later performed outstanding service as head of the rail Equipment Group when CSX merged its Chessie and Seaboard rail groups into a new structure.

. . . . .

When American Commercial Barge Lines company was approved by the Interstate Commerce Commission and released by the courts from its independent voting trust, CSX began to offer coordinated rail-barge service. But there was little success. Water transportation has an inherent advantage; barge lines do not have the need for building and maintaining rights-of-way, so their rates for bulk commodities are less than the railroads. I hoped there would be more areas where we would offer combined services. There were some, but not many.

More important to me, however, was the fact that CSX, with a barge line, a pipeline, and a railroad could offer all of its customers other methods of transporting their goods and materials. This was especially important to our coal customers. Being able to handle coal by rail or water, or both, provided a whole range of transportation options available to our shippers. Depending on price, schedule and equipment preferences or requirements, customers could make their own choice.

But most customers did not avail themselves of this opportunity.

• • • • • • • • • • • • • • • • • • • •

Probably, this resulted from the long history of single modal companies; it was just inconceivable that one could deal with one company on rail, water, and, later, ocean shipping. Transportation companies and their customers' traffic departments had been functioning in one method for decades. There is always a general resistance to change, and they just were not going to change.

Now, contract logistics companies, which provide exactly the sort of coordinated services CSX was trying to market, are the fastest growing segment of the transportation market. And most of them don't own a single asset other than telephones and computers. Thus, an idea that has been around for a long time, and seemed to us at the time to be very logical and advantageous to shippers, is finally gaining acceptance in the shipper community. Change comes slowly and frequently with great difficulty. A good idea then; an even better idea today.

Chapter XXXIV

· ·

The Birth of the "Three-Unit" Structure

Working new ways on the old railroad

B y 1985, after four years of experience with the merged company, it seemed that the time had come to separate the company into discrete business units. The company was reorganized into four major lines of business — transportation, energy, technology and properties. "Transportation" obviously was the rail and barge businesses. "Energy," the Texas Gas units, had no relation to the rail or barge units. "Technology" was becoming increasingly important to us and we needed a separate unit that could take advantage of the economies of scale, providing better advisory services to all the other units. Real estate that had no relationship to any of our other activities was grouped into the "Properties" area.

Although the first three areas were self-explanatory, not many people understood the importance of the Properties unit. To Wall Street analysts, it was difficult to make projections as to a steady stream of income. If we sold a lot of properties in one year, we would report high earnings. The next year, we may have focused on developmental activities and generated

. . . .

lower reported earnings. Since Wall Street always discounted Properties' earnings, that was one more reason we felt it should be separated into an individual unit. The analysts could thus more easily focus on the transportation and energy units, better judging their earnings and long-term potential.

Interestingly, Properties, in a good year, contributed $100 million to operating income; in a "bad" year, maybe $60 or $70 million. Not chicken feed, but not the types of dependable earnings flow that Wall Street understood. It just couldn't be modeled. If we had been a pure real estate company, that would have been different. Basically, what we had were railroad analysts trying to follow different lines of business. They didn't understand the Energy unit either, and didn't care or want to learn about it; they still looked at us as a railroad. Everything else was extraneous. I think that was one of the great failings of Wall Street with regard to CSX, but it was a fact of life.

. . . . .

This also was the time when we separated the two railroads into what became known as the "three-unit structure." By 1984, we were rapidly approaching the time when we should somehow put the two groups together. There had been increasing coordination between the two companies since 1980, but they were still operating separately. During those years, Seaboard had consolidated its operations with the Louisville & Nashville Railroad, formerly operated as a separate unit. Also, C&O, B&O and Western Maryland had been working together much more closely as the Chessie System roads.

• • • • • • • • • • • • • • • • • • • •

To examine the options and make recommendations, a committee was appointed from the two railroads headed by John Collinson, who had been the president of Chessie. Collinson's headquarters were moved to Richmond, he was elected vice chairman of CSX and he began work on this issue with officers from both companies and outside consultants.

The committee worked for several months and developed a number of organizational options. The first was a complete merger of the two rail-roads. Another was to rearrange them into two companies geographically, but without the Chessie and Seaboard designations. The third alternative was a radical new system, a component unit system. The idea was to put the marketing and sales organizations into one unit that would be responsi-ble for interface with customers, combine the transportation activities into a "production" company, and set up a third unit that would be responsible for maintenance and repair of freight cars and locomotive equipment. All three, using transfer pricing, were to have their own profit and loss state-ments.

This was especially appealing in terms of the mechanical operations. On our railroads, in fact on all railroads, equipment had never been viewed as a profit center; it was always considered a supply function. If the sales people were able to market business, then the mechanical department was expected to have the necessary equipment. As a result, railroads generally had excess equipment and inefficient utilization of equipment. This pro-posal would change that, forcing the function to be managed as efficiently as any stand-alone company.

After much debate, concern and trepidation, the three-unit

. . . .

structure was adopted. Using transfer pricing, the equipment people would rent equipment to the transportation unit who, in turn, would produce and sell the service to the marketing and sales organization.

The biggest benefit of the new organization came in terms of the equipment group. Richard Leatherwood, who had come to CSX from Texas Gas and who never had been a railroader, was placed in charge, with Carl Taylor as his assistant. Despite the time and effort and the frustration caused by the three-unit structure, their improvements in utilization and the reductions in the size of the fleet were fantastic.

By establishing equipment as a separate unit, the costs associated with equipment were highlighted as never before. John Collinson and I always knew equipment was costing us a bundle in many different ways, but we could never before quantify how much or exactly in which areas. Separating this function from others completely isolated and identified the costs associated with purchasing, maintaining and furnishing equipment. And that paid off in millions and millions of dollars.

Most of our people would readily, if reluctantly, agree that such a degree of improvement would never have been achieved in the utilization of equipment and in lowering the cost structure had we not adopted the three-unit structure. As far as I am concerned, that and the ease with which we put the two railroads together after the three-unit structure far outweighed the disruption and complaining we faced at the time. Once again, the old adage proved to be true: the greatest fear of us all is change. To me, there is no doubt it was the right choice; well worth it. Looking back, I would do the same thing all over again.

. . . .

However, we were never able to develop an adequate transfer pricing system. Paul Goodwin, the chief railroad financial officer, and his associates worked on the problem for several years, trying various alternatives to produce separate profit and loss statements for each of the three units. It was an excellent concept; we just couldn't make a transfer pricing system work.

There is no doubt there was a lot of frustration and concern within the organization about the three-unit structure. This had never been done by anyone. It was such a radical change that no one thought it would work. But it did work, especially in the equipment area and, more important, in a way that no one expected. Everyone was so concerned about this novel arrangement that they soon forgot if they were from Chessie or Seaboard.

We never had one murmur about losing "my Chessie" or losing "my Seaboard" system. Later on, when it was determined the three-unit structure had served its primary purpose; the three were reassembled into one consolidated railroad. And again, by then everyone had forgotten about Chessie and Seaboard. We were all CSX.

Implementation of the three-unit structure enabled us to make some interesting personnel appointments, in order to provide new areas of experience to our senior officers, and as one more step to eliminating the Chessie, Seaboard loyalty identifications.

In addition to Leatherwood and Taylor, who had been President of Fruit Growers Express, Dick Sanborn, then President of Seaboard System, moved from Jacksonville to Baltimore and was put in charge of sales and marketing. John Snow, who had succeeded John Collinson as President of

. . . .

Chessie, went to Jacksonville to run the operating organization. Jim Hagen, who had joined the company a year earlier from Conrail to combine the sales and marketing departments of the two railroads, became number two to Sanborn and later succeeded him when Dick moved to Conrail as its Chief Executive Officer. He also succeeded him at Conrail after Dick's untimely death.

The primary credit for the success of the three-unit structure and its ultimate benefit for combining the rail operations into one integrated unit goes to John Collinson. A very quiet, thoughtful, conscientious student of transportation and a third generation railroader, Collinson spent a tremendous amount of time on this concept and had strong ideas about its staffing. As later results proved, they were excellent choices.

❖　❖

Chapter XXXV

. . . .

The Acquisition of Rockresorts

"What's the price?" "I don't know, we'll just have to work that out."

For several years before the formation of CSX, my family and I had spent our year-end holidays at Caneel Bay, a Rockresorts property on St. John in the U.S. Virgin Islands. Compared to the harsh Cleveland winters, Caneel Bay was the ideal luxury island vacation. Many times my key Chessie associate, John Collinson, and his family joined us, and we often joked, "Wouldn't it be nice to add Caneel Bay to The Greenbrier as a part of the company."

After CSX was created, and we had moved to the more temperate climate of Virginia, we continued our holiday visits to Caneel Bay. One year we changed to an Easter visit to introduce our two young granddaughters to the charm of the area. Rockresorts at that time operated Caneel Bay and Little Dix Bay, both in the Virgin Islands; the Woodstock Inn in Vermont; The Boulders in Carefree, Arizona; and the Grand Teton Lodge Company in Jackson Hole, Wyoming. After we returned, as was my habit, I wrote to Richard Holtzman, president of Rockresorts to thank him for all he had

• • • • • • • • • • • • • • • • • • • •

arranged for us while we were there. In a very oblique way, I mentioned that it sure would be nice to have Caneel Bay as a part of CSX. I got a letter back that, in an equally oblique way, led me to believe that Rockresorts might possibly be for sale.

Upon receiving the letter, I called Holtzman at his headquarters in Rockefeller Center in New York and asked him if I could visit him in New York, telling him we were interested in expanding our resort holdings. After picking a suitable date, I met with Holtzman and another senior Rockresorts official and expressed our interest in acquiring Rockresorts if there was any desire to sell.

Holtzman was non-committal and did not express his view one way or the other. The other official didn't think much of the idea, but did say he would keep it in mind and that they would mention our interest to Laurence Rockefeller, chairman and owner of Rockresorts. Shortly after that, I got a call from Holtzman indicating that Rockefeller was getting up in years, and that he, Holtzman, was at retirement age, and maybe there would be some interest in selling. The thing to do, he said, would be to meet with Rockefeller, because he was the sole owner and would make the decision.

So it was arranged that Bill Pitt, then managing director and president of The Greenbrier, and I would meet with Rockefeller at the Rockefeller estate north of New York City. I met Pitt at the suburban Westchester airport, and we arranged for a helicopter to take us from Westchester to the Rockefeller estate.

Rockefeller met us in his car and drove us to his house. We sat down and talked about the resort business in general and, finally, he said, "Now, what can I do for you?" So I said, "Mr. Rockefeller, we would like to buy Rockresorts and add it to our resorts activities. You have a high quality operation and we think it would fit quite well with The Greenbrier." He said, "Fine" and then we went on and chatted about other things for a while before leaving. That was it. That was the entire negotiations. We never talked about price or any other detail regarding the transaction.

When I got back to Richmond, I got in touch with Holtzman and told him we had agreed to purchase Rockresorts. He said, "What's the price?" I told him, "I don't know, we'll just have to work that out." He agreed to let us look over the financials on Rockresorts, and CSX Vice President and Treasurer Bill Sparrow went to New York to arrive at a suggested price. He suggested a figure somewhere in the mid-to-high $50 million range. Holtzman, after talking with Rockefeller, gave us a figure that was about $60 million, slightly above what Sparrow thought it was worth, but within striking distance. I called Rockefeller and told him his price was fine. He had one reservation, noting that he and his wife had met and been married at Woodstock and that he would like to reserve it, keeping it personally. The lawyers got together, worked out the details and we closed the deal. I don't know if Sparrow was ever very happy that I had paid a few million more than he had wanted, but I wasn't worried about that. Rockresorts was now part of CSX.

❖ ❖

Chapter XXXVI

. . . .

B&O Railroad Museum Preserved for Posterity

Ensuring its future with a foundation and a grant

A s anyone who knows me well is aware, I am an unabashed rail
fan. Since my first trip at age 10 to my Uncle Alva's caboose at the
B&O's yard in North Vernon, Indiana, I have had a keen interest in railroading and the industry's history. This interest became especially focused
on the Baltimore & Ohio Railroad Museum in Baltimore, which became
part of the Chessie System with the C&O/B&O affiliation. Ever since
then, the B&O Railroad Museum has held a very special spot in my heart. I
am very proud of the 2-10 vote that approved $1 million to fix the museum's
roof. That decision ranks right up there with any we made with regard to
mergers or acquisitions. It is even more satisfying that in the mid-1980s we
were able to make certain the museum, a true treasure trove of America's
industrial history, will endure...will always be there for future generations.

. . . . .

For years, the public relations departments of Chessie, and later CSX, oversaw the museum, but there always seemed to be more pressing needs in other parts of the railroad. As was the case in the vote approving the roof, it was never easy to get budget approval to do much more than keep the door open.

Fortunately, the museum had a very dedicated and talented staff headed by Marion Smith, and they could work miracles. One of the dearest ladies I have ever known, she kept it together for many, many years. There were always problems using railroad labor to make necessary repairs to the equipment and facilities, as well as running the museum. The museum could accept contributions and donations, but they were not tax deductible since Chessie and CSX obviously were not tax-exempt organizations. And the people of the City of Baltimore, even though the museum was one of the bigger tourist attractions in the city, didn't see it as important to the city's heritage. It was Chessie's museum, or CSX's later; not the city's; certainly not of the city's people.

As my tenure began to wind down, I became increasingly concerned about the museum's long-term prospects, especially wondering what would happen to it 15-20 years out? As long as I was chairman, I knew we were going to do the right thing. I had the same confidence about John Snow. But beyond that, one could not be certain.

That led us to the idea that the best way to preserve the museum for years to come, and more closely tie it to the City of Baltimore would be to set it up as a completely separate, charitable, not-for-profit organization. It

. . . .

would be out from under the company, independent, and tax exempt so that it could operate as would any other museum. While this might appear to be easy, it wasn't; the IRS has very strict rules about such things and there were detailed appraisals and a mound of paper to file. In the end, though, our lawyers and tax experts obtained the necessary approvals and established a not-for-profit foundation. The property, equipment and other assets valued at more than $8 million were transferred to the foundation. To many of us, though, they were priceless.

Forming the foundation, however, only solved half the problem. The museum did not generate enough revenue to cover its operating and maintenance costs, and was incurring about a $200,000 operating deficit every year. Having CSX give the foundation not only all the assets, but also a cash endowment grant of $5 million solved that problem. The only restriction was that the museum would have to operate on its own receipts plus the income from the $5 million. It could not touch the endowment for operating expenses; the $5 million was to guarantee the museum would be there for future generations.

This transfer was completed in 1987. Richard Leatherwood, president of the CSX Equipment group, which was headquartered in Baltimore, served as its first president, and I became the first chairman of the foundation. A board of directors, composed primarily of individuals from Baltimore, was elected to oversee the foundation. On an interim basis, the board then hired the City Life Museum of Baltimore to operate the museum while a search was begun for a professional staff, since Mrs. Smith was retiring and most of her staff wanted to stay with the company, not with the museum.

In short order, and most fortunately, we found John Ott, then heading a museum in Atlanta, who was hired as executive director. He assembled a great staff and they have done an outstanding job. After I retired from CSX, Richard Leatherwood succeeded me as chairman of the foundation, remaining in that role until 1998. Richard did an excellent job, expanding the board, bringing it and the museum closer to the city.

The museum contains a priceless collection of equipment, records and railroad memorabilia that must be preserved and enhanced – in my opinion it is the premier such collection in the country. John Ott and the staff have made it an even better and more noteworthy collection while developing its programs and creating an exceptional educational experience for its visitors. In addition to being a great repository of priceless equipment, it also has had great potential as an educational tool. It is the perfect venue to teach people, especially children, who were not familiar with railroads, the importance of the railroad industry over the years to the development of America and our industrial economy.

America's railroads were this country's first major industry. They developed or facilitated many things that came to be taken for granted, including the opening of the West and the industrialization of the interior reaches of this country. The first telegraph, developed by Samuel F.B. Morse, was installed and used along the B&O route from Washington to Baltimore. Standard time and the time zones were developed in 1887 because of the railroads.

There are innumerable engineering firsts attributable to the industry;

• • • • • • • • • • • ◆ • ◆ • • • • • • • •

and railroads carried a majority of products for the American economy until recent years, and still play a very large role in our country and its economy today. John Ott, I am glad to say, also saw that vision and has made education a key mission of the museum.

As a postscript, the museum celebrated its 10th anniversary of independence from CSX and its predecessors in 1997. That year, the museum hosted 94,948 visitors, 15,302 of which were school children and their teachers. At the end of that year, total assets were $23.7 million, with $5.7 million of that in investments and other securities. So, the $5 million is still there and continues to grow. The collections and exhibits were valued at $12.4 million; the property at $4.6 million. It had revenues of $2.3 million in 1997, expenses of $1.9 million, and added $400,000 to its net assets during the year. Today, the museum is essentially debt-free and well situated for even greater value in the new millennium.

Regretfully, because of family commitments, John Ott left the Museum in October 1999 after nearly nine years of outstanding service. He established a lasting legacy, and the B&O Railroad Museum, because of his efforts, will continue to prosper and grow as an attraction and as an institution under its new leadership, headed by his associate, Courtney Wilson. It is a priceless asset, not only of the railroad industry, but also of the whole country. Most important, I know it is going to be there at Mt. Clare Station — the birthplace of America's first railroad — a long, long time.

❖   ❖

Chapter XXXVII

. . . .

Time & Money

The two biggest wastes

O f all things wasted, time and money are the most often abused. In my 40-plus year career, I've probably heard someone say, "Oh, it just cost us a little time and money" a couple thousand times. And it has always bothered me.

. . . . .

Growing up on a small Kentucky farm in the 1930s and early 1940s, there was never enough time and even less money. If you wasted time on the farm, you didn't get something done. I quickly learned that everything had to be done...sooner or later. It was better, far better, to properly manage one's time and get everything done in its own time. An hour later, certainly not the next day, would not do.

And we just didn't have money to spend in those days. Tobacco was the cash crop. For food, we raised hogs, cattle and chickens and tended a garden. We also cut and bailed hay and, later, also for cash, we raised sheep.

. . . .

We learned to make do with what we had, to do more with less.

. . . . .

Those lessons from the 1930s on the farm clearly carried over into my business career. I had no interest in incurring even a nickel more of debt than was necessary – a concern that was shared by all who grew up in the 1930s. Reducing debt and keeping it as low as possible, consistent with good business practices, was always one of my personal objectives. And, when we were required to take on new debt or replace old debt, everyone knew I would be very sensitive to the interest rate.

Taking on more debt was bad enough; paying more than market for it was unpardonable.

. . . . .

Timeliness and punctuality was and still is a hallmark with me. There just is no excuse for anyone being late. If there is anything that gets to me quickly, it is people who don't know how to stay on time, or who waste time. Time is a very scarce commodity. It always should be conserved and used wisely. Unfortunately, I met plenty of people who had absolutely no concept of time.

Prime Osborn was frequently late. He always had things to do; people to see; letters to write. He just didn't worry about time. If he was late, that was too bad. He didn't mean anything disrespectful about it. That was just Osborn; he was obsessed with letter writing, especially answering letters. He is the only person I have ever known who answered every letter he got, even those addressed to "Occupant."

· ·

But he didn't hold a candle to Walter J. Tuohy, head of the C&O from 1949 until his death in 1966. In most things, Touhy was a warm-hearted and considerate person, but when it came to time, he had no consideration of anyone else.

· · · · ·

Every day all the officers of the C&O in Cleveland would meet for lunch in The Greenbrier Suite in the Terminal Tower. Lunch was scheduled from 12:30 to 1:30. Many, many times, Tuohy would come down at 1:25, just as the rest of us were finishing and about to leave. Obviously we could not walk out on the president. Tuohy would sit there, toy with his food (he was a finicky eater) and eat and talk until 2:30 or 3:00 and all the top officers of the railroad had to sit there with him and listen. Usually, he wasn't even talking about company business; mainly he reflected on people he had known or something to do with the coal business, which he had been in before he came to C&O.

Remembering my days in Cleveland, CSX never had an executive dining room. When CSX was first formed and our offices were in the Federal Reserve Building in Richmond, the Fed graciously allowed CSX officers to have lunch in their dining room, but we didn't spend all afternoon there.

· · · · ·

One time, in my early days with the company, we were in New York with Tuohy. We were scheduled to go back to Cleveland on the company plane at 7 p.m. from LaGuardia airport. The four of us who were scheduled to return home with him were at the plane at the scheduled

. . . .

time. Tuohy showed up at 10:30 p.m. He had met someone he decided he would enjoy having dinner with and he did ... without telling anyone.

Someone asked me once, when I told that story, if we had gone out looking for him, or called around to see if we could find him? We didn't. He was the president. I know, though, that his example spurred me on to do things on time. And I never "hitched a ride" with Tuohy after that.

. . . . .

Meetings and travel also can be a great waste of time. In my early days, I used to have stand-up staff meetings. It is surprising how quickly things get taken care of when everyone is standing. Don't put any chairs in a room. It works beautifully.

One of the extra activities that I had during the administration of President Ford was working on the Grace Commission with Peter Grace. We were working on ways to eliminate waste in the Federal government. At our very first meeting, Peter asked me, "Hays, are you still having those stand-up staff meetings?" The word about these meetings got around.

. . . . .

The necessity of traveling to meet people was always a big waste of time and money to me. With telephone, fax machines — and now — electronic mail, most meetings are unnecessary. While one may receive a surge of ego facing a large group, there must be other, and less costly, ways of satisfying one's sense of power. Some travel is necessary, but most problems can be handled in a normal day. Very rarely is there a good reason for delay, or a two or three-day meeting. If travel is required, when you go to see peo-

. . . .

ple, you should have your meeting and move on.

. . . . .

One of the lessons I learned from John Kusik was his passion for keeping letters to one page. He always felt that if an idea could not be expressed in one page, the recipient would soon lose interest.

Likewise, another big waste of time is the preparation of voluminous reports. I always tried to keep the number of reports to a minimum and get those that were needed summarized, with a few key figures. Not only is the preparation costly, but the time and expense of keeping and filing such reports wasteful.

It seems that many people spend large amounts of time saving things, often things that will never again be needed.

Having dealt with several railroad merger cases, I learned very early on that your opponents have the right to come to your office and look at all of your papers. I quickly decided the way to avoid that was to not keep many papers; I still don't. That paid off many times. The opposing lawyers would come in on discovery and find that there were very few papers in my files.

More court cases than I care to remember have been lost when someone on the witness stand found their position disputed by a letter or memo that someone in their very own company had filed away.

. . . . .

Limousines and big offices also make my waste list. They are convenient in a strange city, or when one is pressed for time, but for the

. . . .

home office, no thanks. When we established CSX in Richmond, Osborn suggested we purchase a stretch limousine, a long, silver Cadillac. He thought it befitting a corporation of CSX's stature. It spent a lot more time in the garage than it did on the streets of Richmond. After Osborn retired, we decided there was no need for it in Richmond. We sent it to The Greenbrier where it had a long, useful life.

. . . . .

When the Van Sweringen brothers and their Allegheny Corporation acquired a railroad empire (including C&O) and built the Terminal Tower complex in Cleveland in the late 1920s, they provided themselves with large offices and fancy, antique furniture. During the Great Depression of the 1930s, most of this rail empire was lost, but C&O remained in Cleveland, and inherited the big offices in Terminal Tower.

On the 36th floor Executive Suite were four offices, each with a large "double partners" desk. In later years, one was used by Chairman Cyrus Eaton, one for the railroad president, one for the president's key associate, and one for visiting dignitaries. One day, in the late 1970s, Clement Conger, curator of the White House at the time, was in Cleveland and saw our offices. He spotted my desk and said, "I've been looking for a desk for the President's private study just like that. Would you give it to us?" I said, "No." Then he asked if we would sell it to them? Again, I declined. "Well," he said, "would you loan it to us so we could use it for a while?" I said, "For how long?" He said, "Indefinitely." After talking to the board, we agreed. As far as I know, it is still in the White House "on loan."

A personal concern of mine was always finding a sloppy desk. Having a neat, clean desk was almost a phobia with me. To me, a neat desk was the sign of a neat, quick mind. I always tried to keep as few papers as possible on my desk and keep those that were there as neatly organized as possible so I knew where they were.

As chairman of CSX, my desk had two drawers. That was my way of discipline. One drawer was for pencils, pens and paper clips. The other was for paper and paper supplies. Behind my desk I had a credenza in which I kept the papers I was working on, but that was it.

Mark Aron, just after he joined CSX in 1981, was assigned a small, what was lovingly referred to as a "two-window office." It was probably 10-by-10, not much bigger. I was walking down the hall by his office one day and noticed that he had papers stacked in piles in the hall. Then I looked in his office and saw that he had even more papers strewn around on his desk, the windowsills, a side chair and the floor. So I stopped and commented to him about what looked to me like a mess.

Mark, who was burrowed down in the papers on his desk and clearly preoccupied, looked up and said, "I know this looks like a mess right now. I just don't have time to get more organized, but I do know what is in every one of these piles. I'm working on the MCI deal. Someone promised them we would not be the ones to delay it. And, it will bring us $32 million in cash."

• • • • • • • • • • • • • • • • • • •

    Having been the "someone" who had made the promise to Bill McGowan, the chairman of MCI, I said, "Good," and headed on down the hall. It is easy to be reasonable and overlook a little mess, especially when $32 million in cash is on the line.

❖ ❖

Chapter XXXVIII

. . . .

John Snow Becomes Logical Successor

Served as head of combined railroads, then as president of CSX

O ne of the key responsibilities of every chief executive officer is to think about and plan for succession. By 1985, it seemed clear to me that John Snow was my logical successor, but, first, the board and I wanted to see how he performed in the field, in one of the operating units and, preferably, the railroad. In line with that plan, Snow went to Baltimore in 1985 as President and Chief Executive Officer of Chessie; and to Jacksonville in 1986 to head CSX Rail Transport, the rail operating portion of the three-unit railroad structure. Later, in 1987, he headed the newly formed CSX Transportation as the parent company of the three rail units.

In each job he undertook, he performed well, was outstanding, a natural leader, excellent communicator, and, as one would expect from his background, very capable at handling political and regulatory matters. He also had no problems with the legal issues or numbers, being a lawyer and having a doctorate in economics. In 1988, he returned to Richmond as President of the corporation. He was elected Chief Executive Officer of the company in 1989 and succeeded me as Chairman in 1991.

. . . .

In the first few years of Snow's assignments in Baltimore and Jacksonville, it seemed to some that John Collinson had adopted him. Collinson and I had been close associates for many years in Cleveland, and when I left in 1980 to join CSX in Richmond, Collinson stayed in Cleveland as the head of Chessie. He did an outstanding job and later headed the study group looking at ways to put Chessie and Seaboard together. When Collinson was named Vice Chairman of CSX in 1985, John Snow succeeded him as President and CEO of Chessie.

One of John Collinson's assignments was to work closely with John Snow, to give him the advantage of his experience and expertise. Collinson was an excellent railroader; very quiet; very efficient. He had an engineering and transportation background and he certainly helped John Snow in those areas. But Snow didn't need much help, or, when he did, it wasn't for long. As he developed in these jobs, it became increasingly clear that he had the ability to be the chief executive of CSX.

We were very fortunate to have had three highly qualified candidates as my successor within the organization. There was always the possibility that we could go outside, but as long as we had three competent individuals who had been with the company for a long time, we didn't need to be looking outside. Bob Hintz had been Chief Financial Officer for Chessie in Cleveland, and, after creation of CSX, had the same position in Richmond. Later, he headed the Texas Gas energy group, and after Sea-Land was acquired, became the President of that worldwide company. Because of his financial background, he looked at everything in terms of numbers, which was advantageous as CSX was acquiring and assimilating other organizations.

• •

Alex J. Mandl became Chief Financial Officer for Seaboard Coast Line shortly before the merger, and continued in that role until we brought him to Richmond to create and develop a corporate planning department. Mandl did a lot of great work as the head of the Planning Department, established a new Human Resources Department, oversaw innumerable studies regarding competitive transportation systems and, later, the acquisition of Sea-Land and development and separation of CSX Intermodal. Still later, Mandl followed Bob Hintz as President of Sea-Land where he remained until becoming Executive Vice President of AT&T. I had, and still have a very high regard for Mandl. He is a very able and innovative individual. Bob Hintz also was very able. We selected Snow, though, and he was the right choice.

❖ ❖

Chapter XXXIX

. . . .

Yukon Pacific Corporation

Long shot pipeline project may pale Conrail transaction

The biggest, most challenging project in CSX's future, if not also in its history, may have had nothing to do with Conrail or railroading. More likely, it will involve a little known CSX asset headquartered in Alaska, one that has the potential to earn the company's shareholders an incredible return...or nothing at all.

That asset is a company named Yukon Pacific Corporation that holds the rights — and has all the permits and approvals necessary — to build a natural gas pipeline from the North Slope oil fields of Alaska to the port of Valdez. In addition to the pipeline, Yukon Pacific also has approvals to build and operate a plant that would liquefy the gas and export this gas to foreign markets, primarily Japan, South Korea and Taiwan.

Walter Hickel, Pendleton Thomas and Larry Kelley founded Yukon Pacific in 1983. Hickel was twice governor of Alaska and Secretary of the Interior in the Nixon Administration; Thomas was a retired chairman of

• • • • • • • • • • • • • • • • • • • •

B.F. Goodrich; Kelley was a Houston oilman. Thomas and Kelley also were active in oil and gas exploration and development in Texas. Hickel was an aggressive booster of the Alaskan economy and the three of them had the idea that North Slope gas someday was going to be valuable and Yukon Pacific was the vehicle.

In 1986, CSX acquired a 30 percent interest in the company, increasing that position to about 80 percent by 1990. Initially, CSX's interest in Yukon Pacific was prompted by the opportunity it presented to leverage the expertise of the Texas Gas management team and grow the pipeline business. After the sale of Texas Gas, CSX continued its involvement to consolidate its position and protect its investment. Current estimates put the cost of the project — pipeline, plant and ships — at about $14 billion — a very big project, huge by any standard.

The permits, findings and other approvals Yukon Pacific has obtained over the years are valuable. They will become even more valuable when economic conditions in Asia improve and when the oil companies find an economic advantage to marketing North Slope gas, rather than pumping it back into the ground to ease recovery of the North Slope's oil. Yukon Pacific will then be on the road to becoming a reality. Getting there probably will result in CSX partnering with the oil companies that today own the North Slope reserves.

There has always been a question as to whether or not the project will ever happen. However, the continuing and ever-growing need for energy around the world and the availability of natural gas on the North Slope significantly increases the likelihood that the project — sooner or later — will be built. So, the question probably should be "When," not "If."

• •

Originally, in the late 1980s, we thought the project might get underway before 2000. Obviously, that did not happen. There are a couple of "catches" that will have to be resolved before Yukon Pacific goes forward. First is the Asian economy and the fact that the Asian customers, not surprisingly, won't enter into contracts — regardless of economic conditions — to purchase the gas until they know when it will be available and at what price. Arrangements are fairly well along with customers in Taiwan and South Korea, but the Japanese utilities are the key. For their part, the oil companies won't commit to when they will be willing to market the gas or quote a price until it is worth more to them than North Slope oil. Remember, right now they are in the oil business in Alaska; not the gas business. So Yukon Pacific is caught between the two.

Someday, hopefully in the first 10 years of the new millennium, the balancing act will come together. This will happen if for no other reason than because Alaska will demand it. The oil pipeline today is a large part of the state's economy. As the oil reserves and the revenues from the pipeline diminish, Alaska will exert tremendous pressure to see the Yukon Pacific project built. It will become as critical to the state's economy as the oil pipeline has been and is today.

The project will cost billions and it will be worth billions. These are very big numbers for a railroader, huge numbers. But there really is no way to know exactly how valuable it will be to CSX. That's why we didn't make much of Yukon Pacific back in the 1980s and probably why it remains largely an unknown, unvalued asset of CSX today.

One knows this, though. Energy resources are continually being consumed worldwide. Demand is only going to increase and, at some point,

North Slope gas will be in much greater demand. It will take a huge amount of capital to build the pipeline, the plant, the port facilities and the ships, just like it took a huge amount of capital for the oil companies to build the TransAlaska Pipeline System to transport North Slope crude. But the capital will be there because the revenue stream and the profits will be substantial and they will be so for many years.

❖ ❖

. . . .

Sea-Land —
A Portal on the World

The global economy comes into closer view

O n April 26, 1986, CSX shocked the business world by announcing the acquisition of Sea-Land Corporation. Sea-Land had been a loss company and, to many people, container shipping was a big stretch from railroading. But we saw the acquisition as a logical extension of CSX's business. From the time CSX was created, we looked for ways to develop into a multimodal transportation company. In fact, since the early 1970s I had felt that Chessie could expand into other modes.

In the mid-1980s, after the acquisition of Texas Gas placed us firmly in the barge, pipeline and oil and gas exploration business, we created a corporate planning department for CSX. While the planning function, as such, should be composed of the top officers of the company, we did create a separate planning department in 1985, bringing Alex Mandl, then the Chief Financial Officer of Seaboard, to Richmond as its head. His job was to study other modes of transportation — other than rail, barge and pipeline — and see if there were any good fits.

• • • • • • • • • • • • • • • • • • • •

Mandl assembled a small group of people and started looking at the shipping, airline and trucking industries. After several months of these studies, Mandl and his associates concluded that acquiring a trucking company would not be desirable because we would be competing against some of our customers and ourselves. He did conclude that we should be working much more closely with trucking companies to further develop and grow our intermodal, piggyback business, focusing on handling the longer hauls for them.

That is exactly what CSX Intermodal and the rail industry are doing today. They also concluded that merging with an airline was not compatible, CSX being a freight, not a passenger, carrier. We had some discussions with representatives from some of the air freight companies, but we never found anything that would make a good fit.

The planning people then turned their attention to the shipping industry and concluded that bulk carriers were a specialized transportation business and were not compatible, but that container carriers might have a lot of similarities with rail transportation. As a result, we began a detailed study of the three major U.S. container-shipping companies, Sea-Land, American President Lines and United States Lines.

At about the time of the study, Sea-Land was spun off by RJR Industries as an independent company and both APL and U.S. Lines were stand-alone companies. Bruce Seaton, with headquarters in San Francisco, headed APL; Malcolm McLean, the father of the container-shipping industry and the founder of Sea-Land, headed U.S. Lines; and Joseph Abely was the chairman of Sea-Land.

. . . .

Initially, U.S. Lines seemed to be the only company of the
three that we might be able to acquire at a reasonable price, and there were
several meetings with McLean and his associates. U.S. Lines was implementing a strategy that relied on very large ships to handle Pacific Rim
traffic through the Panama Canal directly to the East Coast, rather than
coming to the West Coast and using the railroads to Eastern markets. The
idea was great, but the additional time that it took the ships – which were
slow as well as big – to get through the Canal and up to East Coast ports
was not appealing to many shippers. When we got into the numbers, we
also found that the debt load being carried by U.S. Lines was just overpow-
ering and that ended those discussions. Later, after U.S. Lines went into
receivership and we had acquired Sea-Land, we acquired 12 of those big
U.S. Lines ships, using them in regular service after repowering them to
increase their speed, but that is getting ahead of the story.

After ending discussions with U.S. Lines, we more closely looked at
APL, but their people made it very, very clear that they had no interest
whatsoever in being acquired; under any circumstances. This left only Sea-
Land. Peter G. Peterson, the former U.S. Secretary of Commerce who had
just established a new company, Blackstone Associates, arranged a meeting
in the winter of 1985-1986 with Abely to see if there might be any com-
patibility between CSX and Sea-Land. We were one of Blackstone's first
customers.

Joe Abely had been Chief Financial Officer of RJR and had been sent
over to Sea-Land to head it and guide the company through the spin-off
from RJR. The meeting at Blackstone went well, but Abely indicated that
he and the board of Sea-Land, having previously seen the company operat-

ed as a subsidiary of RJR, really had no great interest in again being part of a similar arrangement. They wanted to maintain their independence. He was very pleasant, and made it clear that they would be glad to discuss things with us, but they really had no interest. We did agree, however, to exchange limited amounts of information. Conversations with Peterson and his associates indicated that there was a possibility that Sea-Land and we would get together, but it would not be quick or easy.

At the same time as our discussions were underway, Sea-Land's stock was being acquired by one of the so-called "corporate raiders" in Texas, Harold Simmons. In fairly short order, Simmons had a substantial amount of Sea-Land stock and had indicated that he planned a proxy fight to take over Sea-Land early in the spring of 1986. This spurred Abely and the Sea-Land board to express a renewed interest in working with us.

A special all-day CSX board meeting was called at which Mandl and his people presented their findings that container shipping was the most compatible with rail of all the other transportation businesses. We also discussed Sea-Land and expressed our view that combining CSX and Sea-Land would be desirable and profitable.

Sea-Land was then operating at an annual loss of about $70 million, and this generated many questions. Some of our directors wondered if we would be able to turn them around. Our studies indicated that with additional financing for new equipment and some changes in operating practices and a close coordination with our railroad, we would be able to turn the loss into a profit. At the end of the day, the CSX board approved going forward with the acquisition.

• •

Knowing we would need to acquire the Sea-Land stock held by Simmons, I called him to arrange a meeting. We sent Bob Hintz, our chief financial officer, and Mark Aron, our top lawyer, to meet with him and his people. But, things did not go very well in Houston. Hintz and Aron succeeded only in irritating Simmons — apparently within the first 10 minutes of the meeting. He promptly called me, very irate, asking why we had sent those two…using some choice language…and said that if we really had any interest in buying his Sea-Land stock we would have to do something different.

Hearing that, we got together with Peterson and his group to determine what we could afford to pay for Sea-Land stock. We concluded that we could pay up to $28 a share, recognizing that whatever we paid Simmons we would have to pay all other Sea-Land stockholders if we decided to acquire the rest of the stock. The $28 was not acceptable to Simmons. He wanted substantially more. So the discussions came to a screeching halt while we tried to figure out a way to acquire his stock without going over $28 a share. We concluded that the way to do it would be to pay Simmons a fee for the right to purchase his Sea-Land stock at $28 per share at any time during the next several months. We were buying an option to purchase his shares, which accounted for about 40 percent of Sea-Land's shares, at that price within a fixed period of time.

The arrangement accomplished what we wanted and allowed us to do a number of other things. Effectively, it gave Simmons more than $28 a share for his stock. It also gave us time to study making a tender offer for the balance of Sea-Land's outstanding shares and to complete a lot of legal and financial work that was essential if we were going to proceed.

. . . .

That work led us to the conclusion that, having the right to acquire 40 percent of the company by buying Simmons' stock, we had a very good chance of acquiring a majority interest in the company.

During this time, Sea-Land officials were still not being helpful to us. Abely clearly wanted to get rid of Simmons, but he had no interest in being taken over by another company. Thus, we were working to acquire Sea-Land without the approval of its chairman and president, or its board, at the time we entered into the option agreement with Simmons.

Regardless, we purchased Simmons' stock, and put it in a trust, pending Interstate Commerce Commission approval. We also instituted a tender offer for the remaining outstanding Sea-Land shares at $28 a share, conditioned on acquiring enough to give us (including the shares we had bought from Simmons) a majority of Sea-Land's stock. and the Sea-Land board of directors, still wanting to remain independent, but now feeling that we would be successful in our tender offer, reluctantly agreed to announce Sea-Land was in support of our offer. The tender offer was successful and we acquired the remaining outstanding shares. The total cost, including the option to Simmons, was $804 million … for a company that was losing money at the rate of $70 million a year.

After announcement of the successful tender offer, phone calls and letters from disgruntled investors started coming in. Especially vehement was one from the lead analyst of one of our larger stockholders. He told me in no uncertain terms that his company would "dump" all of their CSX stock and have nothing more to do with us. Other analysts were upset, calling it an unwise move.

But we had done our homework and felt quite strongly that,

. . . .

over the long-term, the acquisition of Sea-Land would become a good thing for CSX. Using hindsight 13 years later, it proved highly beneficial to CSX, even with the sale of the international container-shipping portion of Sea-Land's business in 1999.

Sea-Land, an international container-shipping company, handled vast volumes of containers at ports along the Atlantic, Gulf and Pacific coasts of the United States from Europe and Asia and virtually all of the major trade centers of the world. Many of its customers, however, were located in the United States interior and were CSX rail customers. So it seemed logical that those containers could be put on CSX rails and taken to their ultimate customers. We thought there were obvious opportunities for CSX to handle these containers throughout the United States either on its own lines or through connections.

Also, the deal overnight changed CSX from a provincial railroad with a regional outlook, to a worldwide transportation company. Our vision was to create a multimodal transportation company, and doing that required expansion well beyond the rail network of the eastern United States. Sea-Land was that opportunity.

Many things were then changing throughout the world. A global economy was clearly in sight and more and more products were being brought into this country from overseas. At the same time, American companies were outsourcing from foreign markets, completely changing their transportation and logistics patterns and requirements. CSX, in our view, had to change and grow with its customers. CSX had to get to the same markets and sources being reached by its customers. Sea-Land, combined with the railroad, gave CSX that reach, worldwide coverage.

For all these reasons, the acquisition of Sea-Land still seems to me to have been a natural. Of all the activities I have been part of during my business career; this one was the most logical, most desirable, and the least risky. Some thought it was ill advised, but we had done our homework and we were confident it would prove to be in the best interests of our stockholders.

. . . .

Meeting the Challenges of Intermodalism

Turning a $50 million loss into a growing, profitable business

The acquisition of Sea-Land led us to create a new company within CSX, a stand-alone intermodal company, CSX Intermodal. Sea-Land generated vast volumes of containers between both U.S. coasts and from interior points to them. This gave CSX a nationwide presence in the market and offered us an opportunity, by combining the Sea-Land business with our railroads' traditional intermodal business, to dramatically improve efficiency, the economics of the business and, most importantly, service to our customers.

In late 1986 the planning group began to study the feasibility of setting up a completely separate business unit to handle the intermodal business, exclusive of the Sea-Land traffic, moving on our railroad. Their studies indicated we were losing somewhere in the vicinity of $50 million a year after fully allocating all the costs associated with intermodal. We had to make some drastic changes — either we were going to get out of the business, and leave the Sea-Land business as it was, contracted out to other

. . . .

railroads, or find some way to make intermodal, all of it, profitable.

The studies suggested we could grow and improve the profitability of the business by moving it out from under the railroad, especially if we developed an organization that had a closer, direct relationship with customers. The studies indicated that the business, run correctly, could be grown and would operate profitably, but a true picture of its costs and potential could only be obtained by getting it at arm's length from the railroad.

Basically, the studies confirmed the traditional railroader's view of intermodal. The way it was being operated, it just wasn't profitable. As the planning group looked closer, it was clear that the margins certainly were less than they were on carload traffic, but with gross revenues of $700 million, it seemed there must be a way to turn a profit in the business. And it clearly was a growing business.

Once CSX Intermodal had been established, we began looking around the company for someone to head it. Putting a railroader in charge did not appear to be in our best interests. We needed someone who understood that we were competing with trucks, who really understood the economics of the business and could work with the customers and the railroads. That led us to Neil Porter, who had been in the trucking industry with Overnight, Preston and Jones before joining Sea-Land as head of operations in Alaska, then Japan and Hong Kong. He was placed in charge with the charter of doing whatever was necessary to put our intermodal business on a profitable track and grow it.

Neil had absolute authority with customers and the same with

. . . .

our railroad or any other railroad. For example, he had the authority to negotiate contracts with our railroad, or any other railroad to handle the business. If another railroad offered better service or better prices than our railroad, he could go with the other railroad. He also had the authority to add or close intermodal terminals on CSX; add or eliminate service operated by our railroad; and make his own determination as to the other requirements of the business, including how many trailers, or locomotives were needed. In other words, he had the authority to do whatever was required to make CSX Intermodal a profitable, growing company.

One of his first actions was to close a large number of intermodal terminals on our railroad. This upset a lot of people, railroaders and customers. Traditional railroaders were especially upset, feeling that it would cost CSXI traffic. Interestingly enough, one of the terminals he closed was in Richmond, the headquarters city of CSX.

Neil was convinced that intermodal traffic could be better and more profitably handled with a smaller number of more efficient terminals. He took Sea-Land's trade lane concept and converted it to service lanes, concentrating intermodal service on these lanes, all of which connected key city pairs and markets. He also made some very heavy service demands on the railroad's transportation department, which he felt was critical to growing the business and improving its profitability.

Another change he made was partnering with third parties, consolidators, and their customers, the truckers. Railroaders wouldn't go near truckers. They just weren't temperamentally suited to work with them. Railroaders have always been geared to volume at just about any price and

• •

truckers to service, timeliness and low costs and prices. Neil knew nothing about a railroad and the railroaders were not thrilled with him, but that did not bother me. They had not been able to make any money in intermodal and we needed someone who could turn that around. Neil had a lot of new ideas and put them into effect quickly, effectively and profitably.

In short order, by reducing the number of terminals, concentrating service on key lanes and insisting on much, much better service from the railroad, he dramatically improved service, significantly reduced the number of locomotives and other assets needed to handle the business, and turned the corner to profitability.

❖   ❖

Chapter XLII

. . . .

Focusing on Transportation

Turning a profit with timely maneuvers

In 1987, with Sea-Land Service in the family and CSX Intermodal moving forward, it was becoming increasingly clear that CSX primarily was a transportation company. It also was clear that we could not be all things to all people; that the other, non-transportation interests in time would suffer; and, therefore, that we should focus our future on transportation. Additionally, it had been apparent to us for some time that analysts were having a hard enough time figuring out our rail, intermodal, barge and container-shipping activities; the energy and other activities were simply lost in their shuffle. These things combined to prompt us to begin an intensive study of our holdings. The goal was to determine which of the transportation companies really best fit with each other and, therefore, were desirable to keep for the long term and which of the remaining assets might be best sold to bring in funds to finance our future in the transportation business.

Those studies included every business unit of every company, even our coal properties. Railroads had owned coal lands for many years, but were not able to get into the coal mining business. We could only lease these properties to coal companies, who would operate them and then we would haul the coal. Also, virtually all of these properties were adjacent to our railroad. If they were ever mined, we were going to haul the coal whether or not we owned the land. So it didn't make much sense to hold on to those properties. As a result, the first divestiture occurred on December 31, 1986, when we sold Western Pocahontas Corporation to Quintana Minerals, a Texas corporation, for $60 million.

At the same time, Bob Hintz and his associates were studying the oil and gas exploration and development business that we had acquired with Texas Gas. Texas Gas, over the years, had branched out well beyond its pipeline. In fact, just before our merger, it had disposed of its trucking company, leaving three major businesses — the pipeline, a barge line, and oil and gas exploration and development. The pipeline offered us no synergies with our other modes and the oil and gas business clearly was not compatible with our transportation philosophy.

Also, it soon was apparent that oil and gas exploration was very risky and very capital intensive. It seemed we could put that capital to much better use at our railroad and Sea-Land units and began exploring the practicability of selling the oil and gas exploration and production company (CSX Oil and Gas), the natural gas liquids processing plant (CSX Energy), and the pipeline (Texas Gas Transmission). After a considerable amount of work by Hintz and his associates throughout 1987 and into early 1988, we sold CSX Oil and Gas to Total Minatome, a French oil and gas company, in April 1988 for $612 million in cash, recording an after-tax gain of $180 million. At the time we sold those assets, they were contributing about $1 million a year to our net income.

• • • • • • • • • • • • • • • • • • • •

A year later, in April 1989, Transco Energy Corporation purchased Texas Gas Transmission, paying $577 million, which translated into a $23 million after-tax gain. Then, in February 1990 we sold CSX Energy to Enron Gas Processing Company, a subsidiary of Enron Corporation, for an after-tax gain of $52 million.

In other words, we realized $255 million of after-tax gains on the sale of the Texas Gas pipeline and oil and gas interests...and we still owned American Commercial Lines, the Texas Gas barge line. (Later, in 1998, CSX conveyed a roughly two-thirds interest in the barge line to a joint venture with National Marine for $695 million in cash, earning a $155 million after-tax gain.)

In the meantime, in February 1989, we sold our share of Lightnet, a fiber-optic joint venture we had entered into with Southern New England Telephone Company (SNET) for $183 million and an after-tax gain of $73 million. Then, in the third quarter of 1989 we closed on the $145 million sale of Rockresorts, which we had purchased two years earlier for $64 million, to VMS Realty Partners (which did not include the concession contract at the Grand Teton National Park), realizing a $34 million after-tax gain.

More important than the gains on these sales, though, was the fact that CSX, shortly after the turn of the decade, was focused on what it knew best: the transport of raw materials and finished goods for its ever more global network of customers. And, as Hintz's studies had predicted, the stock price clearly reflected the change. When we officially launched the restructuring in September 1988, CSX stock, restated to reflect subsequent

• • • • • • • • • • • • • • • • • • • •

splits, was trading at $13.4375. Five years later, the stock was at $39 a share; not bad, not bad at all.

❖ ❖

Chapter XLIII

. . . .

Retirement Meant Stepping Down... Completely

Applying the lessons learned was easy

It was not at all difficult, when the time came in 1991, for me to retire as chairman of CSX. I had had 42 years of good, satisfying work and I had played a big part in a good regional railroad company, C&O, growing into a major, international transportation company. We had selected and developed a superior successor in John Snow and there was no reason why I could not, in fact, should not retire. In my book, the greatest challenge for any CEO is finding a competent successor and then getting out of his or her way.

Later, after retirement, a number of people asked why I had not remained on the CSX board of directors. Perhaps, in that respect, I am different than many others. I had felt all along — for many, many years, having seen the opposite at other companies — that CEOs should get off the board immediately after retirement. Doing otherwise can be nothing other than a lose-lose situation. If the former CEO stays on the board and doesn't say anything, people think he is sulking. If he does speak up, they think he is trying to tell his successor how to run the business.

As far as I was concerned, that was a no-win situation. So I urged our CSX board, many years before I retired, to adopt a bylaw that required the CEO to leave the board upon retirement from the company. I thought then and I still think today that is an excellent idea.

Even though I wasn't their chief executive, over a period of time I also left the boards of other corporations, civic organizations and educational institutions. I firmly believe that when a person leaves "active service" that he or she loses a certain amount of contact with current events in the business, charitable, educational and other worlds. You don't have the same interests, you aren't building a relevant knowledge base, and no one wants to hear about how things were done "back in the old days." As time progresses, that only gets worse. This prompted my decision to phase out my corporate, civic and college board memberships within three years or so.

One of the activities that I most enjoyed was serving on the board (using the time-honored term "Board of Visitors") of the College of William & Mary in Williamsburg, Virginia. My nine-year term ended in 1993, the 300th anniversary of the college and two years after I retired from CSX. I have always felt that education is very vital to the country and that anything the corporate world can do to support higher education was and is important.

Appointed by Virginia Gov. Robb in 1986, I was honored by serving as Vice-Rector for two years, and as Rector (chairman) for six years. It was a time of extreme activity: selection of a new president (Paul R. Verkuil) in 1986 and another new president (Timothy J. Sullivan) in 1993; successful completion of a $150 million capital campaign in 1993;

• •

additions to campus buildings and endowment funds; and a thrilling 300th birthday celebration. During my time on the board, U.S. Supreme Court Chief Justice Warren Burger served as Chancellor, bringing great distinction to the college. When his seven-year term was up, we were able to secure Margaret Thatcher, Lady Thatcher, as the new Chancellor, who also served with distinction. While the Chancellor's role is largely ceremonial, both have actively and regularly participated in campus activities through the years. William & Mary is consistently rated one of the outstanding public colleges and universities in America, and I am very proud to have been associated with it.

My introduction to William & Mary began when our son, Tom, enrolled there. Tom was the first graduate of his Cleveland area high school to be accepted at William & Mary. His counselors, when Tom was looking at colleges, told him that there was no need to apply to William & Mary because it was difficult to gain admission and no one from the school had ever been accepted there. He was accepted, but went there with considerable apprehension, given what he had heard about the school from his counselors. But he did well.

During Tom's years there I was elected a member of the board of sponsors of the business school and I remained on that board for almost 10 years, leaving only after Gov. Robb appointed me to the board of visitors of the College. After nearly 30 years of association, I still follow William & Mary with great interest, and meet with the president for special activities and ad hoc committee work.

In addition to William & Mary, I continue to maintain high

interest in my alma mater at Bowling Green, Ky., now part of Western Kentucky University. In October 1987, I was honored by being elected to the Distinguished Alumni Hall of Fame. In 1998 the new president, Gary Ransdell, established a 70-member President's Advisory Committee and asked me to serve as co-chairman.

Since retirement I have begun working on my family history, which is the source of the opening portion of this book. It seems more and more people have discovered this hobby and have become very active in genealogy. I always enjoyed being with relatives, but never had enough time to learn about how "Uncle James" and "Aunt Margaret" fit into the family. Tracing the family history has been an interesting and fun project. It hasn't been quite as exciting as 42 years of railroading, but it sure beats farming ... even the gentlemanly type without horses.

❖ ❖

Chapter XLIV

. . . .

Managing to Manage

Done right, it is first based on ethics

I n the annals of commerce, it is hard to imagine anything consuming more ink than theories on management. At various times over the 42 years of my career, one or more of those efforts — and its author or authors — have basked in the spotlight of expertmanship and of best-selling.

Upon reflection, it seems to me that neither the books, nor their authors — the only exception being those by Peter Drucker, who is rightly acknowledged as the father of post-war management — have had much of a lasting effect on the practice of management, or on business. Admittedly, the efforts of some others have attained commercial popularity and their authors have enjoyed personal success. By and large, however, good managers and good businesses today are doing the same things they were doing long before I walked into the C&O's office fresh out of graduate school. None of it is secret and most of it is little more than a variation of Professor Drucker's axioms.

It makes no sense in these pages to repeat the theories, practices and processes of Professor Drucker. His books and articles are as fresh and as insightful today as they were when first published and every prospective and current manager should read them and put them into action.

. . . . .

What does make sense to consider and is usually overlooked, though, are the human aspects of management.

In that regard and first and foremost, good managers and good businesses are ethical. They adhere to a strict moral code and they care about and direct their efforts to serving the best interests of humanity and our society. That is the foundation of their success. Morality alone, however, does not automatically bring commercial success. But those without it, regardless of the quality of their "mouse trap," much more often than not end up as personal or commercial failures, usually both. I have seen many good managers in bad businesses, but very few bad managers in good businesses.

. . . . .

Good managers treat the people they work with, most especially those for whom they are responsible, as equals and they understand that people respond in kind to those who help them. Such managers never assume or act as if their associates work for them. As I came into and advanced in management, I never lost sight of that fact. That was why I always kept an "open door" and insisted on being addressed as "Hays," not "Mr. Watkins." Both, I hoped, set the tone, served as a profession of my faith in and respect for my fellow employees and their work.

The best way I found to guide my conduct as a manager was to follow a simple and long-standing motto: "Be someone you want to work for." To

. . . .

some, that may sound like an over-simplification. Yet, how many people-
have each of us worked with in our careers and wondered how they could
look at themselves in a mirror and be pleased with what they knew was
beneath the suit?

. . . . .

Advancing into management is not difficult. It just seems so.
The first key is mastering ourselves, then learning a skill, and, finally, establishing our reputation, our ability at every opportunity. Before we can know
much about anything, we must first know ourselves. Learning to master our
own frailties is a life-long pursuit and takes honest, introspective effort. It
requires thinking out our values, committing to them no matter what,
knowing our interests and learning and then expanding our personal and
professional limits. The constant in these, throughout our lives, must be our
values. Without them, we deny ourselves the basics around which we develop a personal philosophy and, in business terms, we will come to rely more
on tactics than strategies, a sure recipe for failure.

Another key is doing the best we can do...at whatever we are doing.
All of us have known someone, usually more than a few, who just showed
up for work and went through the motions. What a terrible waste and I am
not talking about the interests of their employer here, but of their personal
interests. Instead of just putting in their time, they should quit and go to
another job that fulfills them, captures their imagination and gives them
purpose. After all, we spend a third of our life at work. If we do not like
what we are doing, are not challenged by it and do not find it enjoyable, we
are squandering our most precious asset, our time. I have never understood
why anyone would throw away a third of his lifetime doing something he

does not want to do or doing it — whatever it is — at less than the best of his ability.

Ultimately, doing one's best, I firmly believe, will prove to be best for our own interests. Good people, doing good work get good, satisfying jobs. And they do it without "running for office," looking ahead to their next assignment at the expense of their current responsibility or role in the organization. The future, as the saying goes, will take care of itself. It really does. I have known people who always were looking at or angling for what they thought should be their next job, ignoring what they were then doing. Generally, they didn't get to the next job. This is not to say each of us should not have personal goals. We should. But we should not flaunt or try to advance them at the expense of our fellow employees or the company.

The best personal goals — and the only ones really worth spending much time thinking about — are lifetime goals. These are value-based and far more important than work, a job, and even a career. They go to the heart of our reason for being and should serve to keep our life in balance. What are we going to do with our life; what is important to us personally and to our family; where can we best direct our skills and interests and, personally and professionally, make a difference? These are the profound questions and I believe they should be addressed in that order — family, work, and community. And then there is a fourth, recreation.

· · · · ·

Recreation, not necessarily of the competitive sort, is exceptionally important to keeping our lives in balance. It cleanses and refreshes us and both sharpens and broadens our instincts and interests, our reality. Some, like myself, find recreation in working The New York Times crossword

. . . .

puzzle, which I have done every day I have been able to get my hands on the newspaper for more years than I can remember, or in quiet, observant walks, another of my personal favorites. Others find recreation in competitive sport, as in golf, or in testing their bodies and their will, as in running. How we "recreate" is really not important. What is, though, is making the time to do it.

. . . . .

Overarching all of these is spiritual enrichment. It is the umbrella, which protects and influences all four. Good managers, though, do not wear their supreme faith in God or their religion on their sleeves. I have known only a few who did anything more to profess their faith than the conduct of their lives. In all instances, though, their faith clearly was at the core of everything that they did every minute of every day. And that held profound meaning among those they managed, as well as the customers they served. It signaled they were free, within the limits of their conscience, to do what was right...for themselves, for the enterprise, for their customers, for society.

. . . . .

Managing and business are all about harnessing and directing the power of people to meet the needs of humanity, of society, at a profit...and that is a high calling. We must not lose sight of that fact. Cyrus Eaton, as noted earlier, strongly believed in free trade, in the global economy, long before the latter term became common to our lexicon. Certainly, he expected to profit from those interests, but he also understood, as he often said,

. . . .

"People doing business usually don't shoot at each other." He was right, of course, and we should not lose sight of that simple fact. It underscores the humanity of business.

❖   ❖

. . . .

Managing vs. Leading... There is a Difference

Leaders must be more uninhibited, creative and set the strategy and the tone

Most individuals who have had the opportunity to lead have worked their way into those positions, advancing through the ranks of the organization. Having demonstrated the ability to master themselves, they are entrusted to manage others. Having accomplished that task with success, a fortunate few earn the opportunity to test their ability to lead. For the most part, they then must stop managing and begin leading. Otherwise, they fail.

Certainly, there is an overlap between managing and leading. Leading requires calling on one's managerial experiences and involves all of the values and skills essential to and developed by managing, most importantly high ethical and moral standards. Leaders who don't have these attributes will sooner or later — more likely sooner — be replaced by those who do.

One major difference between leaders and managers, in my opinion, is that leaders must learn to listen. Leaders use their experience and knowledge to suggest courses of action, to inspire others to find them, are marked by their consideration for the ideas and interests of others and use their abilities to find the right answer and then build consensus around it. They do not direct day-to-day activities and they do not demand. Therefore, listening is critical and successful leaders spend much more time listening than they do talking. No leader knows all the answers; for that matter even all the questions. All leaders need support — new ideas. The best leaders take as much help as they can get ... and give credit. There is an old expression: "There is no limit to what can be done if you don't care who gets the credit."

Leaders must be considerate and that means being prepared to hear good and bad ideas. Even if an idea is bad, good leaders still give it a fair hearing, even if it is a really screwball idea. I have heard some screwball ideas, but I always listened. One just never knows. Leaders have to search out and listen to every view to bring out the best ideas. Then, and only then, should they make their decision.

Every decision, in a perfect world, would result from consensus. Consensus is a wonderful thing, if it is possible, but leaders have to know when to draw the line and, if necessary, make the decision on their own. The Japanese, who are very strong on consensus, seem to me to have at times taken it beyond reasonable limits. There always have been and always will be times when consensus is impossible, when everyone will disagree seemingly just to be disagreeable. Good leaders know when that point has been reached and are prepared, upon reaching it, to take a stand. The problem many leaders have is that they reach that point too soon, before they are fully informed. They lose patience and go with their emotions. Emotions are good when "shown," but they limit objectivity and cut off

. . . .

discussion and debate when "expressed," and that is something leaders cannot afford.

. . . . .

One might think, given the importance of patience, suggestion, listening and consensus, that leaders would do almost anything to avoid change and its discomforts and disruptions. Good leaders do not embrace change for its own sake — which obviously would be counterproductive. They do, however, create and nurture a climate for change. And doing that right is difficult, really difficult.

Change takes all of us, including leaders, out of our comfort zone. Consciously or unconsciously, we resist it above all else. When we see it, our normal reaction is denial. If that doesn't obscure it, then comes outright rejection. It is just human nature. Leaders, therefore, must create a climate where people are at least willing to consider change and know that doing so will not cost them the respect of their associates. Even doing this will not make change especially welcome, but it should keep it from being rejected out of hand and that is the key to getting, developing and applying new ideas, all the while improving the ability of the organization to succeed.

Adverseness to risk is probably the major reason we all resist change. Good leaders are well aware of this and encourage intelligent risk-taking throughout their organizations. And they do it by making certain their associates know risk-taking, after appropriate and complete study of all the alternatives and a thorough vetting, which makes it intelligent, will be respected regardless of the result.

. . . .

Good leaders also do not lose sight of the fact that by cultivating a climate for change and encouraging intelligent risk-taking that they are setting the stage for what I call creative tension within their organizations ... and this is good. Creative is the key word and channeling it is one of a leader's key managerial responsibilities. The alternative is stagnation. Therefore, good leaders are never satisfied with the status quo, never accept, "Well, I can't do this any better" attitudes. The skill they must master is keeping such tension in bounds, making certain it is constructive creative tension, not destructive.

. . . . .

The longer I worked, the more I realized that my intuition was a pretty good guide. To me, intuition is easily defined. It is our judgment based on our experience, insight and intelligence. It is not making blind choices. And, it should not be followed without detailed knowledge and discussions with others. But, basically, I believe most people who have been around a while in a job and an organization develop a built-in compass that generally works pretty well and should be trusted.

. . . . .

A final thought on leadership — being able to communicate is an oft overlooked, but absolute essential for leaders. It requires being able to clearly, concisely and effectively inform and motivate people. Now, I have met a few bad leaders who were wonderful communicators. In fact, they probably advanced to leadership roles because their ability to communicate obscured other failings. Eventually, though, they were found out. On the other hand, I have never met a bad communicator who was a good

• • • • • • • • • • • • • • • • • • • •

leader. Developing a communications style is very important. I worked at being certain I was informal, open and loose. Key to that was being on a first name basis with as many of my associates as possible, regardless of their standing in the company.

❖ ❖

Chapter XLVI

. . . .

The Role of the Chief Executive Officer

Like it or not, every organization reflects the values and style of its CEO

When our son Tom was in the first grade and I was at the Chessie System, someone asked him what his father did for a living? Tom said, "He eats lunch, goes to meetings and talks on the telephone!" Frankly, in terms of the physical activities, he was quite accurate. What he did not understand as a first grader, but now understands as a CEO himself, is that the job involves much more and, when one really gets down to it, is a role more than a job.

Chief Executive Officers are the visible focal point of every organization...internally and externally. Therefore, like it or not, every organization and every person in that organization reflects the CEO's values and style in some way and to some degree. And every individual or organization approaching it comes with that same knowledge.

. . . . .

An unfailing ability to inspire confidence, among all constituencies, is the single most important qualification — beyond knowing the intricacies

. . . .

of the business — required of a CEO. Being able to do it with just employees, or only customers, will not do. A CEO must be able to develop and implement strategies and priorities for every constituency and inspire all of them with confidence.

This first comes into play as a CEO begins to assemble a management team, build on its strengths and skills and, with that team and the board of directors, develop, establish and coordinate policies and a strategic process. These are not easy undertakings and they cannot be done tentatively...or alone. CEO's who attempt to do it alone will soon find themselves isolated from their organizations — and their boards — and looking for work.

. . . . .

Being a Chief Executive Officer is frequently described as the toughest job in corporate America. If this were true, it seems to me that the key words for a CEO to keep in mind are build, develop and work with, not lead, direct, or manage.

Many people believe that CEOs just sit somewhere in a huge office pushing buttons, pulling the strings and sharing their infinite wisdom. That is not the case; not even close. The longer I was around, the more I realized how little I knew and how much I depended on other people. I believe that is one of the key things that those of us who come to the job from such disciplines as accounting or engineering — the sciences, so to speak — have to learn. All of a sudden, nothing is precise, absolute. We find ourselves required to make judgments and must trust other people to do what is right

. . . .

for the organization and its customers. Developing that ability and doing it with confidence is essential.

CEOs do not have to be the smartest people in the world. They must, however, be smart enough to assemble a team, preferably one that is composed of people who are smarter and more talented than they. Give that team direction with general guidelines, get out of the way and let the team do its work. I have always said a good CEO gives the impression of being lazy because he or she has to tell other people what they want and then enjoy letting them do it. But that is the key, giving people responsibility and authority. The two go hand in hand, one requires the other. Then, and only then, can they be held accountable.

. . . . .

One of the key responsibilities that CEOs frequently overlook is the obligation to develop successors. This is understandable. No one wants to face the reality that his career at some point will come to an end, especially when he is at the height of his career. However, I believe the most critical measure of a CEO's tenure may well be how he determines and develops his successor. That, to me, is the ultimate test of a CEO's ability and effectiveness and I was very fortunate with John Snow. I count his selection and the job he has since done as one of my proudest accomplishments. No one can say, though, that he is much like myself and that is one of his strengths and one of the great benefits to the company. Frequently, CEOs make the mistake of going out and trying to find someone in their own image. That is not a good idea. Organizations change, just as do the people within them and the customers they serve. The key is to

. . . .

find someone that can inspire confidence within and outside of the organization, not find a clone of the current CEO.

. . . . .

The greatest asset at the disposal of a CEO cannot be bought or sold. It is the organization's board of directors and the value of that group lies in its objectivity. CEOs must remember that their associates sometimes will have difficulty suppressing their personal feelings regarding the CEO, their other associates, even the organization itself. Customers and other outside constituencies clearly approach the organization and the CEO with biases. Board members, on the other hand, are generally unburdened by such influences or allegiances. Their first and only obligation is to fulfill their fiduciary responsibility to shareholders and that requires complete objectivity. That is a priceless commodity...especially to a CEO.

❖ ❖

Chapter XLVII

. . . .

Expansion of C&O Proudest Achievement

Biggest disappointment — failure to acquire Conrail earlier

L ooking back over my 42 years of active service, I think changing the
C&O Railway into a major transportation company tops the list of
business accomplishments of which I am most proud. As our customers
grew in size and reach, it was very important that C&O also grow and
keep pace with American industry. We began that in the early years, adding
B&O and Western Maryland, and followed that with the
Chessie/Seaboard merger that resulted in CSX. Now, with the addition of
the Conrail lines, CSX has a railroad that can meet the needs of its customers. In service, in facilities — in its ability to serve its customers — I
think CSX has adapted and will continue to adapt very well.

By and large, it has been a very rewarding, satisfying and interesting
career. I was allowed to do a lot of things that I would never have dreamed
of doing; met and worked with many wonderful people; and visited some
incredible places half a world away from Fern Creek and Henry County,
Kentucky.

. . . . .

. . . .

But there also have been disappointments. Reflecting on those
42 years, my biggest disappointment was that we couldn't work out an
arrangement with the Norfolk & Western and, later, the Norfolk Southern to
jointly acquire Conrail and the bankrupts in the 1970s and again in the
1980s. John Snow had the same problems when he took over.

We should have been able to find a way to divide the bankrupts and
Conrail before we had spent $10 billion of our shareholders' money and the
government had spent $7 billion of the taxpayers' money. We may have had
digestive problems back in the early 1970s, but I sure would have liked to
have given it a try.

We would have done a better, much better job at a lot less cost and
the country, the shippers, everyone would have been better off. We certainly
would have saved everyone a lot of money and, I think, we would have
changed the competitive environment between railroads and trucks in the
East.

. . . . .

In early 1999, I read Tom Brokaw's book on the 20th Century,
The Greatest Generation, with a quote from Franklin D. Roosevelt at the
head of the first chapter that talks about my generation having had "a ren-
dezvous with destiny." I can remember President Roosevelt saying that, and
I also remember that the commencement speaker used that quote as his
topic when I graduated from high school in 1942.

I'm certain not many people remember their high school commence-

. . . .

ment speech, but I do, and I remember that I didn't have any idea what it meant. I didn't believe I was anything special. In fact, I've never felt that I was anything other than a rather ordinary fellow who happened to have gotten an extraordinary job.

❖   ❖

· · · · · · · · · · · · · · · · · · ·

The Jeffersonion; Jefferson County, KY
July 1930

Fern Creek's Four Year Old Prodigy in Figures

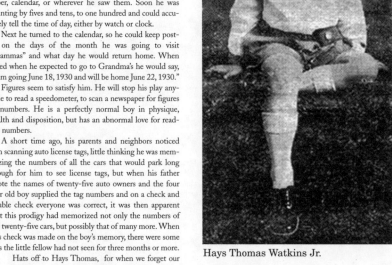

This handsome little fellow says, "I was born January 26, 1926 at Fern Creek." He says his name is Hays Thomas Watkins and his daddy is cashier of the Bank of Fern Creek.

In 1929, when this boy was three years old, one of his neighbors taught him to count to ten. On account of a laughable tongue twisting of the figure seven, he was asked to count again to ten. When we would reach seven everybody would have to laugh.

From this small start Hays Thomas was soon counting to 100, then to 1,000, then onto 100,000. He soon learned to recognize the figures wherever he saw them. He would stand intently admiring the figures on a watch, clock, newspaper, calendar, or wherever he saw them. Soon he was counting by fives and tens, to one hundred and could accurately tell the time of day, either by watch or clock.

Next he turned to the calendar, so he could keep posted on the days of the month he was going to visit "Mammas" and what day he would return home. When asked when he expected to go to Grandma's he would say, "I am going June 18, 1930 and will be home June 22, 1930."

Figures seem to satisfy him. He will stop his play anytime to read a speedometer, to scan a newspaper for figures or numbers. He is a perfectly normal boy in physique, health and disposition, but has an abnormal love for reading numbers.

A short time ago, his parents and neighbors noticed him scanning auto license tags, little thinking he was memorizing the numbers of all the cars that would park long enough for him to see license tags, but when his father wrote the names of twenty-five auto owners and the four year old boy supplied the tag numbers and on a check and double check everyone was correct, it was then apparent that this prodigy had memorized not only the numbers of the twenty-five cars, but possibly that of many more. When this check was made on the boy's memory, there were some cars the little fellow had not seen for three months or more.

Hats off to Hays Thomas, for when we forget our license numbers, as 99 out of every 100 do, he will supply the information free of charge if he has seen the tags.

Hays Thomas Watkins Jr.

Wall Street Journal
July 24, 1970

B&O Sells $27 Million of 11% Securities; Issue Is Tailored for Rail-Leery Market

By Ivan Silverman
Staff Reporter of the Wall Street Journal

NEW YORK — In the first rail bond financing after the Penn Central Railroad's financial collapse, the Baltimore & Ohio Railroad sold $27 million of 11% securities yesterday.

While demonstrating that a market for railroad securities continues to exist, the sale dramatically pointed up the painfully narrow boundaries of that sector. Intimations were provided of the price railroads will be paying for some time— in terms of interest costs and limited financing flexibility—to charm money from investors still stunned by last month's filing by Penn Central Co.'s railroad subsidiary for reorganization under the bankruptcy laws.

First of all, elements of risk in rail financing will have to be slashed to a bare minimum, specialists said. This objective was accomplished on B&O's collateral trust bonds by organizing an unusual financial package. The issuer's parent company, the Chesapeake & Ohio Rail-way, will issue $27 million of 11% mortgage bonds as backing for the B&O securities.

"Normally, C&O would simply guarantee the subsidiary's issue, but here C&O is including buyers of the B&O issue in the circle of its own first creditors," Ernest Kelly Jr., president of Halsey, Stuart & Co., B&O's investment bankers, said.

The collateral bonds will be held by a trustee, Chemical Bank, New York.

Second, yields needed to attract investors will probably have to be higher than would normally be expected even with interest rates hovering near their record peaks. Speaking to this point, Hays T. Watkins, Jr., administrative group vice president of the C&O, said: "C&O-B&O are the innocent victims of the Penn Central (reorganization proceedings). The unprecedented high for the C&O-B&O interest rate is at least two points more than we would expect to pay even in this tight-money market."

In dollar terms, using Mr. Watkins' estimate, B&O will play $3.8 million in extra interest costs over the life of its issue due to the stigma borne by railroad issues as a result of Penn Central's collapse.

Also, C&O-B&O is owed about $5.2 million by the Penn Central Transportation Co., according to information contained in the circular for yesterday's offering. However, a substantial portion of the charges against Penn

Central Transportation may be offset by debts owed to the court-protected line, sources said.

Sacrificial Lamb?

At the same time, Mr. Watkins implied that C&O-B&O was willing to offer itself up as a sacrificial lamb to "reestablish the market for railroad bond issues, a development that benefits the entire railroad industry."

A third implication of yesterday's sale is that the size of railroad issues, and the maturity of rail bonds, may be limited, thereby impairing the financing flexibility of the roads. "You'd have to think in outrageous terms, maybe 12% a year or more, if you tried a long-term issue, say 25 years," Halsey Stuart's Mr. Kelly said. "This might not be acceptable to either management or the stockholders," he added.

The B&O issue falls due in 1977, partly reflecting the railroad's desire to limit interest payments. In addition, the seven-year maturity also was used because it fit into a redemption schedule that was tailored to take into account the proposed merger of C&O with the Norfolk & Western Railway. The merger has been delayed by the Penn Central developments, a C&O spokesman said.

The size of issues that railroads are able to sell may be limited by the unwillingness of certain investors to place orders for rail securities, at least at this time.

"We probably would have liked a $50 million B&O issue," Mr. Kelly stated. "But that would have been too large for the market."

Burlington Northern, a St. Paul Minn. railroad, decided to postpone a planned $60 million public offering of 25-year securities after Penn Central's problems began to surface. The company received a $100 million line of credit from Chase Manhattan Bank, permitting the refunding of debt and the financing of seasonal needs.

C&O-B&O also "had adequate standby credit through a bank loan and short-term paper," Mr. Watkins said. However, the company "didn't want to have large amounts of short-term debt hanging over (it)," he added.

B&O will use proceeds from yesterday's sale to help retire about $39.6 million of mortgage bonds due Aug. 1. The railroad will also use part of a $30 million line of credit extended by banks to pay off the maturing securities. Prior to Penn Central's downfall, the company had planned to raise about $25 million in the Eurobond market, but plans for the foreign financing were undercut by international investor distaste for U.S. railroad issues.

Character of Market

In this country, perhaps one theme emerging from yesterday's sale is that the character of the market for railroad securities is changing, bond specialists say. In the past, the major insurance companies were the prime buyers of rail debt. Many of these insurers are holding large amounts of Penn Central securities that may go into default.

"How can an investment officer go to his board recommending the purchase of railroad bonds when he's got enormous losses on the railroad holdings?" one financing specialist asked.

In addition, the specialists say, insurance companies normally don't buy short-term issues, and railroads may be limited in the near future to selling bonds in a 5-to-15 year range.

Purchasers of the B&O issue included mutual funds, public pension funds and individuals, the investment bankers said. A few insurance companies holding the maturing B&O issue also placed order for the new issue, however, the bankers said.

Relatively high-quality rail bonds—B&O's non-callable issue carried a single-A rating—may continue to attract money from retail investors, at least as long as yields are well-above those available on similar issues sold by nonrailroad operations, the bond specialists say. In addition, high-quality equipment trust certificates aren't expected to suffer from the Penn Central situation.

Yesterday, Salomon Brothers, co-manager with Halsey Stuart for the B&O issue, bought through competitive bidding $4,635,000 of equipment trust certificates sold by C&O. The certificates were then reoffered to yield from 8% for the 1971 maturities to 8.80% for those due 1982-85. Equipment trust issues, however, are considered among the securest of all investments. Financing specialists said they couldn't recall an equipment trust default in recent times.

Railroad executives throughout the country were said to be watching B&O's bond sale with great interest. A considerable amount of railroad securities fall due over the next few years and these maturing bonds will have to be refinanced or paid off from earnings.

"I've spoken with several rail presidents recently and they all want to know how they're going to be able to handle maturing bonds," Halsey Stuart's Mr. Kelly said.

Several hundred millions of rail bonds fall due over the next few years and about $1.5 billion of securities mature over the next decade, Mr. Kelly said.

The Sunday Star
Washington, D.C., May 2, 1971

C&O-B&O CHIEF SPEAKS

Interlocking Transport Is Coming

By Stephen M. Aug
Star Staff Writer

The new president of the affiliated Chesapeake & Ohio-Baltimore & Ohio railroads says one of his principal tasks is going to be "creating a climate for constructive change."

The change that Hays T. Watkins sees is likely to be "more intermodal cooperation" — co-operating among railroads, truckers, barge lines.

"We don't know the transportation demands of the country five or 10 years hence. It may be more intermodal co-operation between different types of carriers... may mean each type of transportation should concentrate on that kind of transportation that each does best... but more intermodal co-operation is coming." he predicted.

Watkins' views, expressed in an interview, could put him at odds with much of the rest of the railroad industry which seeks ownership of other modes of transportation rather than co-operation with them.

The industry, in fact, is seeking legislation that would let down bars to railroad ownership of truck and barge lines. At least one railroad, Southern Railway, has petitioned the Interstate Commerce Commission for authorization to undertake a barge operation.

Rail Moves Fought

All of these transportation diversification moves by railroads are being fought by truckers and barge operators who fear that the railroads may use huge capital resources to drive them out of business.

Reminded of the industry stance, Watkins added that "maybe common ownership, maybe co-operation, maybe some of both" are in the future. Mainly, he said, "I want to make sure that when it does happen we are ready to take full advantage of the changes."

Watkins added that while he is unsure of which course the future holds, "I hope one of my big features is that I have a completely open mind on some things."

Watkins' experience with the C&O— which began in 1949 shortly after he graduated from Northwestern University with a master's degree in business administration— has been mostly in finance.

Hit By P-C Failure

He said that last year's Penn Central bankruptcy actually cost his company far more than the $5 million to $6 million Penn Central owned the C&O-B&O. "We had the misfortune of having this debt ($52 million of B&O bonds) mature a month after Penn Central went bankrupt," he recalled.

As a result, B&O chose to issue $27 million in bonds which came to market in mid-July. The remaining $25 million was refinanced through a short-term loan with the Bank of Nova Scotia. (A C&O subsidiary, the Lake Erie & Detroit Railway Co., Ltd., operates in southern Ontario and C&O has connections with several major Canadian banks.)

We had to pay 11 percent for those bonds which is an unconscionable rate," he recalled. And even to get that interest rate, C&O had to issue its own bonds for use as collateral so B&O could sell its obligations.

"We viewed ourselves as the sacrificial lamb for the railroad industry, but somebody had to prove railroad bonds could be sold," he said. The bonds were sold largely to individual investors, with institutional investors generally spurning them.

"The price Penn Central cost us in addition (to what was owed for freight car rentals) was at least 2 percent in the bond market — between $500,000 and $600,000 a year interest for seven years," he added.

No Total Merger

Watkins said also that he has no plans to fully merge the B&O into the C&O. C&O, which owns 94 percent of B&O, was granted faltering B&O in 1963, although C&O was providing aid in the B&O in 1962.

"There are no material advantages or savings we could achieve by merger," he said. The operations and organization generally have been coordinated wherever possible, but B&O's "credit ratings are still not as good as C&O."

He said that "until we can have B&O's financial position as good as C&O there is no reason why C&O shareholders should suffer in value."

Watkins explained that in financing new equipment, C&O is able to borrow money 1/4 to 1/2 percent cheaper than B&O. Neither railroad has any long-term debt coming due this year. The C&O has nearly $30 million in bonds due in 1973. B&O has $23 million due in 1975 — although its short-term $25 million bank loan is due this year.

Asked what plans B&O has for again paying dividends, Watkins said the subsidiary legally cannot pay dividends because it is $1.9 million in arrears on a sinking fund bond issue. This should be paid off this year, and by 1972 the B&O will no longer have legal restriction on dividends.

But Watkins refused to speculate on whether B&O would even then pay a dividend. If it did, only 6 percent would actually be paid in cash, since its C&O parent owns 94 percent of its stock.

On other matters, Watkins made these points:

■ Now that the proposed C&O merger with Norfolk & Western has been abandoned "we have no intention of talking merger with anyone" in the "foreseeable future."

■ The C&O is "now taking a close look at our facilities" to find, among other things, whether any large-scale track abandonments should be undertaken. The study includes traffic patterns.

■ The B&O, which has small commuter operations in the Washington and Pittsburgh areas, has no plans to expand the services—which currently operate at a loss—unless there are subsidies by some governmental body.

Noting that C&O-B&O earnings for the first quarter were up substantially from the 1970 first quarter, Watkins said "the outlook for the second quarter is good—and for the year it's good. Barring any protracted work stoppage in steel, mining or railroads we should have a better year than 1970."

©The Washington Star

Watkins To Be C&O's 14th President, B&O's 20th

DeVine Named to Board Positions

Forty-Five-Year-Old Hays T. Watkins, Jr., who will take the position of president and chief executive officer of The C&O/B&O Railroads on March 31, will be the fourteenth in C&O's presidential line and the twentieth in B&O's.

He has been C&O/B&O vice president in charge of the administrative group since 1967.

Gregory DeVine, who has been C&O/B&O's top management man since 1966, reaches retirement age on March 20. He will continue as chairman of the executive committee of C&O's board and will also be chairman of B&O's board. He also continues as chairman of the board of the Western Maryland Railway, controlled by C&O/B&O.

The C&O controls the B&O through ownership of 94 percent of B&O stock. Mr. Watkins was also elected a C&O director; the B&O's president and directors constitute that company's board.

Cyrus S. Eaton, board chairman of C&O, said of Mr. Watkins: "This young energetic executive brings to the leadership of the combined C&O/B&O demonstrated executive capacity with a specialty of setting new directions in financial policy. He has literally grown up on the railroad and will apply a thorough knowledge of the company and the industry. There is a new era ahead of prosperity and strength for the railroads, and Hays Watkins is a new leader for this new time.

"C&O/B&O are also fortunate in that they may count on the continuing counsel of Greg DeVine, who has guided C&O/B&O wisely during their coordination program. His acknowledged expertise in coal industry affairs will be of inestimable continued value to the company."

Mr. Watkins, who retains more than a trace of Blue Grass in his soft-spoken speech, was born in Fern Creek, Ky., a suburb of Louisville, on Jan. 26, 1926. His father

was a banker. Later, the family moved about 30 miles east of Louisville to a farm near New Castle. There the railroad president-to-be was brought up and went to high school.

He was graduated from Bowling Green (Ky.) Business University (now part of Western Kentucky University) in 1947 with a bachelor of science degree in accounting. (Campus life was interrupted, however, for two years in the Army, during which he served in the Panama Canal Zone.)

Then it was on to graduate school at Northwestern University, from which he received a master's degree in business administration in December, 1948. His thesis: "Separation of Railroad Operating Expense Between Freight Service and Passenger Service."

Several railroads offered him jobs, but two Northwestern professors he respected urged him to choose Chessie. On Jan. 3, 1949, a few weeks short of his 23rd birthday, he started work at C&O's headquarters in Cleveland as a staff analyst reporting to an assistant to the president.

Advancement came rapidly with the regularity of a time freight's schedule. There were two promotions in 1950, and in the next decade all but two years saw him move up the ladder. In his first five years, he worked in Cleveland, in Detroit (twice) and Richmond, then returned to Cleveland for good.

In 1961, he was appointed treasurer of C&O, and two years later an assistant vice-president. Following affiliation of C&O and B&O, he was named in 1964 vice-president-finance for both railroads.

Charles Day, well-known Cleveland broadcaster and long-time friend, recalls the time ten years ago when an Erie Railroad locomotive engineer unknowingly predicted Mr. Watkins' future. Mr. Day and Mr. Watkins had taken their two sons for a locomotive ride to Youngstown. At the end of the trip, the engineer, who knew only that Mr. Watkins was with C&O, shook hands

with him and said: "You keep that C&O making money. I've got stock in that line."

An associate observed that "Hays is the kind of person who always knows exactly what has to be done — and does it." As an illustration, early in his career he found there was no textbook on basic railroad accounting. So he wrote one, which the Finance Department used in its training program. He himself taught the course five times.

He insists everyone who works with him call him "Hays," and often answers his own telephone, to the consternation of people who are calling his secretary. Mr. Watkins and his wife, Betty, live in Moreland Hills, Ohio. Their 18-year-old son, Tom (Hays Thomas III), is a freshman at The College of William and Mary, at Williamsburg, Va.

For relaxation, C&O/B&O's new chief likes to bowl and play bridge and pursues philately as a hobby. "But I get most of my relaxation," he has said, "puttering around my yard in old shorts."

He is a director of the Western Maryland Railway, the Richmond, Fredericksburg and Potomac Railroad, the Chicago South Shore and South Bend Railroad and the James Center Development Corporation, of Richmond.

Mr. Watkins is a trustee of St. Luke's Hospital in Cleveland, of Goodwill Industries, Inc., a charitable organization, and of The Church of the Saviour (Methodist) in Cleveland Heights.

He is a member of the Financial Planning Council of the American Management Association, the Treasury Division of the Association of American Railroads, of which he is a former chairman, the National Association of Accountants, and the American Institute of Certified Public Accountants.

Mr. DeVine started his railroad career in 1957 as C&O vice-president in charge of coal traffic and development after 30 years in the coal industry. He was elected chief executive officer of C&O/B&O in 1966.

• • • • • • • • • • • • • • • • • • • •

The New York Times
Sunday, March 21, 1971

Running a Railroad

By ROBERT E. BEDINGFIELD

CLEVELAND — Hays T. Watkins Jr. acknowledges that there is a lot he doesn't know about being president of a railroad at the Chesapeake and Ohio Railroad on April 1.

One thing he does know — he emphasized in an interview the other day — is that he will not do the job in the manner of the unfortunate Shakespearean actor who was impaled by a drama critic. After seeing a performance of Richard III, the critic complained that the star had played the king as if he expected somebody else to play the ace.

The 45-year-old Mr. Watkins will take office under the eyes of Cyrus S. Eaton, the 87-year-old chairman of the C&O, who has played more than one ace in his day; Gregory S. DeVine, the outgoing president, who is remaining as chairman of the executive committee and chairman of the board of the B&O, and the durable John E. Kusik, who preceded Mr. Watkins as the C&O's chief fiscal officer and is now vice chairman of the C&O board.

The question of whether he would be influenced by having those strong seniors looking over his shoulder was put bluntly to Mr. Watkins and this was his answer:

"Mr. Eaton has been very strong in his discussions with me, to tell me I do have a free rein. He has said at board meetings that he wants me to have complete authority and responsibility for these railroads. Each of the three has stressed to me that it's my ball game. If I don't manage these companies it's my own fault because I have all the opportunity in the world."

Mr. Eaton, quoted in the new release that announced Mr. Watkins' promotion more than a month ago, praised the new president-elect's "demonstrated executive capacity for setting new directions in financial policy."

Cyrus Eaton watchers took that to mean that the C&O/B&O system had reach the point where it no longer needed to have top coal salesman as its top officer, which has been the policy for about a quarter of a century. Mr. Watkins is quick to concede that he has never sold a ton of coal, but he pointed out that coal still provided nearly 40 percent of the combined roads' revenues and deserved a vice president in charge of coal solicitation.

Mr. Watkins will be spared making one major decision that has been hanging fire for more than five years. That's whether to pursue the C&O's planned merger with the Norfolk & Western Railway. Last week, Mr. DeVine and John P. Fishwick, the N&W's president, met in Washington and decided they would recommend to their respective boards of directors that the merger plan be dropped.

Mr. Watkins asserts that he had no idea before January, or at the earliest December, that he was in line to become president so soon. Outside observers, however, have said they spotted him as the favorite as far back as last July.

"In December and January," Mr. Watkins recalled, "I had an increasing number of questions from both Greg DeVine and Mr. Eaton. The nature of the questions indicated they were looking very carefully at what to do when Greg reached 65 and retired at the end of this month. I gathered from the nature of the questions that I was one of the leading candidates; I won't say this came as a complete surprise."

Mr. Watkins might have been forgiven for thinking the late Walter J. Tuohy was saving him for some top position at the C&O five and a half years ago. Mr. Tuohy, then president of the railroad, had more than enough provocation to throw him off the 34th-floor sun deck of the Terminal Tower Building in Cleveland, and refrained.

It was Aug. 27, 1965, the Friday afternoon before special meetings called for the following Tuesday of both the C&O and N&W boards to act on a merger of the two lines. The idea had been negotiated in secrecy by Mr. Tuohy, with Mr. DeVine, Mr. Kusik and Mr. Watkins, and three top officers of the N&W.

Mr. Tuohy had called Mr. Watkins to brief him on the details.

"I had a sheaf of perhaps 12 papers, stapled together, which I was holding, and there I was going down chapter, verse and line over the numbers and exchange ratios for the proposed merger, all of which were written in longhand," Mr. Watkins recalled. He continued:

"We were on the fourth or fifth page, when suddenly a great gust of wind came along that jerked the papers out of my hand and whisked them over the parapet of the sun roof.

"We ran to the edge of the sun deck and watched those papers float down to the street. Mr. Tuohy leaned so far over the edge of the sun deck that I thought he was going to topple over and fall to the street himself.

"I think I would have—if I could have caught them—jumped myself."

For the next few hours, until dusk halted the search, Mr. Watkins, Mr. Tuohy and four C&O aides who didn't know what they were looking for searched the streets below. When Mr. Watkins returned to the sun deck he said he looked over to the roof of the May Company building, where there appeared to be some papers.

He got the guard of the May Company to allow him to scramble over the roof. "What I had thought were papers were two stone slabs, which actually were about three feet by four feet, but from the 34th floor had looked smaller," he said. "I've never been quite so dejected

and upset in my life, when I returned to Mr. Tuohy's office and had to tell him that it was no use."

Mr. Watkins was born Jan. 26, 1926, in Fern Creek, Ky., a suburb of Louisville. He grew up on his father's farm and said that one the reasons he doesn't smoke is, "I've looked at the anatomy of a horse while plowing tobacco." At New Castle, Ky., High School, from which he was graduated in 1942, he was the valedictorian and voted most likely to become a newspaper editor, "because I was editor of our school paper."

He was only 16 when he finished high school and went to Bowling Green (Ky.) College of Commerce (now the Commerce School of Western Kentucky University) for three years before going into the Army. After the war, he went back to Bowling Green for a semester and got his bachelor's degree, and went on to Northwestern University, where he received his master's in business administration.

His faculty advisers at Northwestern got him to write his thesis on the "Separation of Railroad Operating Expenses Between Freight and Passenger Service." They also encouraged him to apply for a job at the C&O in the fall of 1948, the day after he took—and passed—his CPA exam. The C&O offered him $300 a month as staff analyst in the office of the president.

Mr. Watkins, a lean, 160 pound, six-footer, grinning sheepishly, then told of how the following March he was fired. "There was a coal strike in the spring of 1949 and every department of the C&O was ordered to cut its personnel by 25 percent. There were eight people on my boss's staff. I was one of the two who was dismissed, I guess is the proper word for it."

Within three weeks, the C&O hired Mr. Watkins back at a 10 percent increase in salary. He said that another benefit of the furlough was it gave him time to return to Louisville for three weeks, "where I met the gal who about a year later became my wife."

His rise at the C&O was rapid. By 1961, he was treasurer. He was elected vice president of both C&O and B&O in December, 1964, just before his 39th birthday. His salary last year was $63,000. While he declined to say what his new salary will be—Greg DeVine last year was paid $205,000 — Mr. Watkins acknowledged that he has been promised "a substantial increase."

Mr. DeVine and Mr. Watkins have worked so closely over the years that they have always been on a first-name basis. Mr. Watkins addresses the C&O chairman, however, as "Mr. Eaton" and his old boss John Kusik as "Mr. Kusik." Yet, when some members of the C&O staff addressed him as "Mr. Watkins" after his new appointment was announced, they were quickly informed:

"The name is still Hays. I don't know why I should get any illusions because I have a new title," he explained.

Eaton Replaced as Chessie Chairman

By MICHAEL KELLY AND BRUCE ELLISON

Cyrus S. Eaton, 89, was replaced yesterday as board chairman of Chessie System, Inc. and its subsidiary, Chesapeake & Ohio Railway Co., by Hays T. Watkins Jr., 47.

Action was taken at a special meeting of directors of both companies yesterday in Baltimore.

Neither Eaton, who has been chairman since 1954 and a director since 1943, nor his son, Cyrus S. Eaton Jr., a director since 1954, was present for the meeting, a company officer said.

Watkins had been Chessie president since the holding company was formed this year, and had been C&O president since March 31, 1971. He remains as chief executive officer of the $2.5-billion corporation.

Succeeding Watkins as president was John W. Hanifin, 52, executive vice president since 1971.

Eaton will remain as a director. He is also the largest shareholder.

The sudden announcement caught many persons in Cleveland-based company and in the railroad industry by surprise.

At his last meeting with newsmen on Monday, Eaton gave no indication of the upcoming move. At that meeting — for a visit by Russian railroad officials — Eaton appeared vigorous and in good health.

He merely smiled when the head of the Russian delegation wished him health and a long life.

Eaton's eldest daughter, Mary Eaton LeFevre, said last night her father's departure as chairman "was not expected at all. It's a complete surprise to me, and I don't think Fay knew."

Mrs. LeFevre's husband, Fay, is a Chessie System director, and was present at yesterday's meeting.

When asked at Burke Lakefront Airport about the change, LeFevre said tersely: "I can't give you any comment. No comment at all."

Eaton himself was unavailable for comment. Callers to his farm in Northfield Township were told Eaton was out of town.

Howard Skidmore, vice president for public relations of Chessie System, declined to answer newsmen's questions on whether Eaton was ousted, had submitted a resignation, or knew he was to be replaced.

"Our press release speaks for itself," Skidmore said. "It is clear the board has made provision for succession of management. You have a chairman who is almost ninety who has been succeeded by a younger man who has proved himself the last two years. What's so surprising about that announcement?"

Skidmore described Eaton as "a true renaissance man, a statesman of the world."

The public relations official noted the change in top corporate officers was only one item on the board agenda. But he denied to say what other matters were discussed.

"You've got to remember this is an important time in the railroad business," Skidmore said. "There is legislation now pending in Congress which would change the entire railroad picture in the Northeastern Corridor. Since Chessie is one of the two profitable railroads in this area, we have a vital concern about this."

Eaton was reportedly in Washington Wednesday to confer with U.S. Rep. Harley O. Staggers, D-W.Va., chairman of the House Committee on Interstate and Foreign Commerce, which is studying railroad legislation.

Skidmore confirmed Eaton's trip to Washington, but declined to give its nature.

An executive of another eastern railroad told The Plain Dealer there had been industry rumors for some time that Watkins wanted to promote Hanifin to the presidency of Chessie System.

Watkins, who attended the board meeting, did not return to Cleveland. Instead he and his wife, Betty, went to Williamsburg, Va., to visit their son, Hays Thomas III, 20, a student at the College of William and Mary.

Watkins was unavailable for comment.

Hanifin, questioned at Burke Lakefront Airport on his return from the board meeting, declined to comment on the industry report, or on any other board action.

Watkins joined C&O in 1949 as a staff analyst. He was appointed C&O treasurer in 1961, and became an assistant vice president two years later.

In 1964, after C&O acquired control of the Baltimore & Ohio Railroad Co., Watkins was named vice president for finance of both railroads. He became president and chief executive officer of both lines in 1971.

Hanifin joined the law department of C&O in 1948. He became a vice president and a director in 1972.

Hanifin is a graduate of the University of West Virginia and the University of Virginia Law School. He and his wife, Adele, live in Shaker Heights. They have two children, Elizabeth, 24, now living in Atlanta, and John William Jr., 17, a senior at University School.

• • • • • • • • • • • • • • • • • • • •

The Plain Dealer
Cleveland, Sunday, October 14, 1973

Hays T. Watkins takes the controls at Chessie

This analysis was prepared by members of The Plain Dealer's business and financial reporting staff.

Cyrus S. Eaton, did not step aside voluntarily as chairman of Chessie System Inc. and its subsidiary, the Chesapeake & Ohio Railway Co. That much is clear, although neither side will concede it, or, for that matter, discuss at all Eaton's replacement on Oct. 5 by Hays T. Watkins Jr.

Eaton, 89, whose long career spans the creation and management of several giant corporations, has not returned telephone calls from The Plain Dealer, and declined to talk with a reporter sent to his office. Nor has he allowed his personal staff to talk with reporters.

Chessie's new chairman, Hays T. Watkins Jr., 47, and new president, John W. Hanifin, 52, have been equally inaccessible. They have both been extremely busy this week and their schedules look bad next week," according to Chessie public relations spokesmen.

The power shift is not the type of thing the corporate structure wishes to discuss, or even to have discussed, outside the oak-paneled executive suites on the uppermost floors of the Terminal Tower. Some persons, who may have high regard for Eaton, do not wish to say anything about their new boss, Watkins, and chance the need to look for other work.

From sources outside those executive suites, however, from persons close to Eaton, to Watkins and to Hanifin, it has been possible to reconstruct the story of Eaton's replacement and the reasons behind it.

It was almost a textbook case of an executive power struggle, perhaps compounded by a feeling on the part of Chessie's younger management that Eaton, because of his public position on various issues, and his age, had become an obstacle to the continued profitability — even the continued existence — of the $2.6 billion railroad system.

©The Plain Dealer

The main problem facing Chessie today is the eastern railroad mess: the reorganization of eight roads, including the Penn Central and Erie Lakawanna, and the efforts of government to work out some system of preserving rail operations in a quarter of the nation.

Several salvation schemes have been proposed: one by the Interstate Commerce Commission; one by the House of Representatives; one by Judge John P. Fullam, who is overseeing the Penn Central reorganization. In each "solution," there exists the possibility that the highly profitable Chessie will be forced to merge into some governmentally controlled rail operation.

Eaton and Watkins have opinions on what must be done about the eastern mess, and both have made their views known to Congress. On Wednesday and Thursday of the week of his replacement, Eaton was in Washington conferring with Rep. Harley O. Staggers, D-W.Va., chairman of the House Interstate and Foreign Commerce Committee. Last week, Watkins and Staggers talked.

It is not know if Eaton and Watkins presented the same views to Staggers.

However, on Friday, Staggers told The Plain Dealer that his private meeting with Eaton two weeks ago was their first in 20 years, and that the discussion was more philosophic and general than about specific proposals.

"I'm not really sure what he wanted," the veteran congressman said.

It was on Wednesday, Oct. 3, the day of Eaton's talk with Staggers, that the decision to remove him as Chessie chairman was made.

Chessie System, Inc. has nine directors as does its principal subsidiary, the Chesapeake & Ohio Railway Co. Several of those directors are outsiders, living in Chicago, Maryland, and elsewhere. Calling them all into session takes coordination when that session is not a regular meeting.

Normally that coordination is provided by corporate secretary T. Howard Keelor. It is he who telephones each director, suggesting a meeting date and place, getting

suggestions in return, finally settling on a date convenient to all, or at least a majority of the directors.

For the 19 years that Eaton has been chairman, it has been his custom, if he cannot make a meeting, to tell Keelor either that it should be postponed until he can attend, or to approve holding the meeting without him. As chairman of the board, it is almost his prerogative to call of the meeting should he wish to do so.

The board meeting on Friday, Oct. 5, was different. It was not a regularly scheduled meeting. It was not held in Chessie's corporate headquarters in Cleveland, and it was not attended by Eaton or by his son, Cyrus Jr., also a director. Young Eaton was on a business trip to the Soviet Union.

Nor is it likely that the board chairman Eaton knew his own removal was on the agenda for the Baltimore meeting, to which directors were whisked in two corporate jets.

Keelor, official keeper of the railroad's minutes, declines to say what the vote was on Eaton's replacement, or how the matter was presented on the agenda.

Nor will public relations vice president Howard Skidmore say what happened: "You know we can't discuss things like that; we'd never make public a vote," he said, adding that he was not present at the meeting.

The outcome of the meeting is no secret. Directors voted to name Watkins chairman, and promote John W. Hanifin, an executive vice president, to president. Cyrus S. Eaton was out, and back in Cleveland a stunned aide called the local newspapers. However, the decision had been made two days earlier.

"There's one thing I admire about Hays," says an acquaintance of ten years. "When he makes up his mind to do something, he gets it done, and never reverses himself. That's the kind of man he is."

The decision was so locked up before the Baltimore meeting that public relations man Skidmore called his secretary for biographies of Watkins, Hanifin and Eaton before the session, then closed himself in his Cleveland office to prepare news releas-

The Plain Dealer
Cleveland, Sunday, October 14, 1973

Hays T. Watkins takes the controls at Chessie (cont'd.)

The news of what information Skidmore had requested sent rumors through the corridors, but most speculation centered on the possibility of some important business coup, not on the removal of Eaton.

After the announcement of Watkins' succession, directors scattered. Some returned to Cleveland in the company planes, while Eaton's whereabouts were unknown, or at least undisclosed. Watkins went to Williamsburg, Va. for a relaxing weekend with his wife and son.

In the news announcements, no mention was made of Eaton's retirement or resignation, or removal, for that matter. The emphasis was on the new, youthful management team, and that emphasis was reinforced by Skidmore in an impromptu news conference at Burke Lakefront Airport upon his return from Baltimore. Witness this exchange with reporters:

"Was Mr. Eaton fired?"

"Why would you want to print a thing like that and hurt a nice old man like Mr. Eaton?"

"Did he know he was going to be replaced?" "I really can't answer a question like that."

"OK, Howard, be specific. Did he retire, or resign, or step down or what?"

"Look, our news release speaks for itself. It is clear that the board has made provision for a succession in management. You have a chairman who is almost 90, who has been succeeded by a younger man who has proved himself in the last two years. What's so surprising about that announcement?"

For half an hour Skidmore ducked direct questions. In the background, one could almost hear a folk trio humming "The Times, They Are a'Changin'."

Watkins' rise through the ranks at Chessie, especially in the last three years has been little short of meteoric. He began working for the Chesapeake & Ohio Railway in 1949, after his graduation from Northwestern University. He began as a staff analyst in the accounting department, reporting to an assistant to the president.

Advancement came rapidly with the regularity of a time freight's schedule was the way a Chessie new release announcing his promotion to president in 1971, described Watkins' career.

He was trained by John E. Kusik, once vice chairman of the C&O, a man who established a reputation as one of the foremost financial planners and innovators in the railroad industry.

Kusik, however, never made it to the top post. He lost out to Watkins.

"I pick out a bright young man and give him a tough assignment," Kusik once said of his training course for young executives. "I put him on his own, and it's either make or break. And I am happy when he makes it."

Kusik, 75 last week declined to comment on Watkins' succession to the chairmanship.

Watkins' salary leaped ahead with his promotions. In 1970, according to Interstate Commerce Commission records, he was paid $64,000 as a vice president. As president, his salary surged to $160,500 by the end of 1971. In 1972, according to C&O, his pay had risen to $167,475 — almost triple what it had been 36 months earlier.

Kusik retired after Watkins promotion.

C. Vernon Cowan, senior vice president operations, also retired when Watkins was promoted, as did Kenneth Ekin, vice president for law. One of his younger staff members, then only an assistant general counsel, was John W. Hanifin — the man who now is president.

Some observers think Hanifin might have been the key to Eaton's removal. He is older than Watkins, and as executive vice president was in line to become president —

There was one roadblock. Eaton had been chairman for 19 years, and still looked, acted, was, in perfect health. He was a barrier to Hanifin's career advancement, one so serious that Hanifin probably would have left Chessie if the possibilities of promotion had not been opened up.

All last week Cyrus Eaton remained in the C&O chairman's office in the Terminal Tower. On Monday his staff was still using engraved letterheads that showed him as chairman of the board.

His three assistants — two more than either Watkins or Hanifin have — remain on the railroad's payroll.

But the office and the staff do not go with just a director, and that is a problem Watkins and Hanifin must face this week. There will be a regularly scheduled board meeting tomorrow.

One item reportedly on the agenda is a proposal to name Eaton honorary chairman, or chairman emeritus, or some other such title, to avoid having to ask him to vacate his offices and dismiss his staff.

Whether Eaton would vote in favor of such a scheme or accept such a title if it were offered, is questionable.

He would know he was being shunted aside with an attempt at grace. An honorary chairmanship would have been more appropriate had it come from the board at the same meeting in which Watkins was named chairman. It would also have been more appropriate in December, when Eaton will be 90. He could have been replaced then, with due pomp, ceremony, and honor.

Eaton, with 115,400 shares of Chessie stock worth about $4.5 million, is the railroad's biggest stockholder. He may take his fight to the other shareholders, with whom he is very popular.

He has been a fighter in the past. In many corporations in which he was involved, he clawed his way to the top.

He may do battle yet with Watkins, possibly in the courts. To him, Watkins is one of "those little young men, really not yet out of swaddling clothes when they were elected to the board," as a source close to Eaton describes Watkins.

For the railroad's famed trademark, "Chessie," usually asleep like a kitten, these are troubled times. Her open, watchful eye, alert under the covers in her sleeping compartment, has seen much that is unaccustomed in the last two weeks.

Whether Watkins can now cover that watchful eye and keep himself firmly in the driver's seat, is a question. Whether Eaton will choose to tear back the covers and disturb Chessie's sleep by the glare of a public battle is also a question.

Newspaper Clippings

• • • • • • • • • • • • • • • • • • •

The Washington Post
Thursday, September 7, 1978

Chessie, Seaboard Begin Talks on Combination

By WILLIAM H. JONES

Chessie System Inc. and Seaboard Coast Line Industries have opened negotiations on a possible combination that would create the largest railroad system in the country, the two companies revealed late yesterday.

A three-paragraph joint press release said "exploratory discussions involving a possible affiliation" have begun, and Chessie already owns slightly less than 5 percent of Seaboard's common stock.

Public relations officials at both companies said the formal announcement had been prepared by lawyers and that the spokesmen had been instructed to provide no additional details.

However, informed sources said Chessie had been buying Seaboard stock over recent months and Chessie Chairman Hays Watkins said in a Railway Age interview earlier this year that his company had conducted internal studies on possible combinations with most major rail firms in the nation.

Seaboard stock also has been an attraction for the Southern Pacific Co., a major West Coast railroad firm that currently owns 9.6 percent of Seaboard common in the wake of earlier merger talks that Seaboard ended.

After talks on possible creation of a transcontinental Seaboard-Southern Pacific were ended, Sopac continued to buy shares of Jacksonville-based Seaboard until the Interstate Commerce Commission issued a 70-day cease and desist order on Aug. 8 prohibiting further share purchases.

Seaboard, which opposed a combination with Sopac as not in the interests of the public or its shippers, charged that the Southern Pacific stock purchases violated federal law, but Sopac said it has no intention at this time of seeking control over the East Coast line.

A partnership of Seaboard and Chessie would create a giant rail network with 27,600 miles of routes from Philadelphia and Baltimore south to Miami and New Orleans and to St. Louis and Chicago in the Midwest, involving 20 states, D.C., and Ontario Province of Canada.

Chessie itself is a holding company for three railroads—the Baltimore & Ohio, Chesapeake & Ohio and Western Maryland. Under the name of Family Lines, Seaboard operates two major rail systems — the Louisville & Nashville and Seaboard Coast Line (Seaboard and Atlantic Coast Line merged in 1967).

Railroad industry analysts said yesterday that the Chessie-Seaboard talks could end up in an agreement to merge or with an acquisition of one company by the other.

Chessie's Watkins recently has emphasized a new strategy of developing nonrail businesses that will add to earnings, and he told Forbes magazine last month that he would not object to being a "junior partner" in a business combination.

A combined Chessie-Seaboard most likely would provide continued independent operation of various rail subsidiaries, as Cleveland-based Chessie does now with its three lines, analysts said.

Although the companies' lines now meet in Richmond and at several points in Kentucky or Ohio, there is virtually no overlap in service. The firms employ some 75,000 workers, mostly in railroad operations.

In addition to transportation, Chessie owns 350,000 acres of timber, 2 billion tons of coal, extensive real estate holdings and The Greenbrier resort at White Sulphur Springs, W.Va. A Seaboard subsidiary owns daily newspapers in Jacksonville and St. Augustine, as well as several weeklies.

Seaboard is the larger of the two railroad businesses with 16,000 miles of routes that produced revenues of $1.7 billion last year.

Chessie operates over more than 11,000 miles of routes and reported revenues of $1.5 billion in 1977.

Merger talks and rumors in the railroad industry have been widespread over the last two years following congressional approval of legislation that encouraged some types of mergers and required the ICC to speed decisions on proposed combinations.

Although Seaboard dropped its earlier talks with Southern Pacific, and Southern Railway failed to reach any agreement on a proposed combination with the Missouri Pacific, a number of other combinations are being considered actively and many proposals are being discussed in private. Among the proposed mergers:

- Washington-based Southern is talking with IC Industries about possible acquisition of the Chicago company's Illinois Central Gulf Railroad.

- Burlington Northern and the Frisco have agreed on a merger that the ICC is studying.

- Norfolk & Western and Chessie have proposed joint acquisition of the Detroit, Toledo and Ironton Railroad—and are facing a competing bid by the Grand Trunk Western.

- Union Pacific Corp. is considering acquisition of some lines between Butte, Mont., and the Pacific Northwest from the bankrupt Milwaukee Road.

Hays T. Watkins

Chairman Emeritus
CSX Corporation
Richmond, Va.

Date Employed by CSX (or Predecessor) - 1949
Date of Birth - Jan. 26, 1926
Place of Birth - Fern Creek, Ky.

Education - Western Kentucky University, B.S. 1947
Northwestern University, M.B.A. 1948, CPA

Chronology of Employment
1949 to 1950 - Staff Analyst, Chesapeake and Ohio Railway
1950 to 1953 - Internal Auditor, C&O
1953 to 1956 - Staff Assistant to the Comptroller, C&O
1956 to 1958 - Senior Budget Analyst; Chief of Budget Services, C&O
1958 to 1960 - General Auditor, C&O
1960 to 1964 - Treasurer, C&O; Assistant Vice President, C&O/B&O
1964 to 1971 - Vice President-Finance, C&O/B&O
1971 to 1973 - President and Chief Executive Officer, C&O/B&O
1973 to 1975 - Chairman and Chief Executive Officer, Chessie System Inc.
1975 to 1980 - Chairman, President and Chief Executive Officer, Chessie System Inc.
1980 to 1982 - President and Co-Chief Executive Officer, CSX Corporation, Richmond
1982 to 1989 - Chairman and Chief Executive Officer, CSX Corporation, Richmond
April 1989 to Feb. 1991 - Chairman of the Board of Directors, CSX Corporation, Richmond
Feb. 1991 - Chairman Emeritus, CSX Corporation, Richmond

Civic, Religious and Social Affiliations - Baptist • Country Club of Virginia; Commonwealth Club • Member of the Board, Richmond Symphony Trustee: Musical Arts Association of Cleveland Director: YMCA of Greater Richmond

Business and Professional Affiliations - Director: Black & Decker Corp.; Westinghouse Electric Corp.; Richmond, Fredericksburg and Potomac Railroad; Signet Banking Corp.; Yukon Pacific Corp.; Center for Innovative Technology-Commonwealth of Virginia; Washington Dulles Task Force; *Rector*, Board of Visitors: The College of William and Mary Member; Virginia Business Council; Business Advisory Council, Transportation Center, Northwestern University; National Coal Council; The Conference Board; Business Roundtable; American Institute of CPAs; Trustee: The Johns Hopkins University

Awards - 1975 Honorary LL.D., Baldwin-Wallace College - 1980 Honorary LL.D., Alderson Broaddus College • 1982 Honorary LL.D., The College of William and Mary • 1982 Excellence in Management Award, Industry Week Magazine • 1984 Man-of-the-Year Award, Modern Railroads Magazine • 1984 Silver Award, Financial World CEO of the Year • 1984 School of Business Administration Medallion, The College of William and Mary • 1987 Honorary LL.D., Virginia Union University • 1987 Right-Hand Man Award, The Cooperstown Conference • 1987 Maryland Maritime Medallion, State of Maryland • 1988 Outstanding Industrialist of the Year, Commonwealth of Virginia • 1989 Salzberg Memorial Medallion, Syracuse University • 1989 Distinguished Service Award, Virginia Chamber of Commerce

NEWS

CSX CORPORATION
Corporate Communications
P.O. Box C-32222
Richmond, VA 23251
(804) 355-2894

Richmond, Va., November 1, 1980 — The merger of Chessie System, Inc., and Seaboard Coast Line Industries, Inc., into CSX Corporation was formally consummated today as members of the new CSX board of directors met for the first time in Richmond, Va.

Prime F. Osborn, III, chairman, and Hays T. Watkins, president, termed the meeting "a significant milestone" in the history of the railroad industry. "Our forefathers long dreamed of a strong north-south railroad system that would link the industrial Northeast with the Southeast, tying together these two vital areas of the country. Today that dream is a reality," they said.

In reporting on the meeting, the CSX officials also announced the make-up of the board of directors. The new 24-member CSX board is comprised of 12 directors each from the former companies. They are:

Prime F. Osborn, III, Chairman, CSX Corporation

Hays T. Watkins, President, CSX Corporation

John T. Collinson, President and Chief Executive officer, Chessie System Railroads, Cleveland, Ohio

A. Paul Funkhouser, President and Chief Executive Officer, The Family Lines Rail System, Jacksonville, Fla.

Nicholas T. Camicia, President, Chief Executive Officer and Chairman, Pittston Co., Greenwich, Conn.

J. J. Daniel, Chairman of the Board and Publisher, Florida Publishing Company, Jacksonville, Fla.

Frederick Deane, Jr., Chairman, Chief Executive Officer, Bank of Virginia, Richmond, Va.

Alonzo G. Decker, Jr., Honorary Chairman, Chairman Executive Committee, Black & Decker Manufacturing Co., Baltimore, Md.

Gregory S. DeVine, Chairman, Executive Committee, C&O Railway; Chairman, B&O Railroad, Cleveland, Ohio

Floyd D. Gottwald, Jr., Chairman of the Board and Chief Executive Officer, Ethyl Corporation, Richmond, Va.

Mary Townsend Kimpton, Educator, Author and Consultant, Chicago, Ill.

Fay A. LeFevre, Physician, Medical Consultant, Business Executive, Cleveland, Ohio

John H. Lumpkin, Chairman of the Board and Chief Executive Officer, The South Carolina National Corporation, Columbia, S. C.

Charles P. Lykes, President, Lykes Bros., Inc., Tampa, Fla.

William E. McGuirk, Jr., Chairman of the Board, Mercantile Bankshares Corporation, Baltimore, Md.

Buck Mickel, Chairman of the Board, Daniel International Corporation, Greenville, S. C.

Steven T. Muller, President, The Johns Hopkins University and The Johns Hopkins Hospital, Baltimore, Md.

James L. O'Keefe, Senior Partner, O'Keefe, Ashenden & Lyons, Chicago, Ill.

W. James Price, General Partner, Alex. Brown & Sons, Baltimore, Md.

Robert H. Radcliff, Jr., Chairman of the Board and Chief Executive Officer, Radcliff Marine Services, Inc., Fairhope, Ala.

W. Thomas Rice, Chairman Emeritus, Seaboard Coast Line Industries, Inc., Richmond, Va.

John K. Stevenson, former President, R. M. Stevenson Co., Bloomfield Hills, Mich.

William B. Sturgill, Chairman of the Board, Fourth Street Tobacco Warehouse Company, Lexington, Ky.

Alvin W. Vogtle, Jr., President, The Southern Company, Atlanta, Ga.

CSX Corporation is a company with $7.4 billion in assets. The Chessie System Railroads will continue to be operated from Cleveland and Baltimore and the Family Lines Rail System from Jacksonville, Fla. The combined rail companies will provide single system rail service connecting the East and Midwest regions with the Southeast and create a unified rail network serving 22 states, the District of Columbia and Ontario, Canada.

In addition to the two rail systems, CSX is the parent company of the Florida Publishing Co., The Greenbrier Resort Hotel, Aviation Enterprises, Inc., and other coal-land, real estate and oil and gas enterprises.

286

NEWS

Corporate Communications
P.O. Box C-32222
Richmond, VA 23251
(804) 355-2894

Richmond, Va., November 6, 1980 — Senior officers of the CSX Corporation — the new company created November 1 by the merger of the Chessie System, Inc. and Seaboard Coast Line Industries, Inc. - were announced today at the company's headquarters in Richmond, Va.

In making the announcement, Prime F. Osborn, chairman and Hays T. Watkins, president, said: "The people being named today as top officers of the CSX Corporation are all professionals with solid experience in their respective fields. Together we have the opportunity to create and manage an outstanding new corporation that will have as its centerpiece a single-system rail network that has great potential to serve the growing rail transportation needs of the nation."

The two executives said that CSX corporate activities will center on planning, both immediate and long range; setting overall policy for each of the affiliates; and monitoring internal corporate affairs.

A special group — consisting of the CSX chairman, the CSX president and the presidents of the Chessie and Family Lines Rail systems — will set corporate policy. The CSX corporate departments will consist of (a) internal auditing, (b) finance, which will be responsible for cash management, taxes, financial planning and the corporate treasury, (c) corporate services, which will direct legal activities, corporate communications, government relations and the corporate secretarial functions, and (d) the various non-rail companies including The Greenbrier Resort Hotel, Aviation Enterprises, Inc., and other coal-land, real estate and oil and gas enterprises. Top-level administrative support will be provided by an executive group headed by a vice president.

The presidents of the Chessie and Family Lines rail systems - John Collinson and A. Paul Funkhouser — will report directly to Messrs. Osborn and Watkins, as will J. J. Daniel, chairman of the Florida Publishing Company.

The new officers of CSX are:

Robert L. Hintz, senior vice president-finance. Formerly senior vice president-finance, Chessie System, Inc., he first joined the C&O/B&O in 1963, serving as internal auditor, financial planner, assistant to the vice president-finance, comptroller and assistant to the president.

Gerald L. Nichols, vice president and executive assistant. Formerly assistant vice president-service & equipment planning, SCLI, Inc., he began his railroad career in 1959 with the Louisville and Nashville Railroad, where he subsequently served in a number of positions including assistant chief engineer-design and construction operations, superintendent Louisville Division Operations, assistant general manager transportation operations, and assistant vice president-administration.

John W. Snow, senior vice president-corporate services. Formerly vice president-government affairs, Chessie System, Inc., he began private law practice in 1967, and subsequently served in a number of positions at the U. S. Department of Transportation including deputy undersecretary and finally, presidentially appointed administrator of the National Highway Traffic Safety Administration.

Josiah A. Stanley Jr., senior vice president-audit. Formerly senior vice president-accounting & taxation, SCL Industries, Inc., he had previously served as vice president and comptroller for SCLI and SCL Railroad, as comptroller for the SCL Railroad and as assistant vice president accounting, SCL, at Richmond, Va.

Leonard G. Anderson, vice president and treasurer. Formerly vice president and treasurer, SCLI, Inc., he had previously served as treasurer and general solicitor, SCL Railroad, and as general solicitor, general attorney and assistant general attorney in the law department of the Atlantic Coast Line Railroad.

Edwin E. Edel, vice president-corporate communications. Formerly vice president-corporate communications, SCLI, Inc., his previous appointments have included vice president-public affairs at Amtrak, various positions at the Association of American Railroads, and Director of Public Affairs for the Federal Railroad Administration, U. S. Department of Transportation.

Garth E. Griffith, general counsel. Formerly general solicitor, Chessie System, Inc., he joined the C&O Railway in 1957 where he served as attorney, assistant general attorney, general attorney, and secretary & general solicitor.

Carl C. Hawk, vice president and corporate secretary. Formerly senior assistant vice president and corporate secretary, Chessie System, Inc., he began his railroad career with C&O in 1960 as internal audit officer, subsequently serving as auditor passenger accounts, auditor revenue reports and statistics, assistant auditor revenue reports and statistics, manager financial planning, senior assistant treasurer and general manager financial planning.

James T. Lyon, vice president-taxes. Formerly vice president-taxes, Chessie System, Inc., he joined B&O in 1959 and later served as assistant to the vice president finance, director taxes, and assistant vice president taxes.

Robert C. McGowan, president-CSX Resources, Inc. Formerly president, Chessie Resources, Inc., he joined the C&O Railway in 1951 and held a number of positions including comptroller. When the B&O was affiliated with the C&O he was appointed assistant vice president-finance of the B&O, and later served as vice president planning for the C&O/B&O, and as vice president administration.

Woodruff M. Price, vice president-government relations. Formerly vice president-Washington affairs, SCLI, Inc., he previously served as special assistant to Secretary of Transportation Brock Adams, as his legislative assistant when Mr. Adams was in Congress, and special assistant to the secretary of the Smithsonian Institution.

CSX Corporation is a company with $7.4 billion in assets which will operate two major rail systems — the Chessie System headquartered in Cleveland and Baltimore, and the Family Lines Rail System headquartered in Jacksonville, Fla. The combined rail companies — constituting the nation's largest rail network — will provide single-system rail service connecting the East and Midwest regions with the Southeast across a unified rail network serving 22 states, the District of Columbia and Ontario, Canada.

In addition to the two rail systems, CSX is the parent company of the Florida Publishing Co., The Greenbrier Resort Hotel, Aviation Enterprises, Inc., and other coal-land, real estate and oil and gas enterprises.

NEWS

CSX CORPORATION
Corporate Communications
P.O. Box C-32222
Richmond, VA 23251
(804) 355-2894

RICHMOND, VA — Hays T. Watkins, President of CSX Corporation since its formation in November, 1980, has been elected Chairman and Chief Executive Officer of the company by the Corporation's Board of Directors. At the same time, the Board named A. Paul Funkhouser, now President of the Family Lines Rail System, a major subsidiary of CSX, to succeed Watkins as CSX President. Both appointments are effective May 1, 1982.

As of that date, Prime F. Osborn, CSX Chairman and co-architect of the CSX merger with Watkins, will retire as Chairman. Mr. Osborn, 67, will continue as a member of the Corporation's Board of Directors.

Concurrent with the CSX actions, the Board named Richard D. Sanborn, an executive at Family Lines for over 20 years, to succeed Funkhouser as President and Chief Executive Officer of the Family Lines Rail System.

Watkins started his business career with the Chesapeake and Ohio Railroad in 1949 as a financial analyst. In 1950, he was promoted to internal auditor and, in 1953, was appointed staff assistant to the comptroller of C&O. He became senior budget analyst in 1955, and two years later, was named chief of budget services. He served as general auditor, general staff officer and assistant treasurer, preceding his election as treasurer of the company in 1961.

In 1964, following the affiliation of C&O and B&O, Mr. Watkins was elected vice president-finance for both railroads. He was named president and chief executive officer of both companies on February 15, 1971, and filled that position until his election as chairman and chief executive officer of Chessie System, Inc. in October, 1973. He served in those posts until November, 1980, when he was named president and co-chief executive officer of CSX.

Funkhouser has been President and Chief Executive Officer of the Family Lines Rail System since May, 1980. From 1978 to 1980, he was president of Seaboard Coast Line Industries, Inc. (SCLI, Inc.), the then parent company of Family Lines. SCLI, Inc. merged with the Chessie System Inc. to form CSX.

Between 1975 and 1980, he was executive vice president, senior vice president-executive department and senior vice president of sales and marketing, all of SCLI at its headquarters in Jacksonville. From 1950 until 1975, Funkhouser was employed successively by Hunton, Williams, Anderson, Gay and Moore, a Richmond law firm; the Norfolk and Western Railway; and the Penn Central Transportation Company.

Watkins, 56, is a director of CSX Corporation, the Black & Decker Manufacturing Company, Westinghouse Electric Corporation and The Bank of Virginia.

Funkhouser, 59, is a director of Universal Leaf Tobacco Company, First Kentucky National Corporation and CSX Corporation.

Sanborn has been Senior Vice President- Administration of Family Lines since August of 1980. From 1978 to 1980, he was vice president executive department and assistant to the chairman of Seaboard Coast Line Industries (SCLI), the parent company of Family Lines before SCLI merged with the Chessie System, Inc. to form CSX Corporation in November, 1980.

Sanborn, 45, began his railroad career as an attorney for the Seaboard Coast Line Railroad (SCL) in 1961. He subsequently served as assistant to general counsel and assistant to the vice president-law until January of 1972 when he was promoted to special assistant to the president of SCL. After serving a brief period as special assistant to the president of the Louisville and Nashville Railroad (L&N), he was promoted to vice president-executive department of SCLI, SCL and L&N.

A native of New Hampshire, Sanborn graduated from the University of New Hampshire in 1957 and Harvard Law School in 1960. He is a member of the Massachusetts and Florida Bar Associations.

Sanborn resides in Jacksonville, Florida, with his wife Hilda and daughter Cynthia.

©CSX Corporation
March 11, 1982

WASHINGTON, DC — Agreement was reached today between CSX Corporation and MCI Telecommunications Corporation enabling MCI to install high-speed fiber optic data and voice communication lines using up to 4,000 miles of CSX railroads' right-of-way.

Construction of the first segments of fiber optics links along CSX routes is expected to start within a year, and most of the system is expected to be completed within five years.

Under the terms of the contract, MCI receives the non-exclusive "right of occupancy" for fiber optic cable for 25 years, with four renewal terms. For the first 25 year period, CSX will receive $32 million.

Hays T. Watkins, Chairman and CEO of CSX, said the agreement was a natural for both companies. "Our 27,000 route mile system accesses major metropolitan centers in 22 states. To be able to increase utilization of this asset is a major plus for our company."

The agreement with CSX is the second major fiber optics system announced by MCI this month. On December 1, the company signed a similar occupancy agreement with Amtrak for the right-of-way between New York and Washington.

"The CSX and Amtrak agreements will allow MCI to rapidly expand its capacity among all the major urban areas east of the Mississippi," said William G. McGowan, MCI Chairman.

"A major advantage to MCI is that the fiber optic systems allow major expansions of service in high-traffic areas of the country where microwave frequencies are increasingly difficult to obtain," he added.

MCI's current nationwide long distance network uses microwave technology for intercity voice and data transmission augmented by satellite transmission.

The advanced fiber optics cable to be used by MCI can carry voice, video and data traffic. Infrared signals will be sent through glass fibers slightly thicker than a human hair; a 7/8th-inch thick cable will contain up to 44 individual fibers (22 transmitting in each direction) with an initial capacity of 2,000 circuits each.

The incremental cost of adding capacity to a fiber optic system is lower than with alternate technologies and line quality is improved, since fiber optics transmission is immune to interference, according to MCI.

MCI installed its first fiber optics system in New York City earlier this year, to connect its four major terminals. McGowan said negotiations will continue with other companies to meet MCI's goal of having the most extensive fiber optic network in the nation.

CSX rail routes link Philadelphia and Chicago with all major population centers in the Southeast — including Miami, Atlanta and New Orleans — as well as Detroit, Cleveland, Pittsburgh, Baltimore, Cincinnati, Indianapolis, St. Louis, Louisville and Washington, DC.

©CSX Corporation
December 22, 1982

NEWS

CSX CORPORATION
Corporate Communications
P.O. Box C-32222
Richmond, VA 23251
(804) 355-2894

RICHMOND, VA — The Board of Directors of CSX Corporation today unanimously approved the merger and stock purchase agreements announced Tuesday, June 7, providing for the combination of Texas Gas Resources Corporation and CSX Corporation. Texas Gas' Board of Directors approved the agreement yesterday.

Also, the CSX Board today, consistent with the intent of the agreements and to avoid any diminution in dividends to the Texas Gas shareholders, announced its approval of a 10 percent increase in the quarterly dividend on CSX's Common Stock payable September 15, 1983, to shareholders of record on August 23, 1983. The quarterly rate will be $.78 per share, equal to an annual rate of $3.12 per share, compared to the former annual rate of $2.84 per CSX common share.

The CSX Board also approved a three-for-one split of CSX's Common Stock, subject to shareholder approval, which will be sought at the special meeting where the merger with Texas Gas will be submitted for approval.

Hays T. Watkins, chairman of the board of CSX, said "We are enthusiastic about the opportunities presented by this combination. It is an excellent fit. Together, they present great promise for the future."

Consistent with the agreements, CSX on Thursday, June 9, will commence a cash tender offer for 7.1 million Texas Gas shares (approximately 35 percent of the outstanding shares) at $52 per share net to the seller. Also, CSX has reserved rights to purchase up to 3.2 million additional Texas Gas shares (approximately 16 percent of the outstanding shares) under the tender offer and agreed to purchase another 3.74 million newly-issued Texas Gas shares from Texas Gas. Following those actions and upon approval by shareholders of CSX and Texas Gas, Texas Gas will be merged into CSX with each remaining Texas Gas share converted into .684 of a share of CSX Common Stock.

NEWS

CSX CORPORATION
Corporate Communications
P.O. Box C-32222
Richmond, VA 23251
(804) 355-2894

WASHINGTON, DC, June 6, 1985 — Return Conrail to the private sector but in the process, preserve competition, don't destroy it.

That's the recommendation Hays T. Watkins, Chairman and CEO of CSX Corporation made today to the House Subcommittee on Commerce, Transportation and Tourism, which resumed hearings on the Department of Transportation's recommendation to allow Norfolk Southern (NS) to acquire Conrail (CR).

Watkins said CSX supported the Morgan Stanley public offering proposal as an "effective way to return Conrail to the private sector, to provide a fair return to the Federal Government, to avoid the anti-competitive effects and the adverse effects on employment and on the regional railroads" under a NS takeover.

Watkins said the Department's recommendation was "ill advised" and if the sale to Norfolk Southern were allowed, the government-sponsored merger "would destroy existing head-to-head competition between Conrail and Norfolk Southern in an area of some 100,000 square miles and extend the present Conrail monopoly east of Buffalo and Philadelphia to the South and as far west as Kansas City.

The CSX executive questioned the basic assumption underlying the Department of Justice's claim that "where three carriers compete today, three carriers will compete tomorrow." Whereas the Department of Justice had foreseen competition among three systems — the merged NS/Conrail, the B&O, and the new Guilford system —Watkins said, "The B&O will not be the competitive carrier of last resort if NS acquires Conrail.

"The market power of the NS/CR monopoly will force us to withdraw from service on a large part of the B&O and on other CSX segments," Watkins said. He estimated the immediate impact would reduce rail miles by at least 4,000 and employment by a minimum of 4,000 immediately with additional impact coming "as the newly merged NS/CR rationalizes facilities and begins to use the full power of their monopoly."

That would leave only Guilford and P&LE to compete with NS/Conrail, but Watkins termed the ability of Guilford/P&LE to compete with NS/CR "only an illusion on a map. It will have no reality."

"These weak and under capitalized carriers cannot compete with a combined NS/CR in terms of financial strength, traffic or physical facilities. It will be no contest," he said.

In asking the committee to reject the Norfolk Southern bid. Watkins also took issue with the so-called "deep pockets theory" of DOT. He said "the premise is false. Somehow it assumes that once a business turns sour, the investor will keep pouring money into the investment."

"This is simply not realistic. Only a foolish Investor throws good money at a bad investment." As an example, Watkins pointed to the experience with DERECO, a holding company which was owned totally by NS and controlled the Erie Lackawanna and Delaware & Hudson railroads.

At some point, NS decided that DERECO did not make sense for it and after using DERECO tax benefits, NS let the Erie Lackawanna go into bankruptcy and the D&H wither on the vine."

Watkins concluded, "If an investment goes sour, an investor may give the sleeves off his vest, but he will never dig into his pocket."

NEWS

CSX CORPORATION

Corporate Communications
P.O. Box C-32222
Richmond, VA 23251
(804) 355-2894

RICHMOND, VA, December 11, 1985 — CSX Corporation announced today it is taking major realignment and financial actions to support an accelerated strategic plan to improve profitability, rates of return and shareholder values.

Hays T. Watkins, Chairman and Chief Executive Officer, said the actions were approved "unanimously and enthusiastically" by the CSX Board of Directors today. These actions include:

■ Realignment of CSX's transportation and natural resources businesses into four strategic areas: Transportation, Technology, Energy and Properties.

■ Reorganization of the management of its rail units into three customer and asset focused companies: CSX Distribution Services, CSX Transport and CSX Equipment. The combination of Chessie and Seaboard System railroads' marketing and sales departments earlier this year forms the basis for the Distribution Services Group. High-potential information technology/communication and real estate activities of the railroads will be spun-off to the Technology and Properties groups.

■ Reduction of rail employment levels by some 12 percent by accelerating a voluntary separation program.

■ Writedown of book value and disposition of a number of marginal and unproductive transportation and non-transportation holdings that will result in a special charge in the fourth quarter, and an accounting charge for oil and gas exploration activities.

■ John W. Snow, now president of Chessie, will head CSX Transport, which will assume responsibility for train operations over the entire CSX rail network.

■ Richard D. Sanborn, now president of Seaboard. will head CSX Distribution Services and be responsible for implementing CSX's One-Stop-Shipping concept offering a wide range of shipper services including rail transportation.

■ Richard L. Leatherwood, now vice chairman of both railroads, would lead CSX Equipment, which will assume nationwide responsibility for managing CSX's 200,000 freight cars.

Watkins pointed out the voluntary labor separation program was a continuation of the company's ongoing efforts to lower costs and improve productivity. He estimated some 6,700 contract and non-contract rail employees would be offered the buy-out.

Watkins said implementation of the plan — set to start immediately — will have minimal impact on cash in the short-term. "Most importantly," he said, "the actions will have a very positive effect on future cash flow, earnings and rates of return."

More than 80 percent of a $954 million one-time special pretax charge, excluding the accounting change, is rail-related, with $327 million being a reserve to cover the voluntary buy-out payments and $515 million in writedowns of track, equipment and miscellaneous railroad investments, Watkins said.

The transportation assets being written off include more than 1,000 miles of unproductive track, 600 surplus and outdated locomotives and in excess of 41,000 idle and stored freight cars.

The balance of the special charge primarily reflects writedowns of energy assets, principally coal industry holdings reflecting their reduced value due to weak market conditions. In addition the accounting change from "full cost" to "successful efforts," which is being made to better monitor oil and gas exploration activities, will reduce 1985 pre-tax income by approximately $53 million and result in the restatement of prior years' earnings.

Watkins said the company's actions result from more than a year of extensive study and strategic analysis.

NEWS

 **CSX CORPORATION**
Corporate Communications
P.O. Box C-32222
Richmond, VA 23251
(804) 355-2894

NEW YORK, NY, January 9, 1986 — Laurance S. Rockefeller and CSX Corporation jointly announced today the signing of letters of intent under which CSX would purchase two leading Caribbean resorts, a third resort at Jackson Hole, Wyoming, and Mr. Rockefeller's resort management company, Rockresorts, Inc.

The properties are Caneel Bay, on the Island of St. John in the U.S. Virgin Islands National Park; the visitor facilities in Grand Teton National Park, both owned by Jackson Hole Preserve, Incorporated (JHPI), a non-profit charitable and conservation foundation of which Mr. Rockefeller is President; and Little Dix Bay, on the island of Virgin Gorda, British Virgin Islands, owned by Mr. Rockefeller, personally. These properties are generally considered to be located in two of the most scenically beautiful areas of the world.

Under the proposal, Rockresorts would continue to manage these resorts without change in its management policy of superior standards. Terms were not disclosed.

CSX, the transportation and natural resource company based in Richmond, VA, owns and operates The Greenbrier resort hotel and conference center in White Sulphur Springs, WV. The Greenbrier would continue to operate under its separate management, the joint announcement said.

Mr. Rockefeller said the projected sale to CSX "was influenced significantly by CSX's commitment to the highest resort management standards, as exemplified by The Greenbrier, and by its emphasis on retaining the environmental uniqueness of the three properties." Funds generated by the sales of the Foundation properties would provide Jackson Hole Preserve with additional resources to further its conservation and charitable purposes, while leaving the properties in strong hands for the future, he said.

Hays T. Watkins, CSX chairman and chief executive officer, said the purchase "would be consistent with the long-term strategy of CSX to broaden its resort hotel interests" beyond The Greenbrier, which has received the Mobil Five-Star Award for 25 consecutive years.

He said that Richard E. Holtzman, president and chief executive officer of Rockresorts, and William C. Pitt III, president and chief executive officer of The Greenbrier and CSX Hotels, would work closely together while exploring growth opportunities in the resort industry.

Mr. Watkins said that Rockresorts also would continue to manage The Woodstock Inn and Resort, Woodstock, Vermont, owned by Mr. Rockefeller; and The Boulders, Carefree, Arizona. He said Rockresorts would manage any resort properties which CSX might purchase in the future or bring under management contract.

Caneel Bay's 170-acre grounds are within the 5,000 acre Virgin Islands National Park, made possible by funds contributed primarily by the Rockefeller Brothers Fund, Mr. Rockefeller and other members of his family. The park was donated to the nation in 1956. In 1983, Jackson Hole Preserve made a gift of Caneel's 170 acres to the Federal Government, subject to a 40-year right of continued use by Caneel.

The 170 guest rooms at Caneel are in low-profile buildings with 131 rooms on or overlooking a beach. Rockresorts also operates the nearby Cinnamon Bay Campground, which offers low-cost camping facilities for approximately the same number of occupants as the Caneel Bay resort. All of Caneel's income has gone toward maintenance and operations or furthering JHPI's conservation efforts.

Little Dix Bay, which opened in 1964, covers 550 acres with 84 guest rooms located in cottages with ocean views. A marina accommodates more than 100 yachts, with related boat repair and storage facilities.

The Grand Teton Lodge Company, a Jackson Hole Preserve subsidiary, owns the visitor facilities in the Grand Teton National Park. These include 415 guest rooms at two lodges -Jackson Lake Lodge and Jenny Lake Lodge — and 281 cabin, tent cabin, and trailer sites, at Colter Bay Village.

The Jackson Hole Golf and Tennis Club and related residential real estate, adjacent to the national park and managed by Rockresorts, are included in the CSX transaction.

NEWS

CSX CORPORATION
Corporate Communications
P.O. Box C-32222
Richmond, VA 23251
(804) 355-2894

RICHMOND, VA and EDISON, NJ — April 25, 1986 — CSX Corporation and Sea-Land Corporation today jointly announced they have executed a definitive merger agreement providing for the acquisition of all outstanding Sea-Land shares by CSX for $28 in cash per share. Sea-Land has 23,429,567 shares outstanding and 3,160,587 shares issuable upon conversion of its 11.25 percent Convertible Subordinated Notes due 1998.

As the first step in the transaction, a subsidiary of CSX next week will commence a cash tender offer for all outstanding Sea-Land shares at $28 per share. The offer will be conditioned on, among other things, the valid tender of at least 10,250,000 Sea-Land shares, subject to increase to 13,500,000 shares in certain limited circumstances, and on the informal approval by the Interstate Commerce Commission of an interim voting trust arrangement.

Following completion of the tender offer, the CSX subsidiary will be merged into Sea-Land and each outstanding Sea-Land share will be converted into the right to receive $28. The Sea-Land shares acquired by CSX in the offer and the stock of the surviving corporation following the merger will be held in an independent voting trust pending completion of the required review and final approval by the ICC of the proposed acquisition.

In connection with the transaction, rights under the Sea-Land Shareowner Rights Plan will be redeemed at 10 cents per right, Sea-Land said.

The Board of Directors of CSX and of Sea-Land each have approved the offer and the merger. Dillon, Read & Co., financial advisor to Sea-Land, has rendered its opinion to the Sea-Land Board that the cash consideration to be received by Sea-Land's shareholders in the offer and the merger is fair to them from a financial point of view. Salomon Brothers Inc and The Blackstone Group will act as co-dealer managers for the offer.

CSX previously announced it has purchased call options to acquire approximately 39.5 percent of the outstanding Sea-Land shares from entities controlled by Harold C. Simmons. Sea-Land was not a participant in this transaction.

Hays T. Watkins, chairman of the board and chief executive officer of CSX, said "The combination of CSX and Sea-Land will accomplish several major strategic objectives for CSX. Most important," he said, "it clearly takes CSX Corporation a significant step beyond a primarily railroad focus and in a direction consistent with prevailing trends in merchandise transportation — especially global sourcing, intermodalism and containerization."

Commenting on today's action, Joseph F. Abely. Jr., Sea-Land Corporation chairman and chief executive officer, said 'The people of CSX have had the vision to recognize the long-term strategic advantage in creating a truly international transportation service company, and have boldly stepped at the opportune time to take the lead in this development. All of Sea-Land's people are eager to join with them in this exciting new venture."

Abely further observed. "This merger will integrate an intermodal network covering North America with the Far East, Europe and the remainder of the globe, and it will further extend the concept of ship/rail/truck cargo transfer that Sea-Land pioneered 30 years ago."

Sea-Land Corporation is an international intermodal transportation and trade services company. Its principal subsidiary, Sea-Land Service, Inc., is one of the largest U.S.-flag carriers of containerized goods, operating a fleet of 57 containerships that call at 76 ports and 64 countries around the globe.

Corporate Communications
P.O. Box C-32222
Richmond, VA 23251
(804) 355-2894

RICHMOND, VA — September 12, 1986 — CSX Corporation and Quintana Minerals Corporation of Houston, TX today announced CSX will sell to Quintana nearly all of its coal properties.

Robert L. Hintz, CSX executive vice president, and Corbin J. Robertson, Jr., Quintana's president, said they have signed a letter of intent that will cover sale of about 550,000 acres of coal property, including about 250,000 acres of surface property. The acreage also has valuable timber reserves and about one billion tons of coal reserves.

The property is located principally in West Virginia and Kentucky, and is currently held by several CSX subsidiaries, mostly by CSX Minerals, Inc.

NEWS

 CSX CORPORATION
Corporate Communications
P.O. Box C-32222
Richmond, VA 23251
(804) 355-2894

RICHMOND, VIRGINIA — JULY 20, 1987 — CSX Corporation today announced formation of an integrated CSX/Sea-Land intermodal unit and a logistics management group to take full advantage or the synergies created by the CSX/Sea-Land merger and to move toward full realization or its objective of becoming the world's premier transportation and resource company.

Both the independent integrated intermodal unit and the logistics management group will report to an internal board of directors composed of senior officers of CSX Transportation and Sea-Land. The board, reporting to Hays T. Watkins, chairman and chief executive officer of CSX Corporation, will be chaired by Alex J. Mandl. Mandl will retain his current duties as a senior vice president of CSX and head of the company's Technology Group.

The intermodal unit will include the U.S. intermodal operations of CSX Transportation and Sea-Land, including CMX, CSXT's trucking subsidiary. Sea-Land's trucking units are currently in a voting trust arrangement and will continue in the trust pending Interstate Commerce commission review and approval or CSX's ownership of these units.

Commenting on the integrated intermodal unit, Watkins said, "The key objective of the unit is to realize significant marketplace and operating synergies in terms of service improvements, asset utilization and operating efficiencies. The new unit will be transcontinental in scope and will enable CSX to position itself to participate more effectively in the growth of domestic containerization."

Watkins added, "The combination of the CSX Transportation and Sea-Land intermodal groups creates a large and rapidly growing intermodal business, currently handling in excess of one million trailers and containers annually. The new unit will continue to market aggressively its services to all current and prospective customers of CSX Transportation and Sea-Land as it seeks to accelerate growth of both domestic and international intermodal business through introduction of new services, equipment and systems."

M. McNeil Porter will serve as president of the integrated intermodal unit. Porter, 54, has extensive multimodal transportation experience. Most recently, he was vice president -Asia for Sea-Land Service Inc. In that position and from his Hong Kong base, Porter oversaw operations, marketing and administration for the U.S.-flag containership carrier's services throughout 11 Far East countries.

During his 10-year career with Sea-Land, Porter also has served as vice president, Japan; general manager, Hong Kong; and general manager, Alaska. Prior to joining Sea-Land, Porter held management and operations positions with Jones Motor Company, Preston Freight Lines and Overnite Transportation Company. Porter earned a B.A. degree from the University of Georgia School of Business.

"The logistics management group," Watkins said, "will be responsible for defining the strategies and implementing the initiatives necessary to more fully satisfy the transportation and logistics needs of domestic and international shippers and receivers of merchandise freight."

Hugh L. Randall, 44, will head the logistics management group as senior vice president - logistics management. Previously, Randall was president of Fruit Growers Express, an equipment management firm owned by CSX Corporation and headquartered in Alexandria, Va.

Before joining CSX, Randall was executive vice president and chief financial officer of Ryder-PIE Nationwide. Earlier in his career, Randall held several operating management positions with Consolidated Rail Corporation, including assistant vice president - operations and general manager of Conrail's Atlantic Region and was a management and operations consultant to transportation companies. Randall earned a B.A. degree at Antioch College and an M.B.A. at Harvard University.

NEWS

Corporate Communications
P.O. Box C-32222
Richmond, VA 23251
(804) 355-2894

RICHMOND, Va. — Jan. 23, 1988 — CSX Corporation today announced that The Greenbrier, the world-class resort located in White Sulphur Springs, W.Va., is no longer among the resort assets being considered for sale or monetization by the company.

Concurrently, CSX announced the appointment of Theodore J. Kleisner as president and managing director of The Greenbrier. Kleisner, who previously served as vice president and managing director of the hotel, will report to John W. Snow, CSX president and chief operating officer, and will serve on CSX's management committee.

William C. Pitt III, president of CSX Resorts Inc., will continue to oversee the restructuring of CSX's resort interests. Commenting on CSX's decision to retain The Greenbrier and on Kleisner's appointment, Pitt said, I could not be more pleased for the employees of The Greenbrier and for Ted Kleisner. The proud traditions and high standards for which The Greenbrier has long been known will be preserved under continued CSX ownership and Ted Kleisner's leadership.

CSX's decision to retain The Greenbrier was made largely in response to expressions from shareholders, customers, political leadership and the resort's employees.

"We received an overwhelming response from these and other constituents urging us to keep The Greenbrier," said Hays T. Watkins, CSX chairman and chief executive officer. "While we were fully aware of the strong sentiment about The Greenbrier, we learned that it's widely believed that the identities of The Greenbrier and CSX are inseparably linked.

"Obviously, this relationship has deep historical roots dating back to 1910 when the resort was acquired by the Chesapeake and Ohio Railway Company, a CSX predecessor," Watkins said. "With the exception of World War II when The Greenbrier served as a U.S. Army hospital, the resort has been a member of the CSX family of companies for 78 years. In addition, the 1,400-member staff

at The Greenbrier includes many who are third and fourth-generation employees.

"However, the company's decision to keep The Greenbrier stems from more than sentimentality," Watkins said. "In 1988, The Greenbrier experienced its best year ever in terms of occupancy and had record earnings. It is also the established industry pacesetter in standards and quality of performance, an accomplishment that it has underscored by winning the prestigious Mobil Five-Star Award for 28 consecutive years and the AAA Five-Diamond Award every year since it was introduced. Also, with the pending sales of Rockresorts to VMS Realty Partners and Texas Gas Transmission Corporation to Transco Energy Co., we are certain we can achieve our restructuring and financial targets without a change in our relationship with The Greenbrier.

"We also believe The Greenbrier adds significant value to CSX, and we're convinced that shareholders will benefit in the future from its continuing membership in the CSX family of companies," Watkins said. "The Greenbrier has been a consistently strong earnings performer, and we're confident it will continue on that highly successful course."

Kleisner, 44 and a graduate of the University of Denver School of Hotel and Restaurant Management, began his hotel career with the Albert Pick Hotel Corp., in Greensboro, N.C. He later served as general manager of Hilton Hotels in Texas, Georgia and Missouri and at the Southampton Princess Hotel in Southampton, Bermuda. In 1980, he was named director of operations at The Greenbrier, and in 1984, he became vice president and managing director of the Boca Raton Hotel and Club in Boca Raton, Fla. In 1987, he returned to The Greenbrier, where he assumed his most recent position as vice president and managing director.

CSX Corporation, headquartered in Richmond, Va., is an international transportation company that offers a variety of rail, container shipping, trucking and barge services.

Corporate Communications
P.O. Box C-32222
Richmond, VA 23251
(804) 355-2894

RICHMOND, Va. — March 22, 1988 — Jean-Pierre Donnet, president and chief executive officer of TOTAL MINATOME CORPORATION, and Hays T. Watkins, chairman and chief executive officer of CSX Corporation, jointly announced today that a definitive agreement had been signed for the sale by CSX of its subsidiary, CSX Oil & Gas Corporation, to TOTAL MINATOME for $612 million cash. It is anticipated that the transaction will be closed in approximately 30 days.

CSX Oil & Gas, located in Houston, Texas, is engaged in the oil and gas exploration and production business. Its principal operations are conducted in the United States, primarily in the Texas and Louisiana Gulf Coast and in the North Sea.

TOTAL MINATOME CORPORATION, which also is located in Houston, is engaged in the oil and gas exploration and production business, primarily in Wyoming, Oklahoma, the Gulf Coast area and the Gulf of Mexico. TOTAL MINATOME is an indirect wholly owned subsidiary of TOTAL Compagnie Francaise des Petroles, a major integrated oil and gas corporation based in France with worldwide activities.

Donnet said that this purchase provided an excellent opportunity to expand TOTAL's operations in the U.S. and the North Sea.

Watkins said he was very pleased with the sale which was consistent with CSX's strategic objectives of focusing its resources on CSX's primary transportation, pipeline, property and technology business groups.

NEWS

CSX CORPORATION
Corporate Communications
P.O. Box C-32222
Richmond, VA 23251
(804) 355-2894

RICHMOND, Va. -- April 20, 1988 -- The Board of Directors of CSX Corporation today elected John W. Snow president and chief operating officer and a member of the Board of Directors of the Richmond-based company.

Snow will relocate to Richmond from Jacksonville, Fla., where he has been president and chief executive officer of CSX Transportation. In his new position, he will oversee the company's transportation activities as well as all other CSX operating units.

Snow will report to Hays T. Watkins, chairman and chief executive officer of CSX.

"With the depth and quality of John's experience in key executive positions with CSX and in the federal government, he will play a central and highly visible role in leading the company toward its goal of becoming the premier international transportation and resource company in the coming years," Watkins said.

Snow, 48, joined Chessie System Inc., a CSX predecessor company, in 1977 as vice president-government affairs. He became senior vice president-corporate services-CSX in 1980 and executive vice president-CSX in 1984. In 1985, he was named president and chief executive officer of Chessie System Railroads. With the reorganization of Chessie and Seaboard into Distribution Services, Equipment and Rail Transport in 1986, Snow was named president and chief executive officer of CSX Rail Transport. In 1987, he was promoted to his most recent position as president and chief executive officer of CSX Transportation.

Prior to joining CSX, Snow held a number of posts with the federal government. In addition to heading the National Highway Traffic Safety Administration, he held various senior posts in the U.S. Department of Transportation, including deputy undersecretary, assistant secretary for governmental affairs, deputy assistant secretary for policy, plans and international affairs and assistant general counsel. Before his government service, Snow practiced law in Washington, D.C., was an assistant professor of economics at the University of Maryland and served as adjunct professor of law at the George Washington University Law School.

Snow did his undergraduate studies at Kenyon College and the University of Toledo, earned a doctorate in economics from the University of Virginia in 1965 and received an LL.B. from the George Washington University Law School in 1967.

Snow's civic, business and professional affiliations include the American, Federal, District of Columbia and Virginia Bar Associations. In addition, he is a member of the boards of the University of Maryland School of Public Affairs, Sovran Financial Corp., Best Products Corp., Virginia Museum of Fine Arts, Jacksonville (Fla.) Symphony, The B&O Railroad Museum Inc., Randolph-Macon College, WJCT-Public Television, Center for Excellence in Government, and Richmond, Fredericksburg & Potomac Railroad Co.

Snow currently serves as a member of President Reagan's White House Conference for a Drug Free America. In addition, he is a trustee with the Federal City Council of Washington, D.C., is a visiting fellow with the American Enterprise Institute and was a Distinguished Fellow with the Yale School of Management.

CSX Corporation operates in four major lines of business—transportation, energy, properties and technology.

©CSX Corporation

Corporate Communications
P.O. Box C-32222
Richmond, VA 23251
(804) 355-2894

NEWS

CSX CORPORATION
Corporate Communications
P.O. Box C-32222
Richmond, VA 23251
(804) 355-2894

RICHMOND, Va. — Sept. 19, 1988 — CSX Corporation announced today that its Board of Directors has authorized a restructuring program designed to emphasize the company's commitment to its core business as an international transportation company.

Concurrently, the company announced it was immediately launching an aggressive program designed to significantly reduce operating and overhead costs.

As part of the restructuring program, the CSX Board has authorized the repurchase of up to 60 million CSX common shares (representing approximately 38 percent of the common shares outstanding). CSX will commence a "Dutch-auction" self-tender offer later this week for up to 40 million shares (representing approximately 26 percent of its shares outstanding). After expiration of the tender offer and depending upon market conditions and other factors, the company may repurchase the remainder of the 60 million common shares in the open market, in privately negotiated transactions or otherwise.

Under the provisions of the "Dutch-auction" self-tender offer, each CSX common shareholder will be invited to tender shares at prices specified by the shareholder, ranging from $28 to $33 per share. The company will select a single purchase price and will buy at that price up to 40 million shares tendered at or below such price. The offer will not be conditioned on any minimum number of shares being tendered. Initial funding for the repurchase will come from cash and short-term borrowings.

Additionally, the CSX Board has authorized sale of the company's natural gas transmission and natural gas liquids processing businesses

-Texas Gas Transmission Corporation, Owensboro, Ky., and CSX NGL Corporation, Houston --and the exploration and implementation of alternatives designed to monetize the values inherent in its resort properties, including the sale of certain of those properties.

Hays T. Watkins, CSX chairman and chief executive officer, said, "The restructuring program evidences our continued commitment to increasing stockholder value by concentrating our resources on our core transportation businesses. We strongly believe CSX's common stock represents an attractive investment. However, the repurchase plan will permit stockholders who desire to sell their stock an opportunity to do so at a premium over the current market price."

The company also will redeem four series of preferred stock issued by subsidiary companies. They are CSX Transportation Inc. Series A, B, C and D, formerly Chesapeake and Ohio Railway Series A, B and C and Seaboard Coast Line Railroad Company Series A, respectively.

Wasserstein, Perella & Co. Inc. is advising CSX in connection with the restructuring and will act as dealer manager for the tender offer. The First Boston Corporation and Wasserstein, Perella will assist the company in the natural gas transmission and natural gas liquids processing sale. Wasserstein, Perella also has been exclusively engaged in connection with exploring the alternatives relating to the resort properties.

©CSX Corporation

NEWS

Corporate Communications
P.O. Box C-32222
Richmond, VA 23251
(804) 355-2894

RICHMOND, Va., Dec. 20, 1988 — CSX Corporation and VMS Realty Partners today announced they have signed a definitive stock-purchase agreement which calls for VMS Realty to acquire the stock of the Rockresorts group, a wholly owned subsidiary of CSX Corporation which owns and manages premier resort properties. Terms were not disclosed.

VMS Realty is a group of partnerships owned by three individuals and a subsidiary of Xerox Credit Corporation, a Xerox Financial Services Company. VMS Realty owns and/or manages include several major luxury resorts such as the Boca Raton Resort and Club in Florida and the Sonesta Beach Hotel and Tennis Club in Bermuda. In total, VMS Realty has a portfolio valued in excess of $5 billion, including 56 hotels, and is the second largest owner of hotels in the United States.

"The Rockresorts group is a great strategic opportunity for us," said Joel M. Stone, president of VMS. "It gives us an opportunity to combine the resources of an outstanding organization with our own significant position in the luxury resort business. With our combined resources and our shared commitment to excellence, we expect to continue to grow in a business we know and believe in."

Rockresorts owns and operates Caneel Bay on St. John in the U.S. Virgin Islands, Little Dix Bay on Virgin Gorda in the British Virgin Islands and the Grand Teton Lodge company in northwestern Wyoming. The group also manages the Carambola Beach Resort & Golf Club on St. Croix in the U.S. Virgin Islands, has a joint venture interest in and a management contract for a resort under development near London, England, and has a contract to manage two hotels currently under construction on the island of Lanai in Hawaii.

CSX Corporation, headquartered in Richmond, announced in September that it was exploring a variety of alternatives, including the sale of certain of its resort properties as a part of its restructuring to focus on the company's transportation assets.

Wasserstein, Perella & Co., Inc., which has been advising CSX in connection with the restructuring, was exclusively engaged in connection with the exploration of alternatives relating to CSX resort properties.

NEWS

Houston, Texas — Dec. 23, 1988 — CSX Corporation and Transco Energy Company today announced the signing of a definitive agreement for the sale by CSX of its interstate natural gas pipeline subsidiary, Texas Gas Transmission Corporation, and two related companies to Transco for $571 million, subject to certain adjustments upon closing. Prior to the closing, Texas Gas will pay CSX a cash dividend of $75 million, for total cash proceeds to CSX of $646 million.

It is expected that the purchase will be completed by early spring of 1989 after completion of the pre-merger notification period required by federal law. Transco, headquartered in Houston, through its subsidiary, Transcontinental Gas Pipe Line Corporation (TGPL), operates a 10,000-mile natural gas transmission system that extends from the Gulf of Mexico to a multi-state market area in the eastern United States with capacity of 3.1 billion cubic feet per day. The company also has oil and gas exploration and production, coal and other energy-related businesses.

Transco also announced that it has signed an agreement with CNG Transmission Corporation (CNG) that provides, subject to certain conditions, 250 million cubic feet per day of firm capacity on CNG's pipeline system from Texas Gas terminus in Lebanon, Ohio, to TGPL's Leidy Line in central Pennsylvania. This additional capacity will permit increased deliveries to new markets in the New York/New Jersey area, where TGPL is one of the largest suppliers of natural gas, and permit enhanced delivery service by TGPL and Texas Gas throughout their traditional service areas. CNG also has an option, expiring 30 days after the anticipated closing date of the acquisition, to purchase a one-half interest in Texas Gas.

Commenting on the purchase, George S. Slocum, president and chief executive officer of Transco, said, "We are excited by the opportunity this acquisition offers. Texas Gas is a first-class company long known for its excellent management and dedicated employees who share our commitment to customers and the communities we serve. Moreover, there should be significant opportunities to serve new and growing markets for both Texas Gas and Transco by means of this strategic combination."

The Texas Gas acquisition will be financed with up to $350 million of non-recourse term debt, committed by Manufacturers Hanover Trust Company, and up to $200 million from the sale of a privately placed, new issue of Transco Energy Company convertible preferred stock. Slocum said that a private investor group,

Corporate Partners, has agreed to purchase up to $200 million of convertible preferred stock upon the acquisition of Texas Gas. The convertible preferred stock has a dividend yield of 9-1/4 percent and is convertible into Transco common stock at $41.25 and redeemable in 1999. Slocum explained that Corporate Partners is a $1.5 billion fund organized to make long-term investments in the equity of major publicly held companies, primarily through direct private placements. Transco will use a portion of its existing committed credit facilities to fund the balance of the purchase price. Transco will acquire Texas Gas subject to approximately $256 million of existing long-term debt.

Slocum said "Texas Gas provides an excellent strategic fit with Transco's businesses that will provide immediate and long-term benefits in operating efficiencies, market opportunities and an attractive return on investment for Transco's stockholders." Further, after giving effect to Texas Gas' recently proposed rate settlement, the acquisition should have a positive effect on Transco's consolidated earnings in 1989 that should more than offset the dilutive effect of the sale of convertible preferred stock on earnings per share. He emphasized that this acquisition is indicative of Transco's commitment to concentrate its strategic focus on the natural gas pipeline business and gas-related activities announced this past summer and that it represents an opportunity to acquire a high quality transmission system and a talented and experienced management.

"Texas Gas is an efficient pipeline system with attractive core Midwest markets," Slocum said. "The alignment of TGPL, with its Eastern markets, and Texas Gas provides Transco with additional opportunities to offer diversified access to domestic gas supplies and to expand service to the burgeoning markets in the northeastern United States.

"We intend to operate Texas Gas as an independent entity, maintaining a strong presence and its headquarters in Owensboro, Kentucky. Texas Gas has a unique relationship with its neighbors and this sale will mean that it will long continue to be an important part of the Owensboro and Kentucky communities. The Texas Gas employees are first class and we are pleased with the prospect of working with them and their executive team," he added.

Robert W. Best, president and chief executive officer of Texas Gas, said, "The people of Texas Gas are looking forward to new and exciting opportunities as a part of the Transco family. We are pleased that we will be affiliated with a leader in our industry of

Dec. 23, 1988 (continued)

Transco's caliber. We are especially pleased that Texas Gas will be able to continue its special relationship with its customers, the Commonwealth of Kentucky and community of Owensboro."

Hays T. Watkins, chairman and chief executive officer of CSX Corporation, said, "With this sale CSX completes a major portion of its restructuring. We are pleased that Texas Gas and its outstanding people will be associated with Transco and that Texas Gas will stay in Owensboro."

Texas Gas operates a 6,000-mile pipeline system that extends from the Gulf of Mexico and east Texas through Louisiana, Arkansas, Mississippi, Tennessee, Kentucky and Indiana, terminating in southwestern Ohio, with small-diameter lines extending into Illinois.

Texas Gas is both a wholesaler and transporter of natural gas. The company serves 92 gas distribution utilities and three interstate pipelines with annual mainline volumes currently averaging 600 billion cubic feet per year. Major utility customers include Memphis Light, Gas and Water, which serves Memphis, Tenn.; and Louisville Gas and Electric Co., which serves the city of Louisville, Ky. Other major customers are Southern Indiana Gas and Electric Co., Evansville, Ind.; Indiana Gas Co.; Terre Haute (Ind.) Gas Corp.; Cincinnati Gas and Electric Co.; the city of Hamilton, Ohio; Western Kentucky Gas Co., Owensboro; Jackson (Tenn.) Utility Div.; and Mississippi Valley Gas Co., Jackson, Miss.

CSX purchased the natural gas pipeline system, along with the oil and gas exploration and production interests and barging interests of Texas Gas Resources Corporation, in 1983. In 1984, the Interstate Commerce Commission approved CSX's control of the former Texas Gas barging subsidiary, American Commercial Lines Inc. The oil and gas exploration, development and production interests were sold in April 1988 to Total Minatome Corp. CSX retains the barging unit, certain property interests and the former Texas Gas natural gas liquids processing unit.

CSX Corporation, headquartered in Richmond, Va., announced in September that it would sell Texas Gas as part of a restructuring program designed to emphasize the company's commitment to its core business as an international transportation company.

The First Boston Corp. and Wasserstein, Perella & Co., Inc., which have been advising CSX on the restructuring, were exclusively engaged to assist in the sale of Texas Gas. Lazard Freres & Co. acted as financial advisor to Transco in connection with the transaction.

©CSX Corporation

NEWS

 CSX CORPORATION
Corporate Communications
P.O. Box C-32222
Richmond, VA 23251
(804) 355-2894

NEW HAVEN, Conn./RICHMOND, Va. — Feb. 7, 1989 — Southern Now England Telecommunications Corp. (SNET) and CSX Corporation today announced they have entered into a definitive agreement with Williams Telecommunications Group Inc. (WTG) to sell LIGHTNET, a partnership owned jointly by SNET and CSX subsidiaries, for about $363 million. The sale is consistent with the partners' decisions to focus on their core businesses.

Completion of the transaction is scheduled for early April 1989 and is subject to certain required governmental approvals, officials said.

LIGHTNET, headquartered in Rockville, Md., owns and operates a digital fiber optic network over some 4,500 route miles. The system serves 38 major cities including Boston, New York, Philadelphia, Baltimore, Washington, Pittsburgh, Detroit, Cleveland, Chicago, Atlanta, New Orleans, Jacksonville, Tampa and Miami.

"The combination of the LIGHTNET and WTG networks will represent a much stronger strategic force in the telecommunications industry," said Joe C. Culp, president and chief executive officer of LIGHTNET. "Our customers will benefit further by having a single point of contact and a fully integrated nationwide network."

SNET, headquartered in New Haven, is an independent telecommunications company supplying network services, communications equipment and information management systems to customers throughout Connecticut.

CSX, headquartered in Richmond, is an international transportation company that offers a variety of rail container-shipping, trucking and barge services.

Williams Telecommunications Group Inc., approximately 84 percent owned by The Williams Companies Inc., is one of the nation's leading telecommunications common carriers for long-distance companies and the private networks of large corporations and institutions. The Williams Companies Inc., headquartered in Tulsa, Okla., also is engaged in the pipeline transmission of natural gas and petroleum products.

NEWS

CSX CORPORATION

Corporate Communications
P.O. Box C-32222
Richmond, VA 23251
(804) 355-2894

WHITE SULPHUR SPRINGS, W.Va. — April 20, 1989 — The Board of Directors of CSX Corporation at the Annual Meeting of Shareholders here today announced the election of John W. Snow as chief executive officer of the company. Snow, 49, will continue as president and Hays T. Watkins will continue as chairman, the board said.

Commenting on Snow's new role, Watkins said, "This signals a continuation of the leadership transition we began at CSX a year ago with John's election as president and chief operating officer. John has an innovative, vigorous leadership style that will serve him and the company well in the years ahead."

Recognizing Watkins' 18 years as chief executive officer and 40-plus years of service to CSX and its predecessor companies in a statement read to shareholders during the annual meeting, the board said, "We are delighted Hays will continue his association with CSX as chairman of the Board of Directors as John assumes responsibility for overall management of the company."

The board added it expects no change in the company's strategic direction under Snow's leadership. "CSX," the board said, "will remain focused on its transportation assets and will continue its drive toward becoming the premier international transportation company."

In other actions at today's Annual Meeting of Shareholders, 11 persons were elected to the Board of Directors by the company's shareholders; the appointment of Ernst & Whinney as the company's independent certified public accountants was ratified; and two shareholder proposals were rejected.

Elected to one-year terms on the CSX Board of Directors were Edward L. Addison, Edward J. Boling, Charles K. Cross Sr., Frederick Deane Jr., Bruce C. Gottwald, Clifford M. Kirtland Jr., Steven Muller, W. James Price, John W. Snow, William B. Sturgill and Hays T. Watkins.

The shareholder proposals rejected concerned compensation and length of service on the Board of Directors for outside directors and a proposal which would have required shareholder approval of the company's Shareholder Rights Plan.

Snow joined Chessie System Inc., a CSX predecessor company, in 1977 as vice president-government affairs. He became senior vice president-corporate services for CSX in 1980 and executive vice president in 1984. In 1985, he was named president and chief executive officer of Chessie System Railroads. With the reorganization of Chessie and Seaboard into Distribution Services, Equipment and Rail Transport in 1986, he became president and chief executive officer of CSX Rail Transport. He was promoted to president and chief executive officer of CSX Transportation in 1987.

Prior to joining CSX, Snow held a number of positions with the federal government. In addition to heading the National Highway Traffic Safety Administration, he held various posts in the U.S. Department of Transportation, including deputy secretary, assistant secretary for governmental affairs, deputy assistant secretary for policy, plans and international affairs and assistant general counsel. Before his government service, Snow practiced law in Washington, D.C., was an assistant professor of economics at the University of Maryland and served as adjunct professor of law at George Washington University.

Snow did his undergraduate studies at Kenyon College and the University of Toledo, earned a doctorate in economics from the University of Virginia in 1965 and received a law degree from George Washington University in 1967.

Snow's civic, business and professional affiliations include the American, Federal, District of Columbia and Virginia bar associations. In addition, he is a member of the boards of the University of Maryland School of Public Affairs, Sovran Financial Corp., Best Products Corp., Virginia Museum of Fine Arts, the B&O Railroad Museum Inc., Randolph-Macon College, WJCT-Public Television, Center for Excellence in Government and the Richmond, Fredericksburg & Potomac Railroad Co.

Snow served as a member of former President Reagan's White House Conference for a Drug-Free America. He is a trustee of the Federal City Council of Washington, D.C., is a visiting fellow with the American Enterprise Institute and was a Distinguished Fellow with the Yale School of Management.

CSX Corporation, headquartered in Richmond, Va., is an international transportation company that offers a variety of rail, container-shipping, trucking and barge services.

NEWS

CSX CORPORATION
Corporate Communications
P.O. Box C-32222
Richmond, VA 23251
(804) 355-2894

RICHMOND, Va., Feb. 2, 1990 — CSX Corporation and Enron Corp. today announced they have entered into a definitive stock-purchase agreement which calls for Enron Gas Processing, a subsidiary of Enron Corp., to acquire the stock of CSX Energy Corporation, a wholly owned subsidiary of CSX Corporation. Terms were not disclosed, but CSX expects to report a net gain on the sale. The purchase does not require the assumption of debt by Enron Corp.

Completion of the transaction is anticipated during the first quarter of 1990 and is subject to certain required governmental approvals, officials said.

CSX Energy, headquartered in Houston, produces and markets natural gas liquids from three company-operated plants, including a natural gas liquids extraction plant in Eunice, La.

Enron Corp., America's leading natural gas company with approximately $8.7 billion in assets, operates the nation's largest natural gas transmission system, markets natural gas, gas liquids, crude oil and refined products nationally and worldwide, owns 84 percent of Enron Oil & Gas Company, one of the country's largest independent (non-integrated) natural gas production companies, and also is one of the largest independent producers of electricity.

CSX Corporation, headquartered in Richmond, Va., is an international transportation company that offers a variety of rail, container-shipping, intermodal, trucking and barge services.

NEWS

CSX CORPORATION
Corporate Communications
P.O. Box C-32222
Richmond, VA 23251
(804) 355-2894

RICHMOND, Va. — March 20, 1990 -- CSX Corporation today announced it has asked the Special Committee of the Board of Directors of RF&P Corporation to agree to mutually terminate the RF&P/CSX merger agreement announced on Feb. 20, 1990.

"Our intention," said Hays T. Watkins, chairman of CSX, "was to merge the two companies only with the full and unanimous support of the directors of RF&P who are not affiliated with CSX and only with the support of the Virginia Supplemental Retirement System (VSRS) which had been represented on the Special Committee and the RF&P Board of Directors. Events since announcement of the proposed merger, culminating with the replacement by the VSRS of those of its representatives on the RF&P board who negotiated and endorsed the proposed transaction, indicate the transaction no longer enjoys the unanimous support of the RF&P directors or the VSRS.

"It is absolutely clear," said Watkins, "that the proposed merger is in serious conflict with a wide variety of competing external interests, that it has been the subject of substantial amounts of misinformation, and that the likelihood of the VSRS and the General Assembly favorably ratifying it is in serious question. While we regret this assessment, we must face reality."

"We believe the transaction agreed upon by CSX and the independent RF&P directors is fair and in the best interests of the shareholders of both corporations and represents top dollar for the RF&P minority interest," he said.

"However, in light of the changed circumstances," Watkins added, "it is apparent now that the best interests of the shareholders of both RF&P and CSX will be best served by mutual termination of the agreement. This should be followed," he said, "by the prompt public release by RF&P and CSX of all opinions and evaluations on the merger by their respective advisors."

CSX proposed to the Special Committee that it be reconstituted to include all non-CSX directors, including the two new directors from VSRS. CSX also indicated it would not object if a market test were conducted to determine If there exists a third-party purchaser for the RF&P shares not owned by CSX at a price in excess of $34.50 per share.

"We should now move on," he said. "We see no alternative other than termination to end the disruptive influences of the current situation with respect to RF&P's ongoing business operations and the continuing, and obviously futile, spending of shareholders' funds on a merger which seems impossible to accomplish under the circumstances," Watkins said.

"We feel a sense of great disappointment over these developments which prevent fair and informed consideration of our proposal. We know the many RF&P shareholders who support the merger will share these sentiments. While we do not intend to make a tender offer for RF&P stock, we may, after termination of the merger agreement and depending on market and other conditions, purchase additional shares of RF&P Corporation in the market through local brokerage houses or otherwise," he concluded.

NEWS

CSX CORPORATION
Corporate Communications
P.O. Box C-32222
Richmond, VA 23251
(804) 355-2894

RICHMOND, Va., Sept. 14, 1990 — The Virginia Retirement System (VRS) and CSX Corporation (CSX) (CSX-NYSE) announced today that they had proposed to RF&P Corporation (RF&P) (RFPCK-OTC) a transaction initiated by the VRS in which CSX would acquire RF&P's railroad operations in exchange for a portion of its RF&P shares and the VRS would acquire CSX's remaining shares, in both cases for $35 per share. In addition and subject to favorable government rulings, the proposal includes a self-tender by RF&P for a portion of its shares not held by CSX or VRS at $35 per share in cash.

RF&P is a Virginia-based holding company which owns RF&P Railroad Company and RF&P Properties Inc. RF&P has approximately 17.6 million shares outstanding. CSX Corporation controls, through an affiliate, 62.7 percent of RF&P's voting shares and 38 percent of RF&P's total shares, including dividend obligations. VRS is the second largest independent shareholder of RF&P owning approximately 28 percent of the combined voting and non-voting shares.

This transaction as initiated by VRS is subject to the approval of RF&P's Board of Directors and the Board of Directors of CSX and Trustees of VRS. It is also subject to the execution of definitive agreements among all parties and customary due diligence. The transaction will also require certain governmental rulings and approvals and an appropriate shareholder vote, but would not require approval by the Virginia legislature.

Over the past several months, VRS has sought to enhance its investment in RF&P. To achieve this goal, VRS recently proposed a transaction to CSX which involved the following parts:

1. VRS would support an exchange of the stock of a newly formed RF&P subsidiary which will hold the railroad operating assets of the Richmond, Fredericksburg & Potomac Railroad, exclusive of property not needed for railroad purposes, to CSX for $135 million, which would be paid by exchange of approximately 3.9 million shares of RF&P dividend obligations valued at $35 per share.

2. VRS would buy CSX's remaining RF&P shares for $35 per share in cash.

3. Subject to favorable government rulings, RF&P would make a selftender for a portion of its shares not owned by VRS and CSX at $35 per share in cash.

After CSX indicated that the basic framework of VRS's proposal was acceptable to it, they jointly presented the plan to RF&P.

As contemplated, the proposed transaction would result in RF&P retaining all of its real estate and transferring to CSX only its railroad operations in a tax-free transaction. RF&P directors affiliated with CSX would resign and the VRS would become the largest RF&P shareholder.

Jacqueline G. Epps, chairperson of the VRS, stated: "We conceived and approached CSX with this proposal because it accomplishes our key objective-maximizing the value of our investment in RF&P for the benefit of our beneficiaries and for all shareholders of RF&P.

"RF&P owns some of the best income-producing and developable real estate in Virginia, indeed in the U.S., and the VRS has for some time sought to invest a small portion of its trust fund in prime real estate as a desirable diversification of its portfolio which is primarily invested in securities.

"In conceiving this proposal, we were particularly conscious of the need to keep RF&P financially strong for its real estate development activities. At the same time, we believe it is appropriate to offer shareholders who wish to sell any or all of their RF&P shares, a chance to do so at an attractive price of $35 per share, which is the same price as CSX will receive. This selftender will be non-coercive and most shareholders may very well conclude, as the VRS has, that for long-term investors, RF&P shares are worth significantly more than $35 per share.

"In sum, the proposed transaction meets all of our criteria and the concerns expressed by RF&P management to its Board of Directors -

1. VRS, through RF&P, will increase its ownership of prime Virginia real property at an attractive price.

2. RF&P's shareholders will have the opportunity, at their discretion and subject to favorable government rulings, to sell a portion of their RF&P shares at $35 per share in cash.

3. RF&P will remain, even after the self-tender offer, strongly capitalized, highly liquid and have a substantial and reliable cash flow. Therefore, it will continue to pay regular dividends as well as own and develop its valuable real estate.

4. CSX will provide fair value for the railroad and realize certain synergies. As a result, CSX will be able to operate more efficiently for the benefit of its customers and shareholders.

5. In connection with its acquisition of the RF&P Railroad, CSX will assume the existing agreements of RF&P regarding the right to use track for a planned commuter railway which is currently being developed by the State."

Mark Finn, a VRS trustee and chairperson of its investment committee, stated: "VRS is the largest independent shareholder in RF&P and we would not be making this proposal unless we believed that it was in the best interests of RF&P and its shareholders. But I should remind everyone this is a proposal which the RF&P's Special Committee of the Board will be reviewing before making any recommendation to RF&P's Board of Directors. In addition, there are numerous other matters which are needed before this proposal can be consummated, including a tax ruling. Nevertheless, we are excited about the good business sense this proposal makes for all parties involved. It is rare that a deal can be structured which satisfies all of the competing interests of the parties and their constituencies. This one seems to do just that."

Both Ms. Epps and Mr. Finn serve as VRS's representatives on the RF&P Board of Directors. VRS is charged with administering the pension benefits of employees of the State of Virginia. Through its seven-person board, which includes Ms. Epps and Mr. Finn, VRS manages approximately $11 billion.

©CSX Corporation

NEWS

CSX CORPORATION

Corporate Communications
P.O. Box C-32222
Richmond, VA 23251
(804) 355-2894

RICHMOND, Va., Jan. 9, 1991 — The Board of Directors of CSX Corporation today announced the election of John W. Snow to the additional position of chairman of the board of directors, effective Feb. 1, 1991.

Snow, 50, will retain his duties as president and chief executive officer of CSX. He succeeds Hays T. Watkins as chairman. Watkins, who was elected chairman emeritus of the board of directors, reaches the mandatory retirement age of 65 for CSX officers and inside directors later this month. He has served as chairman of CSX since May 1, 1982, and will retire Jan. 31, 1991, with more than 42 years of active service to CSX and its predecessor companies.

Announcing Watkins' retirement and Snow's election as chairman, the CSX Board of Directors said, "The retirement of Hays Watkins marks the close of one of the most distinguished careers in not only railroading, but all of American business. This company and the transportation industry of the nation have especially benefited from his vision, his commitment to quality and superior customer service and his dedication to serving the best interests of CSX shareholders.

"Hays retires," the Board said, "having provided in the person of John Snow an equally proficient and distinguished manager who clearly will lead this company to even greater heights in the years ahead."

Watkins was chairman, president and chief executive officer of CSX from May 1, 1982, until April 20, 1988, when he relinquished the duties of president and on April 20, 1989, Snow was elected to the additional post of chief executive officer. Prior to being elected chairman, president and CEO, Watkins served as CSX president and co-chief executive officer from the time the company began operations on Nov. 1, 1980.

Watkins began his railroading career in 1949 as a staff analyst for The Chesapeake and Ohio Railway. He was elected president and chief executive officer of The Chesapeake and Ohio and The Baltimore & Ohio Railroad in 1971 and chairman and chief executive officer of Chessie System Inc. in 1973. He continued in that position until the November 1980, Chessie/Seaboard Coast Line Industries Inc. merger into CSX.

Snow joined Chessie System Inc. in 1977 as vice president-government affairs. He became senior vice president-corporate services for CSX in 1980 and executive vice president of the company in 1984. In 1985, he was named president and chief executive officer of Chessie System Railroads and, in 1987, he became president and chief executive officer of CSX Transportation, the CSX rail unit.

Prior to joining CSX, Snow held a number of posts with the federal government. He headed the National Highway Traffic Safety Administration and held various senior positions in the U.S. Department of Transportation, including deputy under-secretary, assistant secretary for governmental affairs, deputy assistant secretary for policy, plans and international affairs and assistant general counsel. In addition to his government service, Snow practiced law in Washington, D.C., hold various academic posts including professor of economics at the University of Virginia; assistant professor of economics at the University of Maryland and as a member of the faculty at the George Washington University Law School.

Snow did his undergraduate studies at Kenyon College and the University of Toledo, earning a doctorate in economics from the University of Virginia in 1965 and an LL.B. from the George Washington University Law School in 1967.

CSX Corporation, headquartered in Richmond, Va., is an international transportation company offering a variety of rail, container-shipping, intermodal, trucking and barge services.

Index

• • • • • • • • • • • • • • • • • • •

. . . .

D

• • • • • • • • • • • • • • • • • • •

• • • • • • • • • • • • • • • • • •

. . . .

Q

R

T

W